La Bonne Soupe Cookbook

La Bonne Soupe Cookbook

Jean-Paul Picot & Doris Tobias

MACMILLAN • USA

MACMILLAN

A Simon & Schuster Macmillan Company
1633 Broadway
New York, NY 10019

Text copyright © 1997 Jean-Paul Picot and Doris Tobias

Design by Rachael McBrearty

Illustrations by Joyce Wynes

Photographs on pages xvi, xix, 1, 31, 52, 77, 166, and
back flap by Thunder Levin

MACMILLAN is a registered trademark of Macmillan, Inc.

Library of Congress Cataloging-in-Publication Data

La Bonne Soupe cookbook / Jean-Paul Picot and Doris Tobias

p. cm.

Recipes by Francis Freund

Includes index.

ISBN: 0-02-860994-8 (alk. paper)

1. Cookery, French. 2. Bonne Soupe (Restaurant) I. Tobias, Doris. II.
Freund, Francis. III. Bonne Soupe (Restaurant) IV. Title.

TX719.P53 1997   96-17765

641.5'09747'1—dc20   CIP

Manufactured in the United States of America

10 9 8 7 6 5 4 3 2 1

iv

To my friend and teacher, Paul Barraud

Acknowledgments

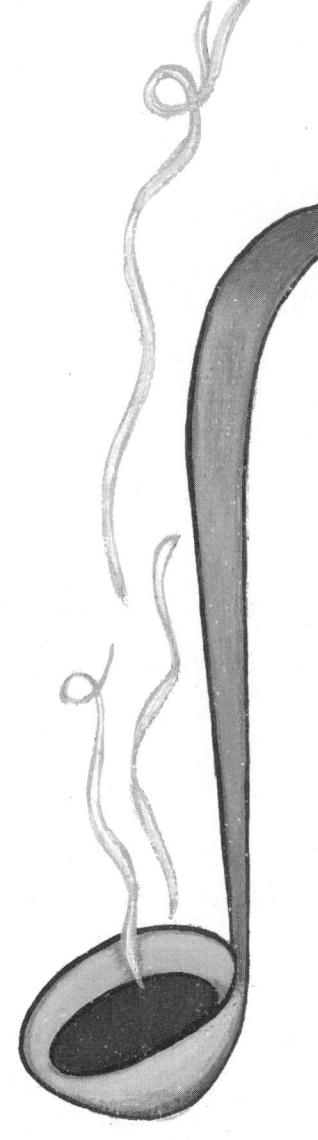

Most radiant and appreciative thanks to my cheering team of pot stirrers—friends, family, and associates—whose sturdy support and guidance made putting together this *piéce de résistance* so rewarding:

To M. David and Glenis Levin, my inspirational friends and cousins, who nourished the concept from the start and saw it through with above-and-beyond emotional and physical hand-holding. To the guiding spirit of Arthur Levine.

To my beloved muses in California: Drs. Judith and H. William Strauss and Marcy Strauss, Dr. David Feigin, Judith Feigin, Matthew and Eric Feigin. Back East: Beatrice, Ed, Laura, and Geoffrey Tobias; Cheryl and David Einhorn; Jane Muccio; my southern muse, Janice Rubin; and the Shapiro family.

To Miriam Malach, the angel, and staunch *sous-chefs* Esther Srole, Marcia Wachspress, Margolit Quitko, Mary Levine, Jo-Ann Levine, Laurie Roberts, Pearl Gordon, Dorothy Margolin, Michael Buller, Eunice Fried, Harriet and Bill Lembeck, Mary Lyons, Catherine Roraback, Elinor Adler, and Ethel Reich.

To Cecile Lamalle, brilliant cook, writer, and comforter, hearty huzzahs for her culinary wisdom, patience, and sentience. Much thanks to Chef Leslie Revsin. And deep appreciation to Nancy Love for her artful guidance and support.

Natalie Petouhoff, without whose computer expertise and diligence the book would never have been, is warmly thanked. Appreciation to Alexis Touchet for her careful and elegant recipe testing.

Special smiles to a superb quintet of *grands becs fins maestros:* John L. Madden, Charles K. McSherry, John E. Sherman, Mark S. Brower, and Lourdes Z. Nisce.

And to the countless friends and devotees of La Bonne Soupe too numerous to list here, a rousing round of thanks.

At Macmillan, a lingering lagniappe to Pamela Hoenig for her percipience and support. To Jane Sigal—*rédacteur en chef*—a standing ovation for her incredible foresight and zeal, and for her innate artistry, virtuosity, and understanding. Special thanks to Amy Gordon for her cheerful helpfulness and support. And bravos to designer Rachael McBrearty and stylist Tracey Moore.

And, finally, thanks to Jean-Paul and Monique Picot, my most gracious collaborators, whose enthusiasm, warmth, and meticulously delineated details and recipes made working with them a joyously memorable experience.

Heartfelt thanks to Chef Francis Freund of La Bonne Soupe for his cheerful cooperation, recipes, and testing and for the countless informative *tête-à-têtes* and tasting over the counter and *à table*.

And loud applause for La Bonne Soupe's wonderful staff— Monique Gutmann, Honoré Pochat, Daniel Lagarde, David Grisevich, Andy Tseng, Marie-Claire Gouzien, Robert Candela, Mariette Thiron, Alcibiades Rodriquez, and Onesimo Vasquez. *Par ici, la bonne soupe!*

Doris Tobias

Contents

4
Les Hamburgers and Filet Mignon
65

How do you give hamburgers and steak a French accent? Add a sauce. Also, find a couple of savory reminiscences.

5
Fish and Shellfish
75

Bistro fish: La Bonne Soupe's inimitable Salt Cod Pureéd with Garlic, Olive Oil, and Cream; Monkfish in Red Wine Sauce; and Baked Haddock with Chives Sauce. And bistro shellfish: Mussels Steamed in White Wine and Jean-Paul's Delightful Mussels on the Half Shell.

6
Poultry and Rabbit
93

Hunter's Chicken and *Coq au Vin* are all-time favorites, along with Chicken Tarragon. Don't miss Monique's Roast Chicken Stuffed with Goat Cheese Croutons and Chicken Roasted with Lemon and Madeira. Rabbit fans will love Madame Davenet's Casseroled Rabbit.

7
Meat
107

"*Boeuf Bourguignon* is a very typical bistro dish," says Jean-Paul Picot. So is Monique's Veal Stew. And try Roast Leg of Lamb with Rosemary and Garlic.

8
One~Dish Meals
117

Great, satisfying meals in a casserole can be done ahead. Just reheat and serve a hearty Alsatian Sauerkraut with Sausages and Meats, savory French Bean Stew, or Chicken in the Pot. For your next get-together, offer Algerian Couscous, a peppery-sauced North African dish starring the grainlike pasta, couscous. Plus read all about French bread.

Pierre Franey Reminisces

Pierre Franey—master French chef, cookbook author, and TV chef personality—has been friends with the Picots more than 20 years. He's been a devotee of La Bonne Soupe since it opened in 1974. For him, the most important thing about this quintessential French-American bistro is the mouthwatering memories it evokes.

[La Bonne Soupe is] so warm, so friendly, so very French, a place that makes me feel welcome and at home. My wife loves to have a bite before the ballet at Lincoln Center, just ten blocks north. She is fond of the onion soup and a salad. I eat there very often. For one, I live very close by, practically next door. Jean-Paul is my landlord, and I must say he treats me very well.

When I sit at one of the red-checkered cloth–covered tables in that bistro atmosphere and order one of the regional dishes, I am really on a nostalgia trip. With a steaming plate of *tripes à la mode de Caen,* a traditional glass of cider and some good crusty bread, I am back in Normandy. I might even finish with a little glass of Calvados [cider brandy].

When I order *brandade de morue,* I am back in Béziers in the Languedoc [southern France]. As I taste the creamy purée of salt cod and potatoes, with just that right touch of garlic and oil, I see in my mind's eye the brilliant blue-green of the Mediterranean and the fresh produce in the market stalls.

When it's Jean-Paul's wonderful *bouillabaisse*, the saffron and fennel aromas take me to Marseilles and its bustling waterfront. And when I'm enjoying a *fondue au fromage* [cheese fondue], I am in Franche-Comté, high in the Alps, breathing the crisp mountain air and sipping white wine and kirsch. Did you know that the fondue pot must be stirred in a figure eight to keep the melting cheese from becoming stringy? Or that if a diner drops his bit of bread into the fondue the penalty for this clumsiness is a round of drinks for the table?

When I take a forkful of *ratatouille,* with its ripe tomatoes, sweet peppers, eggplant, and zucchini, I am sitting at a café on the Cóte d'Azur, bathed in sunlight beside the sea. And when the dish is a hearty *choucroute garnie* [sauerkraut with cured meat and sausages], I am in Alsace, among the houses with the steepled medieval rooftops, lush orchards, and vineyards.

I really enjoy everything on Jean-Paul's menu. What I like especially is that his basic menu remains constant, so that I can always rely on La Bonne Soupe to satisfy my craving for the bistro classics. Yet there are always innovative dishes from Chef Francis to taste and enjoy right here in the heart of Manhattan.

Pierre Franey was a superb mentor, a great chef, and a true friend. We shall miss him.

A Fond Overview by Bryan Miller

∽ ∽ ∽

Bryan Miller, a former restaurant reviewer for *The New York Times,* with brilliant pen and palate, has been friend and neighbor to the Picots for many years and an enthusiastic appreciator of La Bonne Soupe.

If the definition of a good restaurant is one where you are known, then La Bonne Soupe is a veritable family reunion. Anyone who descends the steps on Fifty-fifth Street into the bistro's dining room more than once becomes a member of an extended family.

Of course the soup is *bonne,* and the bread is yeasty and fresh; but it is the spirit of this perpetually packed establishment that makes it special. Presiding over the daily revelry is the owner, Jean-Paul Picot, standing next to the telephone on the bar, wearing his blazer, bow tie, and vigilant expression.

I always refer to Jean-Paul as the "Mayor of Fifty-fifth Street." Like a turn-of-the-century urban politician, he keeps his fingers firmly on the pulse of his domain, which stretches roughly from the Peninsula Hotel on Fifth Avenue to the Chemical Bank office on the Avenue of the Americas. Pressing matters of the day are often discussed at La Bonne Soupe's compact bar over steaming crocks of onion soup or mounds of vegetable couscous. What business is opening on the street? Who is moving? Are taxes going up? Why do the jackhammers start at 1:00 A.M.? How is the French soccer team doing? These are just a few items on the daily gossip menu.

On any given day the bar think tank could include executives from Société Générale, the giant French bank; the chief jewelry designer from Tiffany's around the corner; French merchants and lawyers; chefs and restaurateurs; and sundry movers and shakers who work in this high-powered neighborhood. If the French president were visiting America and wanted to know how he was perceived in America, he would best bypass the United Nations and instead pull up a bar stool at La Bonne Soupe between noon and 3:00 P.M. Moreover, he'd get a well-made *brandade de morue* (purée of salt cod—something that is not exactly a specialty at the UN).

Another part of La Bonne Soupe's appeal is its extraordinary art collection. Jean-Paul Picot and his wife, Monique, must own one-third of Haiti's artistic output over the past ten years. Everywhere you look in the restaurant, upstairs and down, there is another color-drenched primitive painting evoking sun, sand, and serenity. The connection between Caribbean fieldworkers and French cuisine eludes me, but the paintings certainly liven the place up.

A corner table in the upstairs dining room.

Like all great restauranteurs, the Picots have a passion for good food—although Monique sometimes thinks her husband's passion goes a little overboard. When I was the restaurant critic for *The New York Times* I occasionally invited them along as co-tasters. Their opinions were always as informed as they were unequivocal.

"This is way too bland, Jean-Paul," Monique would say.

"Yes dear," Jean-Paul would reply, ever the diplomatic husband. "Yours is much better."

Jean-Paul, a bread expert, always conducted a thorough investigation of the bread basket.

"Oh Jean-Paul," Monique would say. "You don't need any more of that!"

"But Monique, this is quite good and besides, it's my business to know," Jean-Paul replied, reasoning that something well made deserved to be finished.

Dessert usually brought a repeat of the admonitory exchange.

"I'm only eating this to help Bryan," he would say as his wife rolled her eyes.

On the very rare nights that I was not eating professionally, I enjoyed ducking into La Bonne Soupe about 11:00 P.M. for a glass of simple red wine and a plate of garlicky *brandade,* as soothing as a massage on a Mediterranean balcony.

Getting back to the familiar nature of La Bonne Soupe, I remember one incident that underscores how regulars are treated like family, not just credit cards.

One evening I stopped by the bar on my way home, and the bartender said that a few hours earlier a man had come into the restaurant saying that Bryan Miller had been injured in a car accident on Long Island. He said that he was going to pick him up and bring him home but that he needed 20 dollars for gas and tolls because he didn't have any cash.

Jean-Paul suspected a scam but, on the outside chance that it was true, he gave the man 20 dollars cash. Of course the con man was never heard of again. We had a good laugh over that— after I inspected myself for possible injuries. If that is not the definition of a good restaurant, I don't know what is.

The Story of the Picots and La Bonne Soupe

ean-Paul, the heart of the operation, at his host post—the little bar in the center of the main dining room.

You can tell who's *le patron* (the owner) directly on entering La Bonne Soupe. Jean-Paul Picot is the one standing at the end of the little service bar in the middle of the restaurant. He wears a bow tie—always. And his well-upholstered figure exudes confidence in the food he serves. One glance at Jean-Paul shows that he likes food. He has been struggling to overcome this image for years, but his love of food always beats out the diet.

There usually is a smile on Jean-Paul's face, a hand held out in greeting, and you get the feeling right away that here is a man who wants you to feel at home and enjoy yourself. He is the Quintessential Restaurateur.

To see Jean-Paul at La Bonne Soupe, you'd think he'd been born into a family of restaurateurs. But entering the restaurant business was a surprising choice given his background. In fact his decision flew in the face of generations of family tradition.

Jean-Paul Picot was born into a military family in Paris three years before the outbreak of World War II. "My great-grandfather,

Joseph Picot was an *aide de camp* to Napoleon. My grandfather, Yves Picot, was a decorated colonel in World War I, and my father was Admiral Jacques Picot of the French Navy."

During the war Jean-Paul was sent to live with his maternal grandmother, Marguerite Forsans, in a little town near Pau in southwestern France. Jean-Paul loved her wonderful peasant cooking and the robust cuisine of the Basque area. "She had a tremendous sense of the elements essential to fine cooking; I guess it's known as *la cuisine des grandmères*—simple, flavorful, earthy dishes using the natural resources of the countryside.

"*Grandmère* had a big, old, rambling house surrounded by fruit trees and vegetable gardens. During the war, we were displaced by the Gestapo, which took over the main house. We lived in a small cottage to the rear. *Grandmère* continued to cook, but we were minus a lot of things, like good country butter, which the Germans naturally appropriated. Funny, the things one remembers. One time *Grandmère* wanted to make an omelet, or perhaps it was *crêpes,* but there was no butter or oil to cook them in. Being a resourceful and determined woman, *Grandmère* melted a little candle wax to grease the pan. I do recall feeling a bit queasy afterwards.

"When we were back in the big house, as before, *Grandmère* Marguerite made her own butter, and got her cream from the farmer next door. She was back in business! What a gifted cook; I can still taste her delicious onion *tourte* and the fruit tarts that were her specialty. I was her little *gâte-sauce*—someone who runs all the little nitty-gritty errands in the kitchen, but I was also a very good taster, if I may say so!"

Jean-Paul credits his grandmother with instilling in him a passion for cooking. "Yes, it was *Grandmère* Marguerite who taught me to know, love, and respect the art of cooking. She was a perfectionist and she cooked

Jean-Paul's parents, Paulette and Jacques Picot, on their wedding day, May 5, 1920.

Colonel Yves Picot, Jean-Paul's grandpère, a World War I hero, pictured after the war.

from the heart—no recipes—and she was always a bit secretive about the dishes she prepared. It was a little like the famous pianist giving a recital and keeping his fingers very close to the keyboard. Why? He saw a rival pianist in the audience and didn't want him to be copying his fingerwork! So *Grandmère* who, incidentally was a brilliant hostess, also kept her little secrets to herself.

"When the Germans departed from the big house, she turned it into a charming bed and breakfast inn, filled with fresh field flowers and always redolent of freshly baked breads, rolls, and pastries. My grandfather, sadly for me, died before the war, so I never knew him."

Jean-Paul Picot, at two years old, seated in his first Peugeot, with a little cousin in Lagor.

FOLLOWING A PASSION

When Jean-Paul was 15 his father called him back to Paris. "We had a man-to-man talk, during which my father asked me what I wanted to do in life. I replied, 'Oh, travel and do something that involves dealing with people.' He had hoped I would follow family tradition and enter the military, but for me that was out. So I was sent off to boarding school and finally, when I was 17, I knew I wanted to attend a first-class hotel school and pursue a career in the restaurant arena."

Jean-Paul was accepted into the program at L'École Hôtelière in Lausanne, Switzerland, which he found very much to his liking. "All the students had similar interests, and the staff was really inspirational, especially a teacher by the name of Paul Barraud, with whom I immediately bonded. Not only did he teach me the basics of *haute cuisine* but he was also a friend and mentor. Often, after classes, he would take me to a bistro, where we would sit and drink a few glasses of Swiss Fendant or Dole—I was past 18 by then, so it was okay, and I was extremely complimented when Monsieur Barraud said to me: 'Jean-Paul, you are a good student and you also know how to hold your wine!'"

The Switzerland years flew by. "The first year concentrated on restaurant service, the basics of how to deal with people, and how to serve the table, including a complete course on wines.

"For a whole year, we learned cooking techniques, with the entire teaching staff hovering over our shoulders. When we were deemed ready, we were all sent off to real restaurant kitchens." Jean-Paul's first kitchen turned out to be a restaurant in Stuttgart, which did not sit too well with him. "I was made to feel not very welcome," he recalls. "The first word I heard on my arrival was *arbeit*—'work'—and the chef made no bones about the fact that he did not like the French. But I buckled down and even learned the language plus some hands-on cooking procedures."

After Stuttgart, Jean-Paul returned for his final semester at L'École, which concentrated on front-of-the-house procedures and decorum, including diplomacy and dealing with customers. Then it was off to jobs as a trainee at various hotels and restaurants.

"The first was at the grandly eminent Hotel Excelsior in Florence, Italy, and for me it was an immediate and lasting love affair with Italy and its foods." At the Excelsior, Jean-Paul was at the front desk, a key spot, where he wore an elegant uniform complete with white starched shirt, even when the temperature went above 90° in the summer. He greeted celebrities such as Juliette Greco, Darryl Zanuck, and Henry Fonda. "I always felt it was a privilege to be working at the Excelsior," Jean-Paul recalls.

After Italy, Jean-Paul continued his training in France. "There were some valuable experiences I had," Jean-Paul recalls,

Jean-Paul displays his knife-wielding dexterity at L'École Hôtelière in Lausanne, circa 1959.

Forges-les-Eaux, in Normandy, where Jean-Paul and Monique met.

Monique Picot's sister, Yolande Davenet, left, with little Monique, circa 1942.

"but the epiphany came in the spring of 1958 when I was at a hotel in Normandy, where I met Monique Davenet. It was the Hôtel des Thermes in Forges-les-Eaux, where I was doing my training in waiting, and Monique was a cashier at the restaurant. I saw this petite, charming, and adorable person and it was, to use an old expression, love at first sight.

"It was Monique's first job. She was bright and beautiful—a fresh-from-the-country girl—brought up with her sister, Yolande, on a sprawling farm and apple orchard in Normandy. Her father, Léopold, hunted wild hare and duck, which her mother, Augustine, would marinate with wine and wild morels."

Jean-Paul sighs as he remembers his mother-in-law's specialties. "Perhaps it was all that farm cream and apple cider and Calvados, which Monsieur Davenet made himself, but every dish that Madame Davenet made was special. [French people can be extremely formal, and Jean-Paul always called his in-laws ["monsieur" and "madame."] Her roast chicken was divine. Her *tripes à la mode de Caen* were the tastiest and best in the region. And, oh, her wonderful apple tart! To this day I carry with me those unforgettable aromas and tastes of that big, bright, sun-filled kitchen.

"So, back to the Hôtel des Thermes, where Monique and I both worked very hard. I began to help her close her books at the day's end, so that we could go out together. It was a whirlwind romance and we were married in October 1958. After that, I got a job in a small hotel in Paris, where I did a little bit of everything. The owner liked me, and when he was on vacation, he put me in charge for a few weeks, which gave me a lot of confidence."

IN THE ARMY NOW

"Then I was drafted into the army, where I served for nearly three years, mainly in North Africa—Tunisia, Morocco, and Algeria. Since my background had been in hotel school, I was put in charge of food supplies in Tunisia, where I remained for nearly 18 months. I was lucky. I could have been sent to fight in the mountains and been killed. But, really, after the strict discipline of the hotel school, the army was easy! Foodwise and culturally, it was a revelation to me. I learned a lot of things while I was in Tunisia, discovering how friendly the Tunisians are and how different the food is. I was able to visit the ancient city of Carthage, with its relics of Roman culture and civilization. And Tunis is extremely beautiful."

It was in Tunis that Jean-Paul came to love couscous. "Hot and spicy. They do eat it spicy," he says, laughing. "Couscous is a great summer dish because it makes you perspire and then you feel cooler. Well, at least that was the consensus in Tunis!"

BACK TO PARIS

Then came freedom from the army. "The most wonderful feeling in the world. I was so happy and yet still a little disoriented after all that army service. It took me weeks to get myself together and find a job. But with Monique's support, I got through this bad patch and found a job at the Hôtel Lutetia in Paris, a really nice hotel on the Left Bank, and there I stayed, as assistant manager, for two years. By that time I felt confident enough to go out on my own and open my own hotel."

Jean-Paul took out a loan, "which was easy to get from the government and bank because of my École Hôtelière background," and bought a small hotel called Sèvres Azur, on the Left Bank, not far from the Lutetia. "It had 45 rooms, a charming sitting room, and a lovely garden room, where we served a typical French breakfast of *café,* croissants, and *confiture* [jam]. Monique was the chief adviser and decorator, and she did a beautiful job, all in warm, rich colors and with everything geared to our guests' comforts."

"Our idea was to offer personalized service to our customers. I would pick people up at the airport and transport them to the hotel for a weekend or weekday package. I worked with Air France and put together a tour of Paris. We arranged for them to visit all the spots they came to see—the museums, cathedrals, and so forth—and saw to it that they got good theater tickets and ate in fine restaurants.

"It was fun, but not enough for me to do creatively. So after a while, Monique and I agreed this was not our métier; and although business was booming, we sold it. I said to Monique, 'It's time to open a restaurant.'"

LA POMME D'AMOUR

The restaurant turned out to be La Pomme d'Amour, on the Avenue Wagram, not far from the Étoile. It was 1963, and Jean-Paul decided to specialize in seafood. "We even had a small oyster bar out front on the sidewalk, which was a great hit. Monique remembers what a hit it made with their son Yves who, even at the age of four, had a passion for oysters and begged to be taken to the little bar to watch *l'écailler* shuck the oysters.

"We had an excellent chef who did a lot of grilling on a real charcoal stove. He made dishes such as *brochettes de coquilles St. Jacques* (grilled scallops), *bar flambé au fenouil* (sea bass grilled with fennel), and *sole Tante Marie* (sole stuffed with mushrooms). He also did a superb *bouillabaisse* (fish soup). You could smell the aroma of saffron and thyme when you entered the restaurant. La Pomme d'Amour was an immediate success and very popular, and we kept it going for five years.

"But in 1968 there was a kind of revolution in Paris—strikes, unrest, nothing was working well—so Monique and I put our heads together, weighed the pros and cons, and finally agreed to sell La Pomme d'Amour. The buyer turned out to be *the* Jo Goldenberg, famous for his bagels sold in his shop on the Rue des Rosiers, in the Marais. It was time, we thought, to head across the Atlantic to the golden dreams of America."

To the States

Jean-Paul went to New York first to find a job. When things were humming along, he would send for Monique and the two boys, François, who was then six, and Yves, a year younger.

Through a contact made at La Pomme d'Amour, Jean-Paul arranged for a job interview in New York at La Crêpe, a chain of 15 eateries specializing in—what else?—crêpes. His plane arrived, on a boiling hot day, leaving him just enough time for a cab ride to the offices in midtown Manhattan.

"It was on Fifth Avenue," Jean-Paul remembers. "I saw a policeman when I got out of the taxi and asked him in my halting English about the address. He was very kind and even helped me carry my bags to the elevator. I still marvel at that!

"I arrived in the office hot and perspiring and apparently unexpected. Well, when things got sorted out, I was hired and informed that my first assignment was to manage the La Crêpe in Nantucket, someplace I'd never heard of."

Nantucket

When Jean-Paul stepped off the ferry in Nantucket, he took one look and thought, "This is so beautiful, I will never leave. I was met by my new bosses, who took me to the La Crêpe restaurant, which was still closed because the season hadn't quite begun. They said, 'Here is where you get the keys to open the place, and here is where you find the Post Office, and this is the key to your sleeping digs.'

"I was left alone on the beautiful island of Nantucket. Well, in due course, my staff arrived, and the restaurant opened, and we had a terrific summer. The season lasted until Labor Day. Then I packed up and re-

Yves (left) and François in Nantucket in 1969.

turned to New York to manage a La Crêpe branch in Greenwich Village.

At Picot's Place in Hampden, Massachusetts, circa 1969.

"So I had a job, and I was able to send money to Monique in Paris and to pay my debts in France. I felt really good to be able to do this. I returned to Nantucket for a second season, and this time I brought Monique and the boys to stay for a month. We were so happy to be together and the boys loved the seaside.

"It was then that I met a wealthy lawyer who wanted to open a restaurant in Springfield, Massachusetts. We went to look at the place, which was in a small shopping mall in Hampden, a suburb. The mall had a small boutique and space for a restaurant. We decided to call it Picot's Place and hired a French chef by the name of Pierre Chambrin, who later moved on to become the White House chef to Presidents Reagan and Bush and to Clinton for a short spell.

"At Picot's Place he was our star chef and did classic French cuisine with great panache," Jean-Paul recalls. It was a successful operation that lasted about a year. By that time Monique and the boys had finally come to the States to live. But although Hampden was a pretty little town, it was far from the bustle and the opportunities that a metropolis offers. As Monique put it, 'This place seems like the end of the world.'

"So we left the restaurant to the lawyer, packed our bags, and headed back to the Big Apple, where I managed to pick up with La Crêpe."

BACK IN THE BIG APPLE

Jean-Paul was put in charge of La Crêpe's large New Jersey food plant and of opening new branches. "I opened a few La Crêpes in Los Angeles, two in Boston, and one in Virginia Beach. Then La Crêpe went sour. The owners weren't investing their money wisely. They didn't keep up with the trends. There was no evolution. They never changed their format. Little by little the whole enterprise was collapsing like a sand castle."

With the demise of La Crêpe, Jean-Paul and Monique contemplated returning to France, where Monique had a good job opportunity with UNESCO. But there was the space at 48 West Fifty-fifth Street that had been the original La Crêpe, and there was still a two-year lease. "Monique and I agreed it was a little crazy, but we decided to buy the lease. The owner admonished, 'If I didn't make it here, neither will you.' 'Let me try,' I replied.

Monique and Jean-Paul Picot seen through La Bonne Soupe's window, circa 1974.

"And that was 24 years ago! Our concept of a French bistro with American sensibilities really took off. Monique and I loved the idea of serving wonderful soups and hearty bistro dishes at modest prices from lunchtime till midnight. We called it La Bonne Soupe, an expression with a double meaning—'good soup,' of course, but also 'the good life.' We hired a French chef, bartender, kitchen staff, and waiters.

"People could order a special that included a big bowl of soup, a nice tossed salad, good French bread, and a glass of wine, all for $2.25. Or they could order a *plat du jour,* or simply coffee and dessert. But the soups were always big attractions. Monique and I put the menu together, and my good friend Bruce Buchenholz, who had been a regular at our little hotel in Paris, wrote the descriptive material that went underneath the names of all the dishes. In addition to being a doctor, Bruce was an epicurean; he loved good food, and he always helped us. I would just call him, and he was always there when we needed him. He also was a master photographer. Sadly Bruce died during a trip to Paris. We still miss him very much.

"Monique, with her unerring eye for color and decor, designed the original uniforms—blue blouses or shirts, checkered skirts or trousers, and little boots." Monique was the hostess for the first few years, adding charm and luster to the job she found demanding but rewarding. "Monique always has had serious input on the decor and the menu," says Jean-Paul. "Together we selected the Haitian artwork that enlivens the walls, and all the little extra *objets d'art* are her bailiwick."

"And she has a true *bec fin* palate, very critical. I might say, 'Monique, how do you like the soup today?' She never likes to be totally negative, so, *'C'est bon,'* is her reply most times. 'It's good.' Then I know for sure something is amiss. Too salty? Too concentrated? Too heavy on the cream? When she really finds a dish to her taste she will say, 'Excellent, really excellent.'

"I remember the day we opened in 1973. It was kind of cool and rainy and we had a grand total of 12 customers. Bruce Buchenholz shook his head and murmured, 'I'm not sure this is going to work.' I must admit Monique and I also were anxious. Then one day after an iffy three months, a gentleman came up to me in the restaurant. 'My name is Jerome Snyder,' he said. 'I'm a restaurant reviewer for *New York* magazine. I am the "Underground Gourmet." I've been here several times without your knowing it, and I love your place and the food. I'm going to write something about your restaurant, and it will appear next Monday, and it will be very good, so get ready!'

"We rushed to stock the refrigerator, polished up the glasses, and Monique ran to the flower market. Monique was hostessing that day, and we were ready. A rave review, and the place was jammed! Customers were lined up in the tiny foyer and out into the street! And we've been going great ever since!"

Jean-Paul was involved in a second La Bonne Soupe, which he opened with a partner in 1975, but it didn't work out. It lasted two years and then Jean-Paul bowed out; that restaurant eventually closed.

Aside from the magazine article and subsequent good newspaper reviews, Jean-Paul believes his success has been because "We came at the right time with the right idea."

JEAN-PAUL PICOT ON THE FRENCH-AMERICAN COMMUNITY

"Although there are several associations in the French community, the French here keep a low profile. There's no French district in America, to my knowledge. There's no French parade, no French hospital. But there are some 25 thousand French people on the East Coast. I represent them as a delegate of the Ministry of Foreign Affairs, a volunteer position, to help those who need help to get back to France. It puts me in touch with a lot of people and interesting situations."

STEP THIS WAY, LA BONNE SOUPE!

Jean-Paul and Monique Picot took the bistro's name from the avant-garde comedy *La Bonne Soupe* by the French playwright Félicien Marceau. It had a long, successful run in Paris in the 1950s, starring Jeanne Moreau and Marie Bell. The three-act play, which centers on roulette, ends with the words *Et hop! Par ici, la bonne soupe!;* here meaning: "Step up [to the roulette tables], and put your money down, which will give you winnings and ensure you the good life." The play was such a success, it was followed in 1963 by a Twentieth Century Fox film bearing the same title and based on Félicien Marceau's original 1958 play, adapted by Robert Thomas. Among top-ranking stars in the film were Annie Giradot, Jean-Claude Brialy, Claude Dauphin, and Franchot Tone.

The phrase *la bonne soupe* has come to mean the good life, with health, wealth, and happiness. The Picots thought this a

When it opened in 1958, *La Bonne Soupe*, the play by Félicien Marceau, was featured on the cover of *Paris Théâtre*, a popular theatrical magazine.

most appropriate name for their little bistro, and were delighted when they were browsing along Left Bank shops in Paris and came upon a vintage poster for the play. They bought it, framed it, and hung it on the wall next to the staircase at La Bonne Soupe. You can see it there to this day.

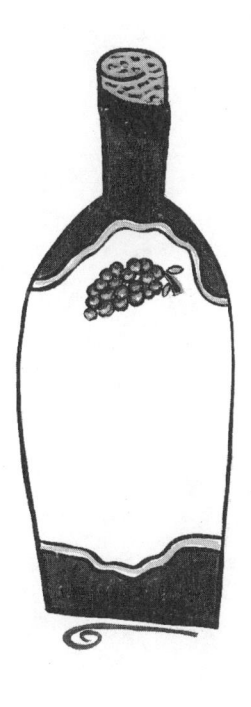

1

Les Bonnes Soupes

A bowl of hearty soup, crusty French bread, and a glass of wine—all for $2.95!

The day's specials are posted on the front window.

It was autumn 1973 and the blackboard menu of the newly opened La Bonne Soupe, on busy Fifty-fifth Street between Fifth and Sixth Avenues, offered one of its specialties, Jean-Paul's Gratinéed Onion Soup. What better way to offer warmth, comfort, and camaraderie than to ladle out Jean-Paul Picot's version of the celebrated onion soup from the Les Halles district of Paris, with its spirit-lifting aroma and deeply concentrated flavor?

Now, after twenty-some years, the onion soup is still number one in the bistro's soup lineup. And the price, although a bit heftier than the prevailing price of the halcyon 1970s, is still a bargain.

"It was a winner from the start," Jean-Paul recalls. "I still tell people this soup should be sniffed like fine Cognac before putting your spoon to the bowl.

"When Monique and I and our little advisory board of friends, including Gretchen and Bruce Buchenholz, were putting our heads together to plan our menu, we naturally zeroed in on soups. After the success of the onion soup, the Buchenholzes said to us: 'You must include two fabulous family heirloom recipes from Gretchen's mother, Helen Friedlander.' So we made her Peasant-Style Mushroom and Barley Soup and her Russian Cabbage Soup, which is tart and tangy. Our tasting panel gave them raves and they've remained on our menu all these years."

Little by little the Picots added fresh, fragrant soups from classic French sources: Jean-Paul's Leek and Potato Soup, Carrot Soup, and Vegetable Soup with Basil and Garlic Sauce, with an ever-expanding and rewarding roster. "And, at the request of some of our customers, we added soups from other countries," Jean-Paul explains.

"Our chefs have always been flexible and very creative," he says. Along with the Provençal Vegetable Soup with Basil and Garlic Sauce, Jean-Paul offers a robust Italian Minestrone. In summer, there's a traditional Chilled Green Pea Soup along with the contemporary Dilled Cucumber Soup garnished with smoked salmon. And, to contrast with another classic, Creamy Cauliflower Soup, the original earthy Carrot and Turnip Soup is featured.

"We now serve a galaxy of international favorites," says Jean-Paul, "and our diners love the concept. They look forward to the day's special soups as they do to the other daily specials. We seem to be keeping everyone happy with our traditional bistro fare—and a little bit more. We feel each of our soups can be an immensely satisfying small meal."

And you can easily replicate this concept at home as the perfect little lunch or supper menu. Just add bread, salad, and a good bottle of wine—and *voilà!* These soups in smaller portions will start off a more elaborate meal with panache. Take a peek at our menu suggestions—and set the soup kettle on the stove.

Homemade Beef Broth

- 2 pounds boneless beef stew meat, such as chuck
- 3 pounds beef bones (shin and marrow bones are good)
- 2 large onions, unpeeled, cut in half (see Note)
- 3 medium-size carrots, peeled and cut into 1-inch pieces
- 1 large parsnip, peeled and cut into 1-inch pieces
- 2 ribs celery with their leafy tops, sliced
- 5 quarts water
- *Bouquet garni:* 6 sprigs flat-leaf parsley, 1 bay leaf, 6 whole peppercorns, and ¼ teaspoon dried thyme tied in a cheesecloth square

Place all ingredients in a 2-gallon stockpot and bring to a boil over high heat. Reduce the heat to medium-low, skim off any froth from the top, partially cover the stockpot, and allow the broth to simmer until it has reduced by one-third. This should take 4 to 4½ hours. Check several times during the cooking period and, using a long-handled kitchen spoon, skim off any scum that rises to the top.

Remove the pot from the heat and allow the broth to cool slightly. Remove and discard the bones. Line a large strainer or sieve with a double thickness of cheesecloth and set it over a very large mixing bowl. Carefully strain the broth into the bowl and discard the solids. (You might want to save the meat for hash.)

Pour the warm broth into pint and quart containers, cover, and refrigerate for up to 5 days or freeze for up to 4 months.

Makes about 3 quarts

Note: Leave the onion skins on when making broth. The skins add both color and flavor.

Tip: No salt is used in our broths to permit seasoning to taste in the final recipes.

Putting the Lid On

Partially covering the stockpot, saucepan, Dutch oven, or whatever cooking utensil you're using to make soup is a handy ploy to prevent over-evaporation of the liquid. To partially cover, place the lid on top of the pan, leaving an air space on one side of about ½ inch. The space needn't be this exact size; just make sure that the steam can escape.

Homemade Chicken Broth

5 pounds chicken parts, including legs, backs, thighs, and wings

1 large, unpeeled onion, cut in half (see Note, page 8)

3 large carrots, peeled and cut into 1-inch pieces

1 large parsnip, peeled and cut into 1-inch pieces

3 ribs celery with their leafy tops, sliced

1 cup dry white wine (optional)

5 quarts water

Bouquet garni: 6 sprigs flat-leaf parsley, 1 bay leaf, 6 whole peppercorns, and ¼ teaspoon dried thyme tied in a cheesecloth square

Rinse the chicken parts thoroughly under cold, running water and, if desired, remove and discard the skins. Place all ingredients in a 2-gallon stockpot. Bring to a boil over high heat. Skim off any foam from the top, reduce the heat to medium-low, partially cover, and simmer until the liquid has reduced by one-third, about 2 hours. Using a long-handled kitchen spoon, skim off any scum that rises to the top as it simmers.

Remove the pot from the heat and allow the broth to cool slightly. Line a large strainer or sieve with a double thickness of cheesecloth and place it over a very large mixing bowl. Carefully strain the broth into the bowl and discard the chicken and vegetables; all their flavor and goodness have now gone into the broth.

Pour the broth into pint or quart containers, cover, and refrigerate for up to 3 days or freeze for up to 4 months.

Makes about 3 quarts

Broth Basics

A good broth is the base of countless soups, stews, and sauces; and a good homemade broth really has it all over purchased canned broth or bouillon cubes. True, it will take a little longer to assemble the ingredients and cook up your own broth than to open a can, but you'll have the pride and comfort of knowing your broth is going to impart more flavor to a dish and is additive free.

Preparing the broth is really not all that labor intensive. Once the ingredients are in the pot and simmering, all that's needed is an occasional check, possibly a little skimming. It's a pleasant project for a stay-at-home afternoon or evening, and the broth has the added plus of freezing well.

La Bonne Soupe's Chef Francis Freund is a purist when it comes to stocks: He first browns the bones to give added depth of flavor and sets the stockpots on the stove in the early morning to ensure that the little bistro always has a freshly made, rich base for its soups and stews. But for the home cook, this cookbook offers a simplified (no browning) yet satisfying version that will stand you in excellent stead.

Soupe Paysanne à l'Orge

PEASANT-STYLE MUSHROOM AND BARLEY SOUP

The Picots gave Helen Friedlander's family recipe a French accent by adding lamb and a bouquet garni. The Picot's result is deeply flavorful. Although La Bonne Soupe's chef relies on fresh white mushrooms, you may follow the lead of many Europeans, who use dried mushrooms for their concentrated, woodsy flavor.

Keep in mind that barley expands voluptuously as it cooks and, most certainly, when stored in the refrigerator, so you will want to check the saucepan and be ready to add additional broth or water, if necessary.

2 tablespoons vegetable oil

1 large onion, chopped

3 ribs celery, thinly sliced

1 large carrot, peeled and thinly sliced

¼ pound boneless lamb shoulder, trimmed of fat and cut into ¼-inch dice

½ pound fresh white mushrooms, sliced, or ½ cup dried mushrooms

2½ quarts Homemade Beef Broth (page 3) or low-sodium canned broth

½ cup plus 2 tablespoons medium-size pearl barley, rinsed and drained

Bouquet garni: 3 sprigs flat-leaf parsley, 1 small bay leaf, and 2 sprigs dill tied in a cheesecloth square

Salt and freshly ground pepper to taste

Heat the oil in a 3- or 4-quart saucepan or Dutch oven over medium-low heat. Add the onion and cook, uncovered, over medium heat until wilted and translucent, 3 to 4 minutes. Add the celery and carrot and cook until the vegetables just start to soften, 4 to 5 minutes.

Add the lamb and cook, stirring, until the meat starts to lose color, 3 to 4 minutes. Add the fresh mushrooms and cook, stirring, just until they start to exude their juices, about 3 minutes. If you are using dried mushrooms, place them in a small bowl, cover with water, and let them stand for 15 minutes. Then drain, add them to the saucepan, and proceed.

Pour in the beef broth and add the barley and bouquet garni. Bring the liquid to a boil, then reduce the heat to medium-low, cover partially, and simmer until the barley and meat are tender, about 1 hour 30 minutes. Check occasionally and skim off any scum that may rise to the top. When the soup has cooked for 1 hour, fish out and discard the bouquet garni, and season with salt and pepper.

The soup can be refrigerated, covered, for up to 3 days. If needed, reheat the soup over medium heat. Ladle into warmed soup bowls.

Makes 4 to 6 servings

Bread: A nicely tart, chewy rye bread is an ideal consort for this soup.

Lunch: A big bowl of this lusty pottage makes a great cold-weather one-dish lunch. And, after all that filling barley and bread, a refreshing salad of seasonal fruits—apples, pears, and orange segments—makes a welcome windup.

Weep No More

If slicing and chopping onions bring tears to your eyes, try this: After removing the papery outer onion skin, peel off the next two layers of onion before cutting it up. You will lose a little of the onion but your eyes will thank you!

Dinner: Serve the soup in small bowls or cups and follow with Calf's Liver with Pommery Mustard Sauce (page 114) garnished with Monique's Garlicky Mashed Potatoes (page 137) and chunky carrots (carrots cut into 1-inch pieces and steamed until tender).

Dessert: A warm compote of stewed apples, pears, and dried figs can be served in pretty dessert coupes; pass a cruet of tawny port for diners to pour over the fruit. Brew a pot of espresso.

Wine: A full-bodied, somewhat assertive red wine, such as a Côtes du Rhône, matches well with both the soup and the stew.

Low-Fat Plan: Omit the oil and the lamb. You'll still have a full-flavored soup, especially if you use the dried mushrooms. Sprinkle all the vegetables with 3 tablespoons defatted beef broth or water, cover partially, and cook over low heat until they start to soften, 4 to 5 minutes. Proceed with the recipe.

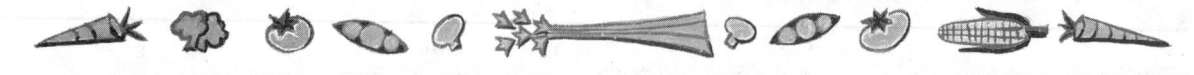

How to Give Canned Broth a Lift

If your supply of homemade broth runs out, canned chicken or beef broth and dehydrated powders or cubes make handy substitutes. Most, unfortunately, contain a few fat globules (which are easily skimmed off) and monosodium glutamate. For those concerned with MSG, brands sold in health food stores and in some health-conscious supermarkets are additive free.

In any case, do buy the low-sodium canned broths to reduce the extraneous salt. Here's how to give canned broths a bit more authority and pizzazz:

Four 14-ounce cans low-sodium chicken or beef broth
1 large onion, peeled and thinly sliced
2 shallots, finely chopped
1 large carrot, peeled and cut into thin rounds
8 sprigs flat-leaf parsley

¾ cup dry white wine
Pinch of dried thyme
Freshly ground pepper to taste

Place all the ingredients in a 2½-quart saucepan and bring to a boil over high heat. Reduce the heat to medium and cook, partially covered, until the vegetables are soft, 15 to 20 minutes. Pour the liquid through a strainer and cool slightly; discard the vegetables.

Pour the broth into pint or quart containers, cover, and refrigerate for up to 3 days or freeze for up to 4 months.

Makes about 2 quarts

Tip: When using this broth as part of a recipe, reduce the amount of salt required in the recipe. Even low-sodium canned broth can contain nearly 700 milligrams of salt per cup.

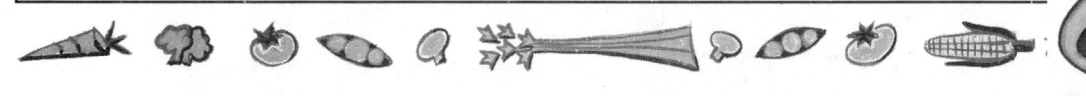

Soupe Crème Andalouse

CREAMY TOMATO SOUP

Quite often French dishes using cooked tomatoes bear Spanish names, for the French associate tomatoes with the sunny south, and just below the Pyrenees lies sunny Spain. The French attitude toward Spain tends to be a romantic one. Think of Bizet and his world-acclaimed chef-d'oeuvre *Carmen. Think of Manuel de Falla, composing Spanish music while sitting in a Paris apartment. Think of Picasso and his leadership of the School of Paris. Then try this sunny tomato soup. The natural thickener is rice.*

- 3 tablespoons unsalted butter
- 2 cloves garlic, minced
- 2 medium-size onions, chopped
- 5 ribs celery, chopped
- 5 large, firm-ripe tomatoes, peeled, seeded, and chopped
- 1 quart Homemade Chicken Broth (page 3) or low-sodium canned broth
- One 6-ounce can tomato paste
- 1 cup raw long-grain rice
- 1 cup light or heavy cream
- Salt and freshly ground pepper to taste

Melt the butter in a 3-quart saucepan over low heat. Add the garlic and onions and cook, stirring occasionally, until softened but not browned, 3 to 4 minutes. Add the celery and tomatoes and cook, stirring, until the celery starts to soften, 3 to 4 minutes.

Add the broth and tomato paste, stirring to blend well. Raise the heat to high and bring the liquid to a boil. Add the rice, reduce the heat to medium, cover partially, and cook until the rice is tender, 20 to 25 minutes.

Remove the pan from the heat and cool slightly. Purée the mixture in a food processor or blender, in batches if necessary.

At this point the soup can be refrigerated, tightly covered, for up to 3 days. If needed, reheat the soup over medium heat until hot but not boiling. Slowly add the cream, stirring to blend, and season with salt and pepper. Reduce the heat to low and cook until the soup is piping hot. Don't allow the liquid to come to a boil. Ladle into warmed soup bowls.

Makes 4 to 6 servings

Tip: If you plan to make the soup ahead and reheat it, don't add the cream until just before serving.

Bread: Cut a crusty peasant loaf into thick slices.

Lunch: Serve wedges of Asparagus Quiche (page 57) and a salad of thinly sliced cooked beets and red onions tossed with a little olive oil, red wine vinegar, and a touch of Dijon mustard.

Dinner: Sustain the sunny aura by serving a smooth, creamy Salt Cod Puréed with Garlic, Olive Oil, and Cream (page 78) and a salad of leafy greens tossed in a light, mustardy vinaigrette.

Dessert: Scoop rich cherry ice cream into dessert coupes and garnish with Lacy Tile Cookies (page 158).

Wine: With the soup, pour small glasses of chilled fino sherry or a young white Spanish Rioja, lightly chilled. For the salt cod, a chilled Rosé de Provence or California White Zinfandel would make a light and pleasingly fruity pairing.

Low-Fat Plan: Omit the butter. Sprinkle 3 tablespoons of defatted chicken broth, water, or white wine over the garlic and onion, cover and cook until the vegetables are softened but not browned, 5 minutes. Repeat this procedure for the celery and tomatoes, but do not add any broth. Substitute skim milk for the cream, or serve the soup without any enrichment. It will still taste ambrosial.

Soupe à l'Oignon Gratinée Jean-Paul

JEAN-PAUL'S GRATINÉED ONION SOUP

Clearly this is the most popular soup at the bistro all year round. "Even on a sweltering summer day diners take comfort in our onion soup," says le patron, Jean-Paul. "It was the same at our La Pomme d'Amour restaurant in Paris. It may sound like boasting, but our chef, Francis Freund, makes a Soupe à l'Oignon Gratinée that most closely resembles its counterpart in Paris's Les Halles as any we've tasted here. And to back me up, just a few months ago La Bonne Soupe's onion soup was voted the best in the entire city of New York by New York's Daily News.*"*

- 3 tablespoons unsalted butter
- 4 large sweet onions (about 1½ pounds total), thinly sliced
- 1 teaspoon sugar (optional, see Note)
- 1 cup dry white wine
- 2 quarts Homemade Beef Broth (page 3) or low-sodium canned broth
- 2 ribs celery with leaves, each rib cut in half
- Salt and freshly ground pepper to taste
- ¼ cup dry fino sherry
- 4 to 6 slices baguette, cut ¼ inch thick, lightly toasted
- ¼ cup coarsely grated Emmental, Gruyère, or other Swiss-type cheese

Melt the butter in a 3- or 4-quart saucepan over low heat. Add the onions and sugar. Cook over low heat, stirring occasionally, until the onions are lightly caramelized, 20 to 30 minutes. (The longer the onions cook slowly the richer the flavor of the soup.)

Which Onions?

When making onion soup, choose only firm sweet onions, such as Bermuda or Spanish. You want sweet flavor and meltability. Large, white California onions never softened enough, even with longer cooking time, nor did they impart the desired sweetness.

Add the white wine and cook over medium-high heat until the wine reduces to about half, about 5 minutes. Add the broth, celery, and salt and pepper and bring the liquid to a boil over high heat. Reduce the heat to low, cover partially, and allow the soup to simmer until the onions are meltingly tender, about 40 minutes. Remove and discard the celery. Add the sherry and simmer the soup for another 5 minutes.

To serve, preheat the oven to 375°F. Ladle the soup into individual ovenproof bowls. Top each with 1 slice of baguette, sprinkle with 1 tablespoon cheese, and place the bowls on a cookie sheet. Heat in the center of the preheated oven just until the cheese melts and bubbles, 5 to 6 minutes. Carefully remove from the oven and serve at once.

Makes 4 to 6 servings

Note: The tiny bit of sugar added to the onions helps caramelize them, but the onions themselves will caramelize if they're sweet enough and if you're patient enough!

Bread: Offer a basket of crisp-crusted baguette cut into chunky slices.

Lunch: A salad of slightly bitter endive and watercress tossed with Jean-Paul's Zesty Vinaigrette (page 146) makes a light and refreshing addition.

Dinner: Follow with Chicken Tarragon (page 97).

Dessert: Serve mix-made brownies topped with a scoop of strawberry sherbet.

Wine: Pour a light French Chardonnay, such as a Mâcon-Villages Blanc with the soup. For the chicken, you could continue with the same wine or switch to an elegant Meursault, if you like.

Low-Fat Plan: Omit the butter. Place the onions in a saucepan, sprinkle with ¼ cup of water or white wine and the sugar. Cover and cook over low heat, stirring occasionally, until the onions are softened, about 30 minutes. Float croutons without the cheese on top and skip the oven procedure.

Croûtons

TOASTED BREAD CUBES

A day-old baguette or ficelle is best for this. Cut the bread into ¼-inch slices. Stack the slices on a cutting board in convenient-to-handle piles of 4 or 5, then cut into ½-inch dice. Place the diced bread in one layer on a cookie sheet and toast in a preheated 400°F oven until golden, 3 to 4 minutes. (Check after 3 minutes, as ovens tend to vary in temperature.)

Cool the bread cubes and store in a tightly covered container up to 1 week.

*Makes 2 to 4 cups,
depending on the size of the loaf*

Note: Some cooks fry their bread cubes in oil, but this may impart an unnecessary oily flavor to the soups and salads you're garnishing with the Croûtons.

Look to Your Laurels

Bay leaf, or in French *laurier*, is widely used in France and in Mediterranean countries. It's also grown here in some of our southern states and in California. Bay leaf is one of the herbs used in the classic *bouquet garni,* along with parsley and thyme, although there are some regional variations. The bay leaves' pungent, faintly eucalyptus-cinnamon flavor perks up soups and stews and is a major pickling herb.

When using bay leaves, there's one caveat: Overcooking can impart a bitter tinge to this herb. When possible, try to fish out and discard bay leaves from your soups and stews after 1 hour of cooking. And you definitely want to avoid serving a bay leaf on a dinner plate or in a soup bowl; the leaf is quite inedible.

Soupe aux Choux à la Russe

RUSSIAN CABBAGE SOUP

When Jean-Paul and Monique were first enjoying married life in Paris, they ran a little hotel on the Rue de Sèvres. "We were running it like a little palace," Jean-Paul recalls. "I picked up our clients at the airport and drove them to the hotel for the weekend. They dined in fine restaurants and went to the theater. It was a lovely package, and we made many friends. Among these were Gretchen and Bruce Buchenholz. When we came to New York and decided to open La Bonne Soupe the Buchenholzes were most helpful. 'We have some family recipes we think would fit right in with your bistro menu,' they said. And that's how this delicious Russian-style cabbage soup and the mushroom and barley soup became top favorites."

- 1 small head green cabbage (about 1½ pounds) or 1 pound prepared sauerkraut
- 1 tablespoon unsalted butter
- 1 quart tomato juice
- 1 quart Homemade Chicken Broth (page 4) or low-sodium canned broth
- Salt and freshly ground pepper to taste
- ⅓ to ½ cup sugar to taste
- ¼ cup red wine vinegar
- 2 teaspoons freshly squeezed lemon juice
- 1 cup golden or dark raisins
- ½ cup sour cream for garnish

Core and thinly slice the cabbage (If you are using a food processor, fit it with the thinnest slicing blade.) If using the sauerkraut, drain it and discard the pickling liquid. Rinse the sauerkraut well under cold running water and squeeze dry.

Melt the butter in a 3-quart Dutch oven or heavy saucepan over medium-low heat. Add the cabbage or sauerkraut and cook, stirring occasionally, over medium heat until it begins to wilt, about 10 minutes. Add all the remaining ingredients except the sour cream. Raise the heat to high and bring to a boil; then reduce the heat to medium, cover partially, and simmer until the cabbage is tender, about 30 minutes. Taste to adjust the seasoning. You may wish to add a bit more sugar or lemon juice. There should be a nice balance of tart and sweetness.

When ready to serve, ladle the soup into warmed soup bowls and spoon a rounded tablespoon of sour cream in the centers.

Makes 6 servings

Bread: Pile a basket with sliced dark and chewy pumpernickel, and pass a crock of whipped sweet butter.

Lunch: All that's needed to make a light lunch is a platter of assorted cheeses and dessert.

Dinner: Have the soup as the start of a hearty meal that includes braised brisket of beef, boiled potatoes, and a big bowl of steamed carrots and bright green peas.

Dessert: Garnish wedges of Apple Tart (page 163) with small scoops of French vanilla ice cream. Or for a low-fat dessert, try Peaches Poached in Red Wine (page 159).

Wine: With the braised beef, a gutsy Gigondas or Châteauneuf-du-Pape from France's Rhône Valley.

Low-Fat Plan: Omit the butter when cooking the cabbage. Sprinkle the cabbage with 3 tablespoons defatted chicken broth, water, or white wine, partially cover, and steam over low heat until soft, 10 minutes. If you are using sauerkraut, simply add it to the saucepan and continue cooking directions. Substitute nonfat sour cream.

Soupe aux Poireaux et Pommes de Terre

JEAN-PAUL'S LEEK AND POTATO SOUP

"As any French chef will tell you, the most important vegetable in the soup cook's larder is the leek, the elegantly elongated member of the onion family," Jean-Paul points out, as he deftly dices a couple of splendid-looking poireaux. *Leek and potato soup certainly has that* je ne sais quoi—*the indefinable something—that sets it apart from a soup made with potatoes and onions. If you're at all skeptical about this, make this soup with onions in place of the leeks. It will be a very good soup. Then make the soup using leeks. Aha! Now you see, or rather, taste, the difference.*

3 tablespoons unsalted butter

2 medium-size onions, chopped

4 medium-size leeks (about 2 pounds total), white and light green parts only, trimmed, washed, and coarsely chopped

1 quart Homemade Chicken Broth (page 4) or low-sodium canned broth

4 medium-size boiling potatoes, peeled and cut into ½-inch dice

1 cup heavy cream

1 cup milk

Salt and freshly ground white pepper to taste

2 tablespoons finely minced fresh chives or scallions for garnish

Melt the butter in a heavy 3-quart saucepan or Dutch oven over medium heat. Add the onions and cook, stirring occasionally, until they are softened but not browned, 4 to 5 minutes. Add the leeks and cook over medium heat just until they start to soften, 3 to 4 minutes.

Add the broth and bring the liquid to a boil over high heat. Add the potatoes, reduce the heat to medium, cover partially, and simmer until the potatoes are falling-apart tender, 25 to 30 minutes.

Remove the pan from the heat and let the mixture cool slightly, then purée in a food processor or in a blender. You may need to do this in batches.

Return the purée to the saucepan and, over low heat, add the cream and milk. Season with salt and pepper and simmer just until heated through. Ladle into warmed soup bowls and sprinkle with the chives or scallions.

Makes 4 to 6 servings

Bread: A crisp-crusted semolina loaf is an agreeable companion with this soup.

Lunch: Follow with wedges of Quiche Lorraine with Bacon and Ham (page 55) and a salad of sliced tomatoes bathed in a shallot-studded vinaigrette.

Dinner: Serve roast chicken garnished with broccoli florets and steamed fingerling potatoes (slender, small, tan-skinned beauties) or other small potatoes.

Dessert: Arrange two different sherbets in glass compote dishes—pineapple and raspberry or lemon and lime—and pass a platter of thin, crisp Lacy Tile Cookies (page 158).

Wine: For the roast chicken a full-bodied white wine, such as a Saint Véran or Pouilly-Fuissé would be a most felicitous match.

Low-Fat Plan: Omit the butter. Sprinkle the vegetables with 3 to 4 tablespoons defatted broth or water, cover, and cook over low heat until they have wilted. Proceed with the recipe through puréeing the soup. At this point, simply return the soup to the saucepan and taste for seasoning. Then slowly add 2 cups of skim milk and heat until piping hot.

Black Bean Soup

"By popular demand we have added black bean soup to our roster of bonnes soupes," said Jean-Paul Picot. On a bone-chilling winter's day, this wonderfully warming mélange of sensuous black beans enlivened with spices and sherry is a perfect warmer-upper. It's hearty enough to be a little meal in itself. Or make it the splendid start of a robust dinner.

¼ pound slab bacon, skin removed, cut into ¼-inch dice

2 or 3 cloves garlic, crushed

1 large onion, chopped

2 ribs celery, chopped

2 medium-size carrots, chopped

1 pound dried black beans, rinsed, picked through, soaked overnight in water to cover, drained, and rinsed again or use the quick soaking method (see "Quick Bean-Soaking Method," page 13)

2 quarts Homemade Beef Broth (page 3) or low-sodium canned broth

1 teaspoon chili powder

1 teaspoon sweet paprika

1 teaspoon ground cumin

Freshly ground pepper to taste

½ cup dry fino sherry

Salt to taste (see Note)

3 tablespoons sour cream for garnish

Cook the bacon, stirring, in a 4-quart saucepan over medium heat until some of the fat is rendered and the bacon is lightly browned, 3 to 4 minutes. Add the garlic, onion, celery, and carrots and cook, stirring, just until the vegetables start to soften, 5 to 6 minutes.

Add the beans, broth, chili powder, paprika, cumin, and pepper. Bring to a boil over high heat, then reduce the heat to medium-low, partially cover, and simmer until the beans are soft, about 1½ hours.

Using a long-handled ladle, take out 3 cups of the soup, cool slightly, and purée in a blender or food processor. Return the purée to the saucepan stirring to blend. Stir in the sherry and taste to correct the seasoning. Simmer the soup for another 2 minutes, then ladle into warm deep soup bowls. Garnish with a spoonful of sour cream.

Makes 6 to 8 servings

Note: When cooking with beans, don't add salt until the beans have become soft. Adding salt too early tends to toughen the beans' outer skins and deter their ability to absorb liquid.

Bread: Arrange chunks of thick-crusted sourdough bread in a napkin-lined basket.

Lunch: The soup is hearty enough to be followed by a simple salad of steamed broccoli florets, green beans, and matchstick strips of red bell pepper tossed in a light, oil-and-vinegar dressing. And keep the bread basket filled!

Dinner: Pan-cook pepper-encrusted minute steaks and surround them with crisp, golden French Fried Potatoes (page 142). Add a salad of thinly sliced cucumbers bathed in white wine vinegar with a dash of sugar, and salt and pepper to taste.

Dessert: Pile Melting Chocolate Mousse (page 162) into dessert coupes and cap with a minimound of lightly sweetened whipped cream.

Wine: With the black bean soup, pour a lightly chilled dry fino sherry for an elegant pairing. With the steaks, offer a Bordeaux Petit Château (a moderately priced château-bottled wine from Bordeaux) or a California Cabernet Sauvignon.

Low-Fat Plan: Place the garlic, onion, carrots, and celery in a saucepan, sprinkle with 3 tablespoons defatted broth or water, partially cover, and simmer over low heat until the vegetables are wilted, 5 to 6 minutes. Proceed with the recipe.

Quick Bean-Soaking Method

If you can't soak the beans overnight, use this alternative technique. Rinse the beans well under cold running water and place in a saucepan large enough to hold the beans and cold water to cover them by 3 inches. Bring the beans to a boil over high heat, then reduce the heat to medium and continue to parboil the beans for 5 minutes. Remove from the heat, cover, and let the beans steep for 1 to 2 hours. Drain and rinse the beans briefly under cold running water. They are now ready for cooking.

Potage aux Pois Cassés

SPLIT PEA SOUP

This classic vegetable soup evolved throughout the centuries, with recipes varying from province to province. Like other vegetable soups, it comes under the umbrella term potages santés, *or healthful soups.*

In this version, a ham bone gives a nice, smoky flavor and textural interest, but if you prefer a meatless soup, leave out the ham and be more generous with the pepper mill. Keep in mind that split peas, along with lentils, do not need to be soaked before cooking.

About 2 quarts Homemade Chicken Broth (page 4) or low-sodium canned broth

1 pound green or yellow split peas, rinsed

1 small ham bone

2 medium-size onions, thinly sliced

2 medium-size carrots, peeled and thinly sliced

2 ribs celery, thinly sliced (save the leafy tops)

Bouquet garni: 4 sprigs flat-leaf parsley, 2 leafy tops of celery, 1 bay leaf, and ¼ teaspoon dried chervil tied in a cheesecloth square

Salt and freshly ground pepper to taste

1 cup light or heavy cream

1 cup *Croûtons* (page 9) for garnish

In a heavy 6-quart saucepan or Dutch oven, bring the broth to a boil over high heat. Add all remaining ingredients except the cream and croutons. Reduce the heat to medium-low, partially cover the pan, and simmer until the split peas are tender, 1 to 1¼ hours.

Remove and discard the *bouquet garni*. Lift out and place the ham bone on a cutting board. Slice off the meat and cut it into ¼-inch dice and discard the bone. Cool the soup slightly, then purée in batches in a food processor or blender. Return the purée to the saucepan, add the ham and cream, and simmer over medium-low heat just until heated through. If the soup seems too thick, thin it with a little more broth or water. When ready to serve, ladle into warmed soup bowls and garnish with the *Croûtons*. The soup will keep up to 3 days in the refrigerator and it freezes very well.

Makes 6 to 8 servings

Bread: The Picots like a bread with good, robust flavor, such as a crusty sourdough or country peasant loaf.

Lunch: Filets of Flounder and Shrimp in Paper (page 90) and a trio of steamed new potatoes makes a satisfying little meal.

Dinner: For an elegant entrée, serve Chicken Tarragon (page 97), garnished with steamed baby brussels sprouts and herbed rice.

Dessert: Warm some made-ahead crêpes (page 151), fill them with pistachio ice cream and finish with a streak of Chocolate Sauce (page 152).

Wine: With the soup and flounder, uncork a fruity white, such as a Saint Véran. With the chicken, you could also serve the Saint Véran or pour a light red Mercurey from Burgundy.

Low-Fat Plan: Skip the cream in the soup and cook the flounder with lemon juice and parsley.

Potage aux Carottes et Navets

CREAMY, EARTHY CARROT AND TURNIP SOUP

This is a great favorite at La Bonne Soupe. Its origins go back to the war years, when the Picots simmered their root vegetables in water. The butter, cream, chicken broth, and fresh ginger were luxurious refinements that were incorporated after the war. In any case, one taste of this bracing pottage, and you'll agree that carrots and turnips make a terrific taste and texture team. Garlic adds another beguiling flavor, and the cream enrichment gives a silken finish.

3 tablespoons unsalted butter

2 medium-size onions, chopped

2 cloves garlic, minced

1 pound carrots (about 4 large), peeled and chopped

1 pound turnips (about 4 medium-size), peeled and chopped

3 ribs celery, chopped

2 quarts Homemade Chicken Broth (page 4) or low-sodium canned broth

1 teaspoon grated fresh ginger or ¼ teaspoon ground

Salt and freshly ground pepper to taste

1 cup heavy cream

Melt the butter over medium heat in a 4-quart saucepan. Add the onions and garlic and cook, stirring occasionally, until softened but not browned, 4 to 5 minutes. Add the carrots, turnips, and celery and cook, stirring, until they start to soften, 3 to 4 minutes.

Pour in the broth, and add the ginger and salt and pepper. Cook, partially covered, over medium heat until the vegetables are very soft, 15 to 20 minutes.

Remove the pan from the heat and purée the soup in batches in a food processor or blender. Return the soup to the saucepan and stir in the cream. Cook over low heat just until the soup is piping hot. Serve in warmed soup bowls.

Makes 6 to 8 servings

Bread: Slice a caraway-flecked rye bread and pass a crock of sweet butter at the table.

Lunch: Cut pretty, wedge-shape portions of Spinach Quiche (page 58) and garnish the plates with a cluster of cherry tomatoes.

Dinner: Prepare Monique's Roast Chicken Stuffed with Goat Cheese Croutons (page 102), served with Monique's Garlicky Mashed Potatoes (page 137) and Monique's Tomatoes with Garlic and Herbs (page 139).

Dessert: Place segments of sweet clementines in glass compotes and add seedless green grapes. Pour a little Rosy Raspberry Sauce (page 164) over the fruit and strew with shards of shredded coconut.

Wine: A glass of chilled fino sherry makes pleasant sipping with the soup. Monique and Jean-Paul enjoy a Bordeaux Petit Château (a moderately priced château-bottled wine from Bordeaux) with the roast chicken, or you could uncork a California Cabernet Sauvignon.

Low-Fat Plan: Omit the butter and forget the cream. Sprinkle all the vegetables with 3 tablespoons of water, cover, and simmer until they start to soften, 5 to 6 minutes. Proceed with the recipe. The soup will be absolutely delicious even without its final enrichment.

Our Darling Clementines

Little tangerine look-alikes, clementines are hybrids of the tangerine and the Seville (bitter) orange developed around 1902 by the Algerian priest Père Clément. These little orange beauties have an extra buzz of sweetness to offset their sprightly tartness, and they're intensely fragrant, with a deep orange, smooth skin and a juicy, seedless pulp that's loaded with vitamin C. You'll find them in supermarkets and specialty food stores from late October until April, imported mainly from Spain and Morocco.

Although clementines are delectable as a table fruit, they're a fine addition to salads or combined with grapes, apples, and pears on a cheese tray. They also make inviting toppings for tarts and cakes.

When buying clementines look for fruit that have blemish-free, shiny, deep orange skins and that are heavy for their size. You'll often find the fruit sporting a couple of shiny green leaves. Pile the clementines in a shallow basket, along with a few grape clusters for a colorful table centerpiece.

Keep clementines in a cool, dry place or in the refrigerator, but bring them back to room temperature before serving.

Soupe au Pistou

Vegetable Soup with Basil and Garlic Sauce

Unquestionably, this is the most popular soup in the region of Nice, according to Jacques Médecin, former mayor of Nice and chronicler of Niçois cuisine in his book La Cuisine du Comté de Nice. *While some say that the word* pistou *is Niçois for basil, Médecin says that the true Niçois term for basil is* balico.

The base of the soup is a mélange of vegetables, but the thickener is vermicelli, thin little cords of pasta. The vegetables may vary, but the essentials are white beans, leeks, celery, carrots, zucchini, and tomatoes. The final enrichment is an addition of pistou—*premium olive oil blended with fresh basil leaves, Parmesan cheese, and more than a suggestion of garlic.*

For the soup

- 1 cup dried white beans, such as navy or pea, rinsed, picked through, soaked overnight in water to cover, drained, and rinsed again or use the quick soaking method (page 13)
- 2 quarts Homemade Chicken Broth (page 4), Homemade Beef Broth (page 3), or low-sodium canned broth
- 1 medium-size onion, chopped
- 1 medium-size leek, white part only, halved lengthwise, washed well, and thinly sliced
- 1 rib celery, thinly sliced
- 2 large carrots, peeled and thinly sliced
- 1 medium-size zucchini, ends trimmed and cut into ½-inch dice
- ⅓ pound green beans, ends trimmed and cut into ½-inch pieces
- 1 large boiling potato (about ½ pound), peeled and cut into ½-inch dice
- 1 cup dried vermicelli or other long, thin pasta, broken into 1-inch pieces
- 2 medium-size tomatoes, peeled, seeded, and cut into ½-inch dice

For the *pistou*

- 3 or 4 garlic cloves, chopped
- 1 cup packed fresh basil leaves
- ¼ cup extra-virgin olive oil
- Salt and freshly ground pepper to taste
- ⅓ cup finely grated Parmesan cheese

Prepare the soup:

Place the beans in a 2-quart saucepan and add enough cold water to cover by 1 inch. Bring the beans to a boil over high heat and simmer, covered, over medium heat until tender, about 45 minutes. Drain the beans in a colander and reserve.

Place the broth in a 6-quart Dutch oven or heavy casserole and bring to a boil over high heat. Add the onion, leek, celery, carrots, zucchini, green beans, and potato; reduce the heat to medium and simmer, partially covered, until the vegetables are tender but not falling apart, about 20 minutes. Add the vermicelli, tomatoes, and reserved beans and simmer, partially covered, until the vermicelli is tender, about 10 minutes.

Prepare the *pistou:*

While the vermicelli is cooking, make the *pistou.* In a small food processor or blender, purée the garlic and basil with the oil and pep-

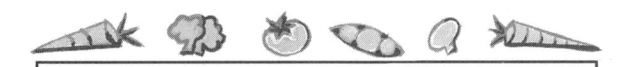

per. Add salt, if necessary, and stir in the cheese until well-blended. Transfer the *pistou* to a small sauceboat or bowl.

Ladle the soup into warmed soup bowls and pass the pistou separately.

Makes 6 to 8 servings

Tip: When preparing the pistou, *you might want to double or triple the recipe and store some as a zippy sauce for pasta or as a tangy dip for* crudités. *It will keep, tightly covered, for up to 2 months in the refrigerator.*

Bread: The Niçois would cut a big, round country loaf into good thick chunks and pile it into a wicker bread basket.

Lunch: Keep the Provençal mood by cooking large shrimp in a little olive oil with chopped garlic, chopped tomatoes, salt and pepper to taste, and lots of chopped fresh flat-leaf parsley.

Dinner: Jean-Paul's Grilled Tuna by the Sea (page 84) makes a fine entrée, with a side dish of Monique's Garlicky Mashed Potatoes (page 137) and a salad of thickly sliced tomatoes dressed with a touch of extra virgin olive oil and chopped fresh basil leaves.

Dessert: Splurge with Fondue au Chocolat (page 157) and cubes of seasonal fruit.

Wine: With the shrimp, a nicely chilled Rosé de Provence makes perfect sipping. For the tuna, see Jean-Paul's suggestion on page 86. A fruity Rosé d'Anjou or Bandol Rosé from Provence will partner the zingy *pistou* very nicely.

Low-Fat Plan: For the *pistou*, substitute ¼ cup white wine or defatted chicken broth for the oil and use a low-fat hard cheese in place of the Parmesan.

Lentil Lore

Lentils cook faster than other legumes and need not be soaked before cooking. Rinse them thoroughly and look for any little pebbles or detritus that may cling to them. Brown lentils are the most widely available variety. The smaller, Mideastern green lentils and Indian red lentils are extremely quick cooking and can easily become mushy. And, although the French green lentils are flavorful and make a delicious soup, they're harder to find than the brown lentils, which are perfectly fine for this satisfying soup.

Soupe aux Lentilles
(Potage d'Esau)

LENTIL SOUP

"When I was quite a small boy, I was assigned to many kitchen chores by Grandmère Marguerite, who was a fabulous cook and a bit of a martinet in the kitchen. Among my least favorite chores," says Jean-Paul, *"was cleaning and picking through what always seemed to be endless piles of lentils to find any little stones that might be lurking there.*

"I knew Grandmère's soup was wonderful, and everyone in the house looked forward to lentil soup day. But, standing there in the big kitchen, I would grit my teeth and wish I were out in the fields playing ball with my friends. Of course, much later, when everyone at the dinner table applauded Grandmère's lentil

amily group in Lagor: Grandmère Marguerite Forsans (second from right) with Jean-Paul Picot and his brothers, Henri and Robert.

soup and asked for seconds, I was patted on the back for my contribution. The soup tasted absolutely divine, and I even felt a little proud of my culinary achievement."

4 slices bacon, cut into ¼-inch dice
1 large onion, finely chopped
3 or 4 cloves garlic, crushed
2 ribs celery, finely chopped
2 medium-size carrots, peeled and chopped
2 quarts Homemade Beef Broth (page 3) or low-sodium canned broth
Salt and freshly ground pepper to taste
¼ teaspoon ground red pepper
⅓ teaspoon each dried thyme, chervil, and marjoram, mixed
6 sprigs flat-leaf parsley
1 pound lentils, rinsed and picked over (see "Lentil Lore," page 17)
2 tablespoons red wine vinegar

In a 6-quart Dutch oven or saucepan, cook the bacon over medium heat until some of the fat has rendered and the bacon begins to crisp, about 5 minutes. Add the onion, garlic, celery, and carrots and cook, stirring occasionally, until the vegetables start to soften, about 6 minutes.

Add the broth, turn the heat to high, and bring to a boil. Reduce the heat to low and add all the remaining ingredients. Simmer, with the lid partially on, until the lentils are tender, 30 to 40 minutes. Remove and discard the parsley.

Using a long-handled ladle, spoon out 3 cups of the lentils, with a little of the liquid. Place in a food processor or a blender and purée until smooth.

Return the puréed lentils to the soup pot and stir to blend well. Taste and adjust the seasoning; the soup is ready to serve. Or store, covered, in the refrigerator for up to 4 days. The flavor improves upon reheating.

Makes 4 to 6 servings

Bread: Country rye or a five-grain loaf and a big mound of whipped sweet butter make good munching.

Lunch: When spooned generously into deep bowls, all that's needed is a salad of sliced cooked beets and thinly sliced red onion rings in a zesty vinaigrette.

Dinner: Follow with an herbed roasted rack of lamb served enticingly pink, with creamy mashed potatoes and a cluster of crunchy bright green broccoli florets.

Dessert: Serve Pears Poached in White Wine (page 159) garnished with a pouf of crème fraîche.

Wine: With the lentil soup, sip a hearty Côtes du Rhône or French country wine such as Madiran or Minervois. With the lamb, serve a red Bordeaux or California Cabernet Sauvignon.

Low-Fat Plan: Omit the bacon and cook the vegetables in 3 tablespoons of defatted beef broth.

Of Stockpots and Casseroles

A stockpot is a good, basic cooking utensil for making stocks, or broths, as we are calling them, and for large amounts of soup. Its tall, narrow shape, smaller around the rim than most other top-of-stove pots, lets the stock simmer for a long time, encouraging the slow melding of flavors without losing too much liquid to evaporation.

Stockpots come in an array of sizes, from 4 to more than 20 quarts. The larger sizes are great if you're going to reduce a lot of liquid to a *glace de viande,* the jellied meat concentrate French chefs use (sparingly) to enrich sauces. For most home purposes, however, a 10- to 14-quart size is adequate. Stockpots come in aluminum or other medium-gauge metal and they needn't be expensive. Just be sure the bottom is thick and heavy compared to the sides, so that vegetables or bones don't burn.

For making the soups in this book, we found that a 4-quart saucepan worked very well for the amounts given, whether aluminum with a nonstick finish, stainless steel, or enameled cast iron.

As for the casserole recipes, it's a matter of taste. We like enameled cast iron because it's heavy, cooks evenly, and is attractive enough to bring to the table. But there are beautiful heavy stainless-steel and superb nonstick-surface casseroles that can fill the bill very well, indeed.

Incidentally, when the utensil Dutch oven is mentioned, we are referring to a round, heavy, top-of-the stove casserole with handles on either side, which is exactly what a casserole is!

Potage Crécy

Carrot Soup

In French cuisine, anything à la Crécy will undoubtedly star carrots, honoring the little town outside Paris known for its top-quality carrots. But some folks attribute the celebrated carrots to the town of Somme, close to where the famed Battle of Crécy took place in 1346.

Whatever their town of origin, carrots bring a fresh, sweet flavor to this puréed soup. The classic herb here is chervil, but by unanimous agreement of the kitchen bunch at La Bonne Soupe, it's been superseded by dill. "We just love the play of fresh dill's zingy tartness against the sweet resonance of the carrots, and the undercurrent of cumin, which gorgeously intensifies the deep orange color of the soup," says Chef Francis Freund.

Potage Crécy doubles as a warming brisk-weather soup and refreshing cold soup in summer. Ladle it into shiny black or white soup bowls for a dramatic presentation.

2 cups thinly sliced carrots (6 to 8 medium-size)

2 tablespoons grated onion

1 quart water

¼ teaspoon ground cumin

Salt and freshly ground pepper to taste

3 tablespoons finely chopped fresh dill

½ cup sour cream (nonfat is fine)

Place the carrots, onion, and water in a 2-quart saucepan, and bring to a boil over high heat. Reduce the heat to medium, partially cover, and cook until the carrots are very soft, 12 to 15 minutes. Check the saucepan from time to time and skim off any orange scum that may rise to the top. Remove from the heat and cool slightly.

Purée the soup in batches in a blender or food processor. Return the mixture to the saucepan and add the cumin, salt and pepper, and dill. Reheat until piping hot; or if serving cold, pour into a large pitcher or bowl and chill, covered, for 2 to 3 hours. Ladle into warmed soup bowls or mugs and top each with a rounded spoon of sour cream.

Makes 4 servings

Bread: Choose a chewy, robust multigrain bread from your supermarket or local bakery.

Lunch: Chunky chicken salad zipped up with capers and hot pepper sauce looks pretty when piled into curvy red-tipped lettuce leaves.

Dinner: A *magret* of duck is a meaty, ready-to-cook duck breast meat, available in some supermarkets and in specialty meat shops. Score the top fat layer crisscross with a sharp knife and broil the duck for 10 minutes on each side. Slice it thinly and serve with French Fried Potatoes (page 142).

Dessert: Spoon Dr. Vassaux's Rice Pudding (page 156) into dessert coupes and, if desired, garnish with a dollop of whipped cream.

Wine: For the soup, a lightly chilled herbal Sauvignon Blanc makes a pleasing partner. A lightly chilled Beaujolais, such as a Morgon or Moulin-à-Vent, is a felicitous choice for duck; the deep and fine acidity counterbalance the richness of the duck meat.

Low-Fat Plan: This soup is low-fat, especially if you use nonfat sour cream or omit the sour cream entirely.

Soupe de Légumes Pépé Jean

PÉPÉ JEAN'S VEGETABLE SOUP

Cecile Lamalle, who is both a cook par excellence *and a friend, gave us the recipe for this satisfying soup. "My grandfather, Pépé Jean, was a* charcutier, *a pork butcher," says Cecile. "Nonetheless he believed that meat was too rich for everyday fare; meat was for Sundays and holidays. Every evening during my visits to Villa Les Ifs [Villa of the Yews] in Lons-le-Saunier in the Jura Mountains in eastern France, we'd sit down to vegetable soup, followed by an omelet, a gratin of potatoes or vegetables, or* les macaronis au gratin. *We always finished with a platter of cheeses and whatever fruit was in season.*

"Whenever I think of Les Ifs, I picture my grandparents, Pépé Jean and Mémé Marie, sitting on the back stoop, off the kitchen, preparing the vegetables for the soup. Mémé was the sous-chef, Pépé was the chef.

"There were always chopped leeks, of course. No French person would ever dream of making a soup without leeks. Then there might be carrots, string beans, onions, garlic—whatever was in the garden or at the big open-air market in town. But no beets. They would color the soup. And no members of the cabbage family. They would smell. The vegetables boiled in water, plain water, for perhaps an hour. Then the broth was tasted, and salt was added. An egg of butter (that is, a piece of butter the size of a small egg) was added along with a big handful of chopped fresh flat-leaf parsley and some freshly ground pepper. The soup was poured into the big tureen and taken into the dining room, to be eaten with bread, never butter, but always lots of bread."

3 medium-size leeks, white and light green parts only, trimmed, washed, and coarsely chopped

2 medium-size tomatoes, peeled, seeded, and cut into ½-inch dice

1 medium-size turnip, peeled and cut into ½-inch dice

1 medium-size parsnip, peeled and cut into ½-inch dice

1 large onion, chopped

2 cloves garlic, minced

2 ribs celery, chopped

2 quarts water

1 cup fresh or thawed frozen shelled peas

¼ cup unsalted butter (½ stick)

½ cup chopped fresh flat-leaf parsley leaves

Salt and freshly ground pepper to taste

Place all the vegetables except the peas in a 3-quart saucepan and add the water. Bring to a boil over high heat, then reduce the heat to low and simmer, partially covered, for 1 hour. Add the peas, butter, parsley, and salt and pepper. Simmer for 10 minutes and serve piping hot in warmed soup bowls.

Makes 6 to 8 servings

Bread: Pépé Jean and Mémé Marie always set out big loaves of country bread, thickly sliced, to enjoy with their vegetable soup.

Lunch: Whip up a fluffy omelet, seasoned with some chopped shallots and fresh thyme.

Dinner: Cecile recalls her grandparents' dish of *macaronis au gratin,* a French version of macaroni and cheese. Our suggestion is to serve a pasta dish, such as Pasta Quills with Vodka Sauce (page 39) and a salad of escarole, chicory (curly endive), and thinly sliced red onion tossed with extra-virgin olive oil, red wine vinegar, and finely chopped shallots.

Dessert: The Lamalles always finished the meal with a big platter of assorted cheeses and a bowl of seasonal fruit.

Wine: With the soup, the Lamalles often enjoyed a wine of the Jura area, *vin jaune*, a late-harvest, long-aged white wine with a yellow color and a nutty flavor similar to sherry. Since this wine is rarely found in the States, serve a glass of lightly chilled sherry with the soup. For the pasta, you might switch to a medium-bodied country red wine, such as Corbières.

Low-Fat Plan: Omit the butter from the soup and serve the penne with a low-fat tomato sauce.

Fancy Greens

To make the spinach *chiffonade,* rinse and pat dry about 10 fresh spinach leaves and remove the stems and any of the tough "spines" at the base of the leaves. Make little stacks of the leaves, 5 to a pile, then roll the pack into little cigar shapes. Using a sharp knife cut the little cigars into thin julienne strips.

Soupe aux Tripes

HOT AND TANGY TRIPE SOUP

Here's another enticing contribution from our friend and La Bonne Soupe devotee, Cecile Lamalle. She encourages Jean-Paul to put it on the list of plats du jour *on wintry days, when a soul-satisfying soup is just what everyone is looking for.*

"I'm not 100 percent certain that my mémé [grandma] and pépé [grandpa] Jean originated this recipe," says Cecile, "but I can say that it's really very easy to prepare and wonderfully comforting. Tripe tends to be on the bland side, so I like plenty of pepper, gobs of garlic, and a pungent jolt of ground cumin to pep it up."

- 2 tablespoons olive oil
- 2 large onions, chopped
- 8 cloves garlic, chopped
- 2 pounds tripe, rinsed under cold running water, drained well, and cut into bite-size pieces
- 2 cups canned plum tomatoes with juice
- 1 tablespoon ground cumin
- 2 cups dry white wine
- 2 cups Homemade Chicken Broth (page 4) or low-sodium canned broth
- Salt and freshly ground pepper to taste
- ½ cup fresh flat-leaf parsley leaves, chopped

Heat the oil in a 3- to 4-quart saucepan over medium heat. Add the onions and garlic and cook until they become softened but not browned, 3 to 4 minutes. Add the tripe, tomatoes, cumin, white wine, and broth and bring to a boil over high heat. Reduce the heat to low and simmer the soup, partially covered, until the tripe is tender, 1 to 1½ hours. Check for tenderness and season with salt and pepper. If the tripe is not fork tender, simmer the soup for another 20 minutes or so. (The soup may be cooled and refrigerated at this point for up to 2 days; it reheats beautifully and also freezes well.)

When ready to serve, ladle the soup into warmed soup bowls and sprinkle with the parsley.

Makes 6 to 8 servings

Bread: Cecile puts out a capacious basket of country bread with a nicely dense crumb alongside curls of sweet butter nestled in a bowl of cracked ice.

Lunch: A big bowl of this lusty soup and plenty of crusty bread and butter makes a dandy cold-weather lunch. You can add a small greens salad tossed with extra-virgin olive oil, chopped shallots, and red wine vinegar, if you like.

Dinner: Serve the soup in small bowls as a first course. A fine entrée would be linguine with meat sauce. Toss a salad of spinach leaves and sliced mushrooms dressed with Jean-Paul's Zesty Vinaigrette (page 146).

Dessert: Baked Anjou pears glazed with melted currant jelly wind up this meal perfectly.

Wine: Pour a gutsy red wine with both the soup and the pasta. A Gigondas or other Côtes du Rhône is an amicable choice.

Low-Fat Plan: Tripe is not very calorific, about 100 calories for 3½ ounces, so omit the oil and proceed with the recipe.

Crème de Cresson

CREAMY WATERCRESS SOUP

The late, great Nika Hazelton, eminent food authority and cookbook author, was a devotee of bistro cuisine and loved dining and chatting with the Picots at La Bonne Soupe. "I love all of those full-of-flavor, peasant-y soups and dishes," she often said. She was especially partial to Savory French Bean Stew (page 120) and Chicken in the Pot (page 131). But in the spring, when the dark and crispy shoots of watercress poked through the woodland streams, she expressed a longing for some Crème de Cresson, with its fresh, tangy flavor and silken texture.

3 tablespoons unsalted butter

2 medium-size onions, chopped

4 ribs celery, thinly sliced

1 quart Homemade Chicken Broth (page 4) or low-sodium canned broth

3 bunches watercress

1 cup heavy cream

Pinch of ground nutmeg

Dash of hot pepper sauce

Salt and freshly ground pepper to taste

Melt the butter in a heavy 2-quart saucepan over medium heat. Add the onions and celery and cook, stirring occasionally, until they soften, 4 to 5 minutes. Add the broth and bring to a boil over high heat. Reduce the heat to medium and cook, covered, until the vegetables are very soft, 10 to 15 minutes. Add the watercress and cook, covered, over medium heat just until the leaves are wilted, 2 to 3 minutes.

Remove the pan from the heat and transfer the contents of the saucepan to the container of a food processor or blender. Process until smooth and puréed. (You may need to do this in several batches.)

Return the mixture to the saucepan and, over low heat, add the cream slowly, stirring well, then add the nutmeg, hot pepper sauce, and salt and pepper. Simmer the soup just until warmed through but no more than 5 minutes, as over-cooking can bring out a bitter essence from the watercress. Ladle into warmed soup bowls.

Makes 4 servings

Bread: Lightly toast fresh slices of golden brioche and pile into a napkin-lined basket. Pass a tub of sweet country butter for those who wish to intensify the richness of the dish.

Lunch: Whip up a light and frothy omelet flavored with chopped scallions and a little grated Swiss cheese and pass a bowl of crisp, golden French Fried Potatoes (page 142).

Dinner: In keeping with spring's bounty, fresh-caught shad or halibut, gently cooked in a little butter and white wine, with a sprinkling of chopped chervil makes a beguiling dish. Garnish the plates with steamed basmati rice and briefly blanched sweet peas tossed with a little melted butter or margarine.

Dessert: Quickly assemble a really luscious strawberry shortcake: Tuck slices of angel food cake into dessert coupes. Spoon sugared strawberries on top and swirl lightly sweetened whipped cream over all.

Wine: With the soup pour chilled fino sherry into small glasses (the Spanish call these *copitas*). With the fish we like a big, buttery California Chardonnay, which stands up to the richness of the fish.

Low-Fat Plan: Omit the butter. Sprinkle the onions and celery with 3 tablespoons of water, partially cover, and cook, covered, over low heat until they start to soften, 5 to 6 minutes. Omit the cream and, if desired, garnish the bowls with a tablespoon of nonfat yogurt.

Gazpacho de Bonne Soupe

CHILLED SPANISH RAW VEGETABLE SOUP

"That first summer on Fifty-fifth Street was a very hot one and although a surprising number of our diners still ordered a hot soup, many more longed for something refreshing and cold," Jean-Paul recalls as he adds a bit more pepper to his cooling liquid salad, also known as gazpacho. *"This was the first of our cold soups.*

"Gazpacho, with its healthy, summer's bounty of ripe tomatoes, cucumbers, and bell peppers and the tang of vinegar, was described on our menu as being as 'fragrant as the flowers of Granada, as Tangy as the sea air of Malaga, and as delicious as the fruit of Seville.'" Of its many versions, this one, specially researched by the Picots, is the envy of all Andalusia.

5 large, ripe tomatoes, peeled, seeded, and coarsely chopped

1 large cucumber, peeled, seeded, and coarsely chopped

1 large onion, coarsely chopped

2 to 3 cloves garlic, smashed with the flat side of a knife or put through a press

1 red or green bell pepper, cored, seeded, and chopped

½ cup chopped cilantro leaves

⅓ cup extra-virgin olive oil

1 tablespoon freshly squeezed lemon juice

1 tablespoon red wine vinegar

Dash of ground red pepper or to taste

Salt and freshly ground pepper to taste

1 quart tomato juice

1 cup Homemade Chicken Broth (page 4) or low-sodium canned broth

In a large bowl, combine the tomatoes, cucumber, onion, garlic, bell pepper, cilantro, olive oil, lemon juice, and vinegar. Transfer the mixture to a blender or food processor and process until finely chopped but not puréed. You want to retain a bit of crunch. Return the mixture to the bowl or pour it into a large pitcher. Season with ground red pepper and salt and pepper and stir in the tomato juice and broth.

Cover and chill for at least 3 hours. Ladle the soup into chilled bowls or mugs and add an ice cube, if desired.

Makes 4 to 6 servings

Tip: *For a festive fillip add a tomato or vegetable juice ice cube to each serving of gazpacho. Pour the juice into an ice cube tray, place a tiny sprig of parsley in each cube, and freeze.*

Bread: Here's a great opportunity to turn leftover baguettes into garlic bread. However, if you feel this is *de trop* (a bit too much), serve chunks of plain baguette.

Lunch: Warmed wedges of Quiche Lorraine with Bacon and Ham (page 55) garnished with cherry tomatoes seem just right.

Dinner: Serve Fillets of Flounder and Shrimp in Paper (page 90). Offer a *chiffonade* (see "Fancy Greens," page 22) of fresh spinach leaves filmed with a little olive oil and red wine vinegar.

Dessert: Apple Tart (page 163) makes an elegant finale, especially when accompanied by cups of double espresso.

Wine: A lightly chilled red wine from the Midi in France makes delightful sipping.

Low-Fat Plan: Omit the olive oil from the gazpacho and enjoy!

Potage à la Dubarry

CHILLED CAULIFLOWER SOUP

We have the Comtesse du Barry to thank for this suavely sensuous soup. History tells us that the favorite inamorata of King Louis XV was inordinately fond of cauliflower. To please her, the royal chefs created special dishes aggrandizing the crunchy, creamy-hued vegetable. À la Dubarry also connotes any dish that is garnished with the pretty little florets, which are often filmed with a rich Mornay sauce (white sauce enriched with grated cheese) to add a fillip of elegance.

Cauliflower was a favorite of Mark Twain, who referred to it as "the cabbage with a college education," because the name derives from the Latin caulis *(stalk) and* floris *(flower). Whatever the derivation, this is a superb summer soup.*

1 tablespoon extra-virgin olive oil

1 large onion, chopped

2 cloves garlic, chopped

4 ribs celery, thinly sliced

1½ quarts Homemade Chicken Broth (page 4) or low-sodium canned broth

1 tablespoon freshly squeezed lemon juice

1 large cauliflower (about 2 pounds), separated into florets

3 medium-size boiling potatoes, peeled and sliced

Salt and freshly ground white pepper to taste

Dash of ground nutmeg or to taste

1 cup heavy cream

⅓ cup minced fresh chives or cilantro

Heat the oil in a heavy 3-quart saucepan over medium heat. Add the onion and garlic and cook until softened but not browned, about 4 minutes. Add the celery and cook over medium heat until softened, 2 to 3 minutes. Add the broth, lemon juice, cauliflower, and potatoes and bring to a boil over high heat. Reduce the heat to medium-low, cover partially, and cook until the cauliflower and potatoes are tender, about 30 minutes. Transfer the contents of the saucepan to a food processor or blender and purée in batches.

Season the soup with salt, pepper, and nutmeg and transfer to a large bowl or pitcher. Cover and refrigerate for at least 3 hours or up to 2 days. When ready to serve, stir in the cream and taste to adjust the seasonings. Sprinkle with the chives or cilantro.

Makes 4 to 6 servings

Bread: Thin slices of dark pumpernickel bread—even some of the packaged Westphalian pumpernickel breads—make an ambrosial pairing with the soup.

Lunch: With this silken, creamy pottage all you need to complete the meal is good bread and a crunchy salad. Try a *Salade Niçoise* (page 44).

Dinner: As an elegant start to a warm-weather dinner, pour the soup into thin porcelain cups. Follow with slices of cold roast veal loaf garnished with a tangy chutney and warm potato salad.

Dessert: Lemon Tart (page 160) makes a fine finish.

Wine: For the soup, uncork a chilled Sauvignon Blanc from France's Loire Valley or from California. With the veal, a sturdy French country wine, such as Corbières or Minervois, would make a pleasing partner.

Low-Fat Plan: Instead of cooking in oil, sprinkle the onions and garlic with 3 tablespoons of water, cover, and steam over low heat for 5 minutes. Substitute skim milk for the cream. For dessert, serve Peaches Poached in Red Wine (page 159).

Heard of Curd?

Did you know the white part of cauliflower is called the curd? When buying a head, look for a compact, blemish-free, white or cream curd, with fresh-looking green leaves.

Potage Froid aux Petits Pois

Chilled Green Pea Soup

The great Italian composer Gioacchino Rossini was a fastidious gourmet and bon vivant. He lived in a luxurious apartment in Paris and summered in Passy, a Parisian suburb, where he entertained le beau monde—*the rich and beautiful of the art world—in grand style. He adored fine food and wine. The elegant Tournedos Rossini, beef fillets under a coverlet of foie gras and truffles, was created just for him by an admiring chef. And we know for certain that he doted on sweet green peas. One of his last collections, called* Péchés de Vieillesse (Sins of My Old Age), *includes a charming piano piece titled "Ouf! Les Petits Pois" (Oh! The Little Peas).*

But please don't wait until your vieillesse *to try this lovely, suave soup, with its fresh green pea flavor set off with a hint of cumin and thyme.*

1 quart Homemade Chicken Broth (page 4) or low-sodium canned broth

1 small head of Boston or romaine lettuce (about ½ pound)

6 scallions, trimmed, white and green parts, thinly sliced

3 pounds fresh green peas in the pod, shelled (about 3 cups)

½ teaspoon sugar

Salt and freshly ground pepper to taste

½ teaspoon fresh thyme or ¼ teaspoon dried

¼ teaspoon ground cumin

1 cup heavy cream

Bring the broth to a boil in a heavy 3-quart saucepan over high heat. Reduce the heat to medium and add the lettuce, scallions, peas, and sugar. Reduce the heat to low, and cook, partially covered, until the peas are tender, 8 to 10 minutes.

Remove the pan from the heat and season with salt, pepper, thyme, and cumin. Allow the soup to cool, then purée in a food processor or blender. Refrigerate, covered, for at least 2 hours. When ready to serve, stir in the cream, and blend well.

Makes 4 to 6 servings

Note: Frozen peas are a pleasing alternative if you can't find the fresh. One 10-ounce package yields nearly 3 cups, and they'll need 3 to 5 minutes additional cooking time.

Bread: A ficelle (a long, skinny baguette) or crisp, slender breadsticks are elegant with the soup.

Lunch: A warm-from-the-oven Quiche Lorraine with Bacon and Ham (page 55) garnished with cherry tomatoes and a few sprigs of curly endive makes an eye- and taste-appealing little meal.

Dinner: Dust baby lamb chops with freshly cracked pepper and finely minced rosemary and place under the broiler until brown and crusty outside and pink inside. Steamed new potatoes bathed in extra-virgin olive oil and showered with chopped flat-leaf parsley are superb with the chops.

Dessert: Fresh chunks of rhubarb simmered with sliced strawberries and sugar make an attractive spring dessert.

Wine: With the sweet pea soup, a chilled, softly fruity Vouvray from the Loire Valley picks up the floweriness of the peas beautifully. With the chops, a Bordeaux Petit Château makes a fine consort.

Low-Fat Plan: Skip the cream for the soup; if it seems a bit too thick, add additional broth.

Jean-Paul Picot's Soupe au Corail

JEAN-PAUL PICOT'S COLD CORAL SOUP

Coral is the gorgeous color of Jean-Paul's creamy, dreamy cold tomato soup. It was featured in the sleek fashion newspaper W back in the days before it metamorphosed into its present glossy magazine format. I [the author, Doris Tobias] was the food writer then, under the watchful eye of publisher John Fairchild. We were doing soups for a summer issue, and Jean-Paul gave us this colorful and refreshing recipe. We made it, photographed it, and enjoyed it with great relish.

3 large cucumbers

1 small onion, sliced

1 cup tomato juice

1 tablespoon tomato paste

1 cup Homemade Chicken Broth (page 4) or low-sodium canned broth

1 quart sour cream

¼ cup dry fino sherry

12 small fresh basil leaves for garnish

Peel the cucumbers and slice in half lengthwise. Spoon out and discard the seeds. Place the cucumbers in a blender or food processor. Add the onion, tomato juice, and tomato paste, and process until puréed.

Pour the mixture into a large bowl, add the broth, then whisk in the sour cream and sherry, beating until well incorporated. Cover and refrigerate for 3 to 4 hours.

Ladle into chilled soup bowls and float 3 basil leaves in each.

Makes 4 to 6 servings

Tip: For an elegant presentation, pour the soup into a big porcelain tureen and ladle into the soup bowls at the table.

Bread: Cut small brioche rolls in half and lightly toast. Pass a dish of whipped creamery butter.

Lunch: For a meal with Asian flavor, follow the soup with cold soba noodles tossed with sesame seeds seasoned with light soy sauce. Pass a platter of thinly sliced cucumbers flecked with finely chopped cilantro.

Dinner: Set out a beautiful platter of cold poached salmon garnished with steamed fresh asparagus, crisp red radish roses and tiny ebony Niçoise olives. Pass a sauce boat of mayonnaise, homemade or prepared, zipped up with a Dijon mustard and minced chives.

Dessert: Offer wedges of Apple Tart (page 163).

Wine: With the soup, try a lightly herbal French Sauvignon Blanc. With the salmon, you can continue with the same wine or switch to a big, full-bodied Hermitage Blanc.

Low-Fat Plan: Use nonfat sour cream and serve chunks of baguette with it.

Sous chef Robert pours the soupe du jour.

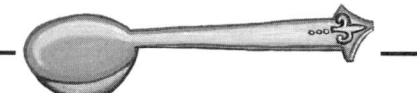

A Day in the Life of La Bonne Soupe

5:00 A.M.

As the sun begins to cast a glow over the East River in New York, bakers at France Croissant are shaping the baguettes that will arrive at La Bonne Soupe in a few hours. Meanwhile, at the little bistro on East Fifty-fifth Street, the *plongeur* (cleaning person) opens the latch and awakens La Bonne Soupe with a brisk and thorough scrubbing.

7:00 A.M.

Chef Francis Freund and his staff slip in and don their whites; the kitchen starts to hum. Almost simultaneously stove burners ignite, stockpots simmer, and busy hands peel, chop, slice, dice, and shred the aromatic vegetables. Little brown crocks are set out for Jean-Paul's Gratinéed Onion Soup (page 8).

8:00 A.M.

The day's deliveries roll in. An under chef checks them and stores them in accessible cubicles. He then whisks fresh salad greens to the sink, washes, dries, and readies them for the day's salads. Potatoes are peeled and cut into proper-size batons, or thin sticks, for the *pommes frites* (French fried potatoes) that fly out of the kitchen so fast. A minor crises arises: The skate, billed as the day's fish special, is unavailable. Monkfish is sent in its place. "No problem," says Chef Francis in a soothing voice. "The caper sauce we've made for the skate will be absolutely wonderful with the monkfish. Everyone will love it."

9:00 A.M.

The kitchen goes into high gear. Chef Francis rolls out pastry for the quiches and tarts. The *sous-chef* purées the codfish and potatoes, lacing the *brandade* with just the right amount of olive oil and garlic. In one corner of this amazing little kitchen the air is fragrant with caramelized sugar (for the *crème caramel*) and melted chocolate (for the chocolate mousse).

continues

10:00 A.M.

Two of the wait staff hurry in along with the morning's supply of baguettes from France Croissant. (Baguettes for the evening arrive in late afternoon.) They set the tables with traditional red-and-white checkered cloths, arrange flowers, and half fill white wine buckets with ice and water. Cutlery and glassware are eyeballed for spotlessness and set out.

11:00 A.M.

All remaining personnel arrive, including the maître d'hôte and affable bartender, Honoré Pochat, who at once checks his stocks behind his cozy four-stool bar. He sees that ice is plentiful, sets out cocktail garnishes, and inspects wineglasses and carafes. The telephone is already ringing off the hook. The staff has a bite of lunch, usually one of the day's specials.

11:30 A.M.

Jean-Paul Picot strolls into the bistro and heads for a bar stool, a favorite perch where he can meet, greet, chat, oversee, and even sip an espresso. Although he likes to regard himself as a kind of *éminence grise*, he confesses: "I never really tell my staff when I'm going to show up. I just appear." Most lunches, dinners, and late evenings, however, he is definitely there.

Noon

The maître d' shows the first of the lunch bunch to their seats and makes them comfortable. If it's overcoat weather there are hangers up front or an informal old-fashioned rack upstairs. (Jean-Paul and Monique don't believe in forcing diners to pay extra for checking gear.) The main floor quickly fills up and diners are directed to the upstairs rooms, with their displays of Haitian art and rustic beamed ceilings. In mild weather a tiny terrace can seat a happy handful of street observers. The lunchniks are mainly businesspeople—execs discussing deals over a bowl of soup, shoppers taking a midday breather, and tourists.

The pace steps up and the line waiting in the vestibule grows longer. The maître d' assures the customers that the wait won't be more than ten or fifteen minutes. The bistro is alive with multilingual conversation as the staff maneuvers up and down narrow aisles and winding stairs to keep things moving.

2:30 P.M.

Things have quieted to the point that you can hear the hissing of the espresso machine. The last of the lunch bunch files out.

3:00 P.M.

Le patron (the owner) Jean-Paul sits down with Chef Francis to discuss the menu specials for the next few days. The innovative chef outlines ideas for new dishes that he feels will enhance the basic menu. "I'd like to try a lighter version of *cassoulet* that cuts out the heavy fats but still has plenty of pow flavor," says Francis, referring to France's ultimate pork-and-bean dish. *Le patron* nods approval, and the talk continues until it's time to call purveyors with fill-in orders.

The chef returns to the kitchen to place bones in the oven to brown for the rich beef and veal stocks and get ready for the dinner crowd. Jean-Paul heads to his office to telephone. He calls Bossangue: "My favorite Italian butcher, who has the best meat in town." He also calls Cambridge, his backup butcher: "I'm afraid one day my Italian butcher may disappear." He orders prime steaks—filets and sirloins—and lean shoulder to grind as needed for the hamburgers.

He buys free-range chickens and ducks from Polarica; "And when we want something a little more elaborate, say, *magret* of duck (duck breast), quail, and turkey, we contact D'Artagnan in New Jersey. Fresh fish from Hampton Bays, Long Island, comes in three times a week. Eggs and milk products are sent fresh daily from Seelig, and our baguettes arrive twice daily from France Croissant."

3:30 P.M.

Jean-Paul finishes his orders; strolls off to chat with Monique; takes care of some chores; and, perhaps, relaxes before the evening's action.

Jean-Paul takes a moment to gaze with pride at the La Bonne Soupe window.

continues

4:00 P.M.

The night staff arrives. Tables are spruced up for the evening and the staff has dinner before the action accelerates. Genial bartender Daniel Lagarde settles in at the little bar, ready for the evening action.

6:00 P.M.

Enter the first of the early diners—the pretheater crowd, solo diners, some armed with a favorite book to peruse while sipping a glass of wine and awaiting their meal. They are never rushed and can really feel at home here. Many of the pretheater diners will return after the performance to have dessert and coffee. "It's a nice touch we like to encourage," offers Jean-Paul. "This way they enjoy an appetizer and entrée before and, afterwards, leisurely air their views across the table."

8:00 P.M.

Dinner at a more relaxed pace is the order of the evening from now on. "Many of our European customers are accustomed to dining at eight or later," explains Jean-Paul. They mostly order wines by the bottle, and this lengthens the meal pleasurably. Eventually they are joined by the after-theater returnees."

10:30 P.M.

The late diners linger while the early late-nighters arrive. By eleven there's a pleasant peppering of friends of the Picots and chefs who come in to wind down and talk, talk, talk with Jean-Paul Picot over a bowl of *bonne soupe* or a light snack. Look, there's a radiant Nello Santi, straight from the Metropolitan Opera House where he conducted Puccini's *Turandot*, bringing some friends for a collation and a glass of wine. There's Jean-Jacques Rachou, who just closed the doors of his elegant restaurant, La Côte Basque, sitting down for a light bite and heavy conversation.

Midnight

The last drops of wine are sipped. The last stories are told. It's good-night time at La Bonne Soupe.

A Quintet of Easy No-Cook Cold Soups

When the temperature and humidity soar to uncomfortable highs, (read New York summers), Chef Francis often quickly assembles reviving soups that need no cooking. They're refreshing to start off a light meal or to enjoy after a game of tennis or a swim. The two fruit soups felicitously double as dessert. "These may not seem very French," Jean-Paul Picot explains, "but the people who come to our little bistro to cool off from a sweltering heat wave love them. And, of course, we always say a few French words over the soups as they are served," he adds with that inimitable twinkle in his eyes.

Dilled Cucumber Soup

The tang of lemon and yogurt melded with the refreshing flavor of cucumber and perky fragrance of fresh chopped dill make this easy-to-make soup a warm-weather delight.

4 medium-size cucumbers, peeled, seeded, and chopped

2 shallots, chopped

2 tablespoons freshly squeezed lemon juice

½ cup plus 1 tablespoon finely chopped fresh dill

2 cups cold Homemade Chicken Broth (page 4) or low-sodium canned broth

2 cups low-fat yogurt

Salt and freshly ground pepper to taste

In the bowl of a food processor or in a blender, place the cucumbers, shallots, lemon juice, and ½ cup of the dill and process until well puréed.

Transfer the purée to a large bowl or pitcher. Add the broth and yogurt, stirring to blend. Season with salt and pepper. Cover and chill in the refrigerator for 3 to 4 hours.

When ready to serve, still well, then ladle or pour into chilled bowls. Garnish with the remaining dill.

Makes 4 servings

Variation: For a colorful and flavorful touch, you can garnish the soup with tiny cubes of smoked salmon. Two thin slices cut into small dice will do very nicely.

Spicy Guacamole Bisque

Although this may not be a true bisque—a thick, creamy soup usually made with shellfish and thickened with rice—the richness of the avocado blended with the citrus juices, spices, cilantro, and sour cream make it quite bisquelike and delicious.

3 ripe avocados, peeled, pitted, and diced

3 tablespoons freshly squeezed lemon juice

3 tablespoons freshly squeezed lime juice

2 tablespoons finely chopped onion

½ cup finely chopped cilantro

⅛ teaspoon hot red pepper sauce

⅛ teaspoon chili powder

Pinch of ground cumin

Salt and freshly ground pepper to taste

2 cups cold Homemade Chicken Broth (page 4) or low-sodium canned broth

2 cups nonfat sour cream

2 tablespoons finely diced red bell pepper

2 tablespoons finely diced red onion

2 tablespoons thinly sliced scallions

Corn Chips

Place the avocados, lemon and lime juices, chopped onion, cilantro, hot red pepper sauce, chili powder, cumin, and salt and pepper in a food processor or blender. Process until puréed and smooth.

Transfer the mixture to a large bowl and add the broth and sour cream. Stir well to blend. Cover and chill for 3 to 4 hours.

When ready to serve, ladle the soup into chilled soup bowls. Garnish with the bell pepper, red onion, and scallions and serve with the corn chips.

Makes 4 to 6 servings

Herb-Scented Tomato Soup

The zing of basil, mint, red wine vinegar, and hot red pepper sauce and Worcestershire sauces lift this fresh tomato soup to tangy heights. Add the crabmeat (see the variation) for a luxurious touch.

2 pounds ripe tomatoes, peeled, seeded, and quartered

3 shallots, chopped

2 cloves garlic, chopped

½ cup basil leaves (reserve 4 for garnish)

½ cup fresh mint leaves (reserve 4 for garnish)

2 cups tomato juice

1 cup cold Homemade Chicken Broth (page 4) or low-sodium canned broth

1 cup heavy cream

¼ cup red wine vinegar

3 tablespoons freshly squeezed lemon juice

¼ teaspoon hot red pepper sauce

¼ teaspoon Worcestershire sauce

Salt and freshly ground pepper to taste

Place the tomatoes in a food processor or blender. Add the shallots, garlic, basil, and mint and process until puréed.

Transfer the mixture to a large bowl or pitcher. Add all the remaining ingredients, except the reserved herbs, stirring to blend well. Taste and correct seasoning. Cover and chill for 3 to 4 hours.

When ready to serve, ladle into the chilled soup bowls, and garnish with the reserved basil and mint.

Makes 4 servings

Variation: For added elegance you can garnish the soup with ready-to-use lump crabmeat or the meat from crab claws cut into bite-size pieces. You can find these at your fish market or supermarket, and ¼ pound will suffice.

Sparkling Berry Soup

The pleasurable plus of chilled fruit soups is they can double as summertime desserts.

2 cups fresh raspberries

2 cups fresh blackberries or blueberries

2 cups fresh strawberries

1 cup freshly squeezed orange juice

¾ cup superfine granulated sugar

½ cup freshly squeezed lemon juice

2 cups chilled sparkling wine or nonalcoholic sparking wine

Rinse the berries and remove the hulls or stems. Pat dry with paper towels to remove excess moisture. Reserve 12 berries for garnish.

Place the berries, orange juice, sugar, and lemon juice in a food processor or blender. Process until puréed and smooth. Transfer the mixture to a large bowl or pitcher, cover, and chill for 3 to 4 hours.

When ready to serve, add the chilled sparkling wine and stir quickly to blend. Ladle into chilled cups or small soup bowls and garnish with the reserved berries.

Makes 4 servings

Icy Melon Soup

Cool, refreshing, and a breeze to prepare.

1 large ripe cantaloupe or other sweet-fleshed melon (about 2 pounds), peeled, seeded, and diced

Juice of 2 limes

About ½ cup freshly squeezed orange juice

1 teaspoon grated fresh ginger or ¼ teaspoon ground

½ cup fruity white wine, such as Chenin Blanc

½ cup crème fraîche

4 thin slices of lime for garnish

Place the melon, lime and orange juices, ginger, and wine in a food processor or blender. Process until smooth and puréed. If the mixture seems too thick, thin it with a little more orange juice. Transfer to a large bowl or pitcher and chill for 3 to 4 hours.

When ready to serve, ladle the soup into small chilled bowls or cups. Garnish with crème fraîche topped with a slice of lime.

Makes 4 servings

2

Pasta and Salads

"In France, pasta is not quite as prevalent as it is in Italy," says Jean-Paul Picot. "But it's an easy dish to cook and extremely popular here in the States." Jean-Paul tells how pasta dishes became mainstays at La Bonne Soupe: "When we first opened, pasta was the furthest thing from our minds. But then we began to attract a group of Italians who worked down the block at the RAI [the Italian national radio and television network] who asked if we'd include a couple of pasta dishes for them from time to time. The chef was happy to accommodate, and today, pasta dishes, such as Fusilli with Tuna, Sun-Dried Tomatoes, and Olives; Pasta Quills with Vodka Sauce; and others continue to captivate so many of our patrons."

And that's how the Picots adapted their French menu to accommodate multiethnic American tastes.

Salads translate so well from French to American because in cafés, similar salads are often enjoyed as a luncheon entrée.

"For our initial salad offerings, we did *Salade Niçoise*, Chef's Salad, and Spinach Salad, based on fresh spinach. These are great meal-in-a-bowl lunches and have always been popular choices. They have been supplemented by Chef Francis Freund's French-American composed salads, which are light and flavorful and fit in with today's health-conscious lifestyle requisites."

Fusilli Provençale

FUSILLI WITH TUNA, SUN-DRIED TOMATOES, AND OLIVES

Pasta in Provence benefits from the inherent lushness of Mediterranean produce, especially in the Pays Niçois—the area bordering Italy around Nice. There, it is not at all unusual to find variegated pastas sauced with red-ripe tomatoes, garlic, fresh herbs, and ebony Niçoise olives.

For this racy sauce, Chef Francis Freund adds nuggets of fresh tuna, slivers of sun-dried tomatoes, and tender artichokes.

¼ cup extra-virgin olive oil

½ pound fresh tuna fillet, skin discarded and flesh cut into ½-inch cubes

4 cloves garlic, finely chopped

½ cup sun-dried tomatoes in olive oil (about 6 ounces), drained and cut into julienne strips

One 16-ounce can Italian plum tomatoes, undrained

One 6-ounce jar marinated artichoke hearts, drained and cut into ¼-inch lengthwise pieces

½ cup fresh basil leaves, chopped, or 1 teaspoon dried

¾ cup Niçoise or other flavorful black olives (about 5 ounces), pitted (see "How to Pit an Olive," page 44)

Pinch of hot pepper flakes

Salt and freshly ground pepper to taste

1 pound fusilli

Heat 2 tablespoons of the oil in a small skillet over medium-high heat until hot but not smoking. Add the tuna and cook, stirring, until the cubes are lightly browned on all sides, about 2 minutes. Remove the skillet from the heat and reserve.

Heat the remaining oil in a 1½- to 2-quart heavy saucepan. Add the garlic and cook over low heat until the garlic is softened but not browned, 1 to 2 minutes. Add the sun-dried tomatoes and cook over low heat until they start to soften, 1 to 2 minutes. Add all the remaining ingredients (except the fusilli) one at a time, stirring. Bring to a boil over high heat, then reduce the heat to medium and cook until all the elements have amalgamated and sauce is reduced to 3½ cups, 8 to 10 minutes. Add the reserved tuna and season with salt and pepper. Keep the sauce warm on low heat while you cook the pasta.

Bring 4 quarts of water to a boil in a 5- to 6-quart kettle over high heat. Add a pinch of salt and the fusilli and bring the water back to a boil. Cook, stirring occasionally, until tender but still firm to the bite, about 8 minutes. Drain the fusilli in a colander and turn into a large warmed bowl. Spoon the sauce over the pasta and toss well. Divide among 4 warmed oversize soup bowls.

Makes 4 servings

Bread: A freshly baked baguette suits this pasta admirably.

Lunch: Add a salad of thinly sliced cucumbers and cherry tomatoes tossed with a light vinaigrette.

Dinner: Start with Vegetable Soup with Basil and Garlic Sauce (page 16) and follow with a big salad of seasonal greens tossed with Jean-Paul's Zesty Vinaigrette (page 146).

Dessert: Place scoops of peach ice cream in dessert coupes and ladle Rosy Raspberry Sauce (page 164) on top.

Wine: A Beaujolais, served chilled, is an excellent accompaniment with this robust sauce.

Low-Fat Plan: Omit the oil and lightly brown the tuna under the broiler. Sprinkle the garlic with 1½ tablespoons of water and cook, covered, over low heat until softened but not browned, then proceed with the recipe.

Pasta Presto

Pasta is so versatile and accommodating. We see it as the grown-ups' security blanket. With a larder stocked with a variety of pastas (dried, fresh, and frozen), plus the fixings for a quick sauce (cans of Italian plum tomatoes, tomato paste, and tomato purée; extra-virgin olive oil; perhaps some olives; and capers) along with some fine aged grana (Italian hard cheese such as Parmigiano-Reggiano or Romano), you'll never be fazed when suddenly it's mealtime and the question of what to prepare pronto arises!

Penne à la Vodka

PASTA QUILLS WITH VODKA SAUCE

"When I dash down from the upstairs office for my midday meal, which is generally about 2:30 in the afternoon, I'm ready for a bowl of comforting pasta," says Monique Gutmann, who takes care of the myriad details that constantly besiege an office manager. French-born, tall, and willowy, Monique is charming and multitalented. Often she fills in as maître d' at the bistro, which she enjoys a lot. *"I love chatting with our diners and seeing that they are comfortably settled and enjoying themselves. When I finally get to my own lunch, it's usually one of the* plats du jour; *and if there's a special pasta, that's for me!"* One of Monique's favorites is this quick, simple, piquantly sauced penne (short, slant-cut quills).

2 tablespoons extra-virgin olive oil
4 cloves garlic, finely chopped
2 pounds plum tomatoes, peeled, seeded, and chopped (3 cups)
½ cup vodka
1 cup tomato sauce
⅓ cup chopped fresh basil or ½ teaspoon dried
1 cup heavy cream
Salt and freshly ground pepper to taste
1 pound penne

Heat the oil in a 2-quart heavy saucepan over medium heat until hot but not smoking. Add the garlic and cook over low heat, stirring, until the garlic has softened but not browned, 1 to 2 minutes. Add the tomatoes and cook over medium heat, stirring occasionally, until they have softened, about 5 minutes. Add the vodka, raise the heat to medium-high and cook until the vodka is totally absorbed into the tomatoes, 8 to 10 minutes. Reduce the heat to medium and add the tomato sauce, basil, heavy cream, and salt and pepper. Cook, stirring until the sauce is reduced to 3 cups, about 12 minutes. Remove the sauce from the heat and keep warm.

Bring 4 quarts of water to a boil in a 5- to 6-quart kettle over high heat. Add a pinch of salt and the penne and bring the water back to a boil. Cook the penne, stirring occasionally, until tender but still firm to the bite, about 12 minutes. Drain the penne in a colander and turn into a large warmed bowl. Spoon the sauce over the penne and toss well. Divide among 4 warmed dinner plates or oversize soup bowls.

Makes 4 servings

Bread: Monique likes a bâtard (a fat baguette) with this richly sauced pasta.

Lunch: Just add a salad of oak-leaf lettuce and sliced red radishes, dressed with extra-virgin olive oil and a little balsamic vinegar.

Dinner: Start off with Carrot Soup (page 20) and follow with a salad of arugula and sliced endive dressed with extra-virgin olive oil and a little freshly squeezed lemon juice.

Dessert: Serve wedges of Apple Tart (page 163) and cups of steaming espresso.

Wine: A fruity Chardonnay from California or France, such as Saint Véran, is a pleasing match for the rich sauce.

Low-Fat Plan: Omit the olive oil. Sprinkle the garlic with 1½ tablespoons of water and cook, covered, over low heat, stirring, until softened but not browned, 1 to 2 minutes. Omit the cream and increase the tomato sauce to 2 cups.

Linguine with Shrimp and Sugar Snap Peas

Thin, flat linguine is the perfect foil for this delectable amalgam of rosy pink shrimp and bright green, crunchy sugar snap peas. We also like angel hair pasta, which is so thin and ethereal (it soaks up the sauce, though, so beware); it's a joy to prepare and a delight to present. We enjoy the fresh versions of these pastas, which are generally available packaged and dated. However, dried linguine or angel hair pasta is eminently suitable for this quick and delightful dish.

¼ cup extra-virgin olive oil

2 shallots, finely minced

½ red bell pepper, seeded, tough ribs removed, and cut into ¼-inch dice

1 pound small shrimp, peeled and deveined

½ pound sugar snap peas, trimmed

1 cup heavy cream

Salt and freshly ground white pepper to taste

Dash of Worcestershire sauce or to taste

1 pound fresh or dried linguine

8 fresh basil leaves or parsley sprigs for garnish

Heat the oil in a large, heavy skillet over medium heat until it is hot but not smoking. Add the shallots and bell pepper and cook until the vegetables start to wilt, 3 to 4 minutes. Add the shrimp and cook, stirring, until they turn pink on all sides, 3 to 4 minutes. Add the sugar snap peas and cook, stirring, until they are warmed through, about 1 minute. Stir in the cream and season with salt and pepper, and Worcestershire sauce. Cook, stirring, just until the cream has thickened slightly, 2 to 3 minutes. Remove from the heat and keep warm.

Bring 4 quarts of water to a boil in a 5- to 6-quart kettle over high heat. Add a pinch of salt and the linguine and bring the water back to a boil. Cook fresh pasta, stirring, just until it firms up, about 1 minute, and dried pasta until it is firm to the bite, 6 to 8 minutes. Drain the pasta in a colander and turn into a large warmed bowl.

Add the shrimp sauce to the pasta and toss gently. Divide the pasta among 4 warmed plates and garnish each with 2 basil leaves or a sprig of parsley.

Makes 4 servings

Bread: We like a crusty, grainy country loaf or a baguette with all of our pasta dishes.

Lunch: All you need to add to this elegant little dish is a seasonal salad of field greens tossed in a light vinaigrette.

Dinner: Start off with Chilled Green Pea Soup (page 27) and follow with a salad of arugula and endive dressed with extra-virgin olive oil and balsamic vinegar.

Dessert: Slice peeled, ripe peaches into dessert coupes and ladle Rosy Raspberry Sauce (page 164) on top. Spoon a small mound of peach ice cream in the center of each.

Wine: A chilled Pouilly-Fuissé, with its fruitiness and crisp finish, is ideal with the cream-rich linguine and shrimp.

Low-Fat: Omit the oil, sprinkle the vegetables with 2 tablespoons water or white wine, and cook, covered, over medium-low heat until softened but not browned. Omit the cream and substitute ¾ cup defatted chicken broth and continue with the recipe.

Variation: Scallops—either tiny bay or the larger sea scallops—cut into bite-size pieces work well in place of the shrimp.

Pasta Tips

When buying fresh pasta, look for the expiration date on the label to be certain you're getting the freshest.

It's provident to keep a selection of dried pasta—from thin angel hair to broad lasagna noodles—in your larder, ready for a quick, satisfying meal.

Salade du Chef

CHEF'S SALAD

"Our trio of composed salads—Chef's Salad, Salade Niçoise, and Spinach Salad—have been mainstays through the years," explains le patron *as he sits down to enjoy his own favorite: Chef's Salad. "These are mainly luncheon dishes enjoyed as a one-dish meal. We present them in large individual salad bowls, and the colors and textures are vibrant. With some crusty baguettes and a glass of wine they make a really satisfying light meal."*

1 head romaine or other lettuce, washed, dried, and torn into bite-size pieces

¼ pound sliced boiled ham, cut into julienne strips

¼ pound sliced smoked turkey, cut into julienne strips

2 ounces Gruyère or other Swiss-type cheese, cut into julienne strips

2 medium-size tomatoes, peeled and cut into quarters lengthwise

4 hard-cooked eggs, cut in half lengthwise

24 small flavorful black olives, preferably Niçoise

Salt and freshly ground pepper to taste

Jean-Paul's Zesty Vinaigrette (page 146)

Mound the lettuce in a large salad bowl or individual bowls and arrange the ham, turkey, and cheese in little spokelike groups around the bowl. Place the tomato quarters and egg halves in between and strew with the olives. Add the salt and pepper. Pass the Zesty Vinaigrette separately.

Makes 4 servings

Bread: A crusty baguette is excellent, or offer thick chunks of country bread and a little crock of sweet country butter.

Lunch: As Jean-Paul Picot says, just add bread and wine and perhaps a little dessert, if you feel it's in order.

Dinner: You could start off with a hearty bowl Lentil Soup (page 18). With the salad, you could set out a platter of French Fried Potatoes (page 142), if you wish.

Dessert: Go all-out and whip up Crêpes with Orange Butter (page 152) and pass cups of steaming double espresso. Or for a less caloric dessert, mound raspberry sherbet in dessert coupes and garnish with thinly shaved dark chocolate.

Wine: Since the vinaigrette in the salad will dull a fine vintage, uncork an acidic white, such as Sauvignon Blanc. For red wine buffs, a young fruity Beaujolais or Zinfandel is a pleasing option.

Low-Fat Plan: Substitute low-fat ham and turkey and a low-fat cheese such as Alpine Lace Swiss cheese. Replace the oil in the dressing with chicken broth.

Some Salad Tips

- Be sure to dry your greens well before adding the dressing. If you don't have a salad spinner, shake off excess water and place the leaves between layers of paper towels. Place the towel-wrapped greens into plastic bags and store in the vegetable compartment of the refrigerator for up to two days. They'll stay nice and crisp.

- In general, it's best to tear large lettuces and other greens into bite-size pieces. Even Belgian endive leaves, unless you're using them as stuffing shells, should be broken into manageable segments. However, endive does brown quickly when exposed to air. To discourage browning, place cut endive in a bowl and sprinkle with lemon juice. Tightly cover the bowl with plastic wrap and refrigerate until ready to use.

- Vary your mixed greens. Today there's such a pleasing plethora—from Bibb, romaine, oak-leaf, red tip, and other loose-leaf lettuces to escarole, endive, *frisée* (curly endive or chicory), watercress, arugula, radicchio, and mâche. Many fine produce sections offer mixed mesclun greens to buy by the pound.

- For salad dressings Jean-Paul Picot prefers a mildly flavored extra-virgin olive oil. He feels a less-assertive olive oil blends more harmoniously with the other ingredients of the dressings. But if your palate craves a heavier, fruitier olive oil or your diet demands canola oil, you can still prepare a satisfying dressing!

Salade Niçoise

MEDITERRANEAN VEGETABLE SALAD

One of the perks of putting together a Salade Niçoise *is that you really can add any ingredient you fancy, as long as it has a Niçoise counterpart. And since Nice is in the market garden of France, this means green peas, beans, asparagus, artichokes, endive, celery, radishes, mushrooms, potatoes, and even truffles. You get the general idea! Here's La Bonne Soupe's version.*

1 large head romaine lettuce or other lettuce, washed, dried, and torn into bite-size pieces

Two 6-ounce cans white meat tuna, drained and broken into bite-size chunks

1 red bell pepper, cored, seeded, and cut into julienne strips

3 ribs celery, thinly sliced

1 medium-size cucumber, peeled and thinly sliced

⅓ cup Jean-Paul's Zesty Vinaigrette (page 146) or to taste

2 medium-size tomatoes, peeled and cut into quarters lengthwise

4 hard-cooked eggs, cut in half lengthwise

12 canned anchovy fillets, well drained

16 black olives, preferably Niçoise

Salt and freshly ground pepper to taste

Place the lettuce in a large salad bowl or 4 individual bowls along with the tuna, bell pepper, celery, and cucumber. Add the Zesty Vinaigrette and toss well. Decorate the salad with the tomatoes, eggs, anchovy fillets, and olives. Offer a pepper mill and salt at the table.

Makes 4 entrée or 8 appetizer servings

Bread: Offer a basket of small warmed brioches with the salad.

Lunch: The salad and buttery brioches make a sumptuous light meal.

Dinner: With the salad as the first course, a pasta, such as Fusilli with Tuna, Sun-Dried Tomatoes, and Olives (page 38) is most satisfying.

Dessert: Poached Pears with Ice Cream and Chocolate Sauce (page 157) makes a sweet conclusion.

Wine: A *vin ordinaire*—blended red wine—from France or California suits the salad and the pasta.

Low-Fat Plan: Use tuna canned in water and replace the oil in the salad dressing with chicken broth.

How to Pit an Olive

The easiest way to pit olives, especially the tiny Niçoise fellows, is to lay the flat side of a heavy broad knife on top of them and pound down with your fist a few times. The olives will be a bit bruised, but you can then remove the pits with your fingers.

Salade Popeye

SPINACH SALAD

The adventures of Popeye, the feisty cartoon sailor, are as popular in France as they are here. Popeye got his energy eating a can of spinach, which he opened with his bare hands. Only then did his biceps and deltoids rise to the occasion so he could properly pummel Brutus, the bad guy, and protect his girlfriend, Olive Oyl.

Well, La Bonne Soupe's salad emphatically does not come out of a can, but we know Popeye would love this fresh-tasting raw spinach salad as everyone at the bistro does. He might even enjoy the snappy dressing and crumbled bacon that makes it so special.

For the dressing (see Note)

1 clove garlic, finely minced

1 shallot, finely minced

⅓ cup white wine vinegar

1 tablespoon Homemade Chicken Broth (page 4) or low-sodium canned broth

1 teaspoon Dijon mustard

¾ cup soybean or other vegetable oil

Salt and freshly ground pepper to taste

For the salad

1½ pounds fresh spinach or two 10-ounce plastic bags fresh spinach, washed, stemmed, and dried

½ pound mushrooms, stemmed, thinly sliced

4 strips bacon, cooked until crisp, drained, and crumbled

4 hard-cooked eggs, cut into quarters lengthwise

¾ cup Croûtons (page 9)

Prepare the dressing:

Place the garlic, shallot, vinegar, broth, and mustard in a small bowl. Using a wire whisk or fork, slowly add the oil, whisking continually, until the dressing is smooth and slightly thickened. Season with salt and pepper.

Prepare the salad:

Pile the spinach leaves evenly into 4 oversize soup bowls. Add the mushrooms and strew with the bacon. Mix the salad dressing and pour 2 to 3 tablespoons into each salad. Gently toss to mix well and thoroughly coat the spinach. Arrange the hard-cooked eggs in groups on the top, bottom, and each side and sprinkle with the croutons.

Makes 4 servings

Note: Makes 1 cup dressing. You can make the salad dressing ahead and keep it stored in a tightly covered jar in the refrigerator for up to 2 weeks. You might even wish to double the recipe. It's great on other salads, too.

Bread: A French-style rye bread, or *pain de seigle*, goes very well with the spinach salad.

Lunch: You could follow the salad with a platter of fresh fruit and cheese, such as Reblochon or Brie.

Dinner: Start out with scaled-down portions of the spinach salad and follow with red snapper fillets cooked in lemon butter (melt a couple of tablespoons of butter and blend with 1 tablespoon freshly squeezed lemon juice), sprinkled with chopped cilantro and garnished with steamed little new potatoes.

Dessert: Crêpes with Chocolate Sauce (page 151) make a luscious finale.

Wine: Pour a *vin ordinaire*—an inexpensive blended red or white wine.

Low-Fat Plan: Omit the bacon and the egg yolks, omit the oil in the dressing and increase the broth to ½ cup.

Salade de Fenouil à la Maltaise

FENNEL AND BLOOD ORANGE SALAD

You may regard the blood orange as a fruit suited to the macabre images of Halloween, when in fact it is a gentle and decidedly delectable member of the orange family. The blood orange is immensely popular along the Mediterranean. Its State-side appearance, however, is generally limited to mid-December through mid-May.

Blood oranges, however, are well worth seeking out for their lovely garnet color and juicy, almost berrylike flavor. They mesh perfectly with wafer-thin slices of crunchy anise-flavored fennel in a salad Jean-Paul Picot adores. "We serve it as a light first course and often following the entrée as a refreshing palate picker-upper. It's so simple to prepare and can be made ahead, wrapped well with plastic wrap, and stored in the refrigerator for up to a day."

- 1 large fennel (about 1 pound)
- 2 blood oranges, peeled, pitted, and thinly sliced crosswise (see Note)
- 2 tablespoons extra-virgin olive oil
- 1 tablespoon balsamic vinegar
- Freshly ground pepper to taste
- ¼ cup thinly shaved Parmesan cheese

Trim the fennel at its base and save the feathery green and stalks to flavor soups. Cut the fennel in half lengthwise, then in quarters and cut into very thin slices. Arrange the fennel and orange slices in an overlapping pattern on each of 4 salad plates. Drizzle with the oil and vinegar and sprinkle generously with pepper. Top with curls of Parmesan.

Makes 4 servings

Note: *If you can't find blood oranges, substitute any well-flavored, juicy orange.*

Low-Fat Plan: Omit the olive oil and drizzle 1 tablespoon of defatted beef, chicken or vegetable broth over the fennel. Omit the cheese or substitute a finely grated low-fat Gruyere.

More on the Blood Orange

The skins of these flavorful oranges with their dark-red pulp and rich flavor run the gamut from pale orange to blush and are sometimes orange streaked with red. Specialty fruit stores import Italian blood oranges with names like Moro and Tarocco and a Spanish variety called Sanguinelli. In California, the blood orange harvests start in late fall; and although the crop is not gigantic, the fruit is generally available in local markets from late fall until late spring.

Yogurt Low-Fat Salad Dressing

For those pursuing low-fat regimens, this dressing is especially felicitous with the spinach salad and works very well with weightier lettuces, sliced cucumbers, and cole slaw. Use it as a nifty dip for crudités.

¾ cup plain nonfat or low-fat yogurt
Juice of 1 lime
2 shallots, finely minced
1 teaspoon Dijon mustard
Dash of Worcestershire sauce
2 tablespoons finely chopped cilantro
Salt and freshly ground pepper to taste

In a small bowl, whisk all the ingredients together until smooth and well amalgamated. The dressing should be the consistency of heavy cream. If it seems too thick, thin with a little skim milk.

Makes about 1 cup

Haricots Secs en Salade

SAVORY WHITE BEAN SALAD

This salad is another of Monique Picot's specialties that's simple to prepare and makes a pleasing side dish for baked ham, rabbit, poultry, and fish. It also doubles as a peppy participant in an array of hors d'oeuvre. Serve it, too, as a first course at dinner or for a light lunch or brunch. Simply add such appetite-whetters as tiny black Niçoise olives, a slice or two of prepared cold saucisson sec (French salami), thinly sliced cucumbers, a cluster of caper-stuffed anchovies, and a basket of croutons.

For the beans

1 pound dried white navy or pea beans, rinsed, picked through, soaked overnight in water to cover, drained, and rinsed again or use the quick soaking method (page 13)
3 sprigs fresh thyme or ¼ teaspoon dried
3 bay leaves
3 cloves garlic, roughly chopped

For the vinaigrette

1 tablespoon balsamic vinegar
4 tablespoons extra-virgin olive oil
1 Vidalia or other sweet onion, finely chopped
⅓ cup finely chopped fresh flat-leaf parsley
Salt and freshly ground pepper to taste

Prepare the beans:

Place the beans in a heavy 3-quart saucepan, add the thyme, bay leaves, garlic, and cold water to cover by 1 inch. Heat the water to just below boiling, then reduce the heat to medium-low, partially cover, and simmer until the beans are tender, about 1 hour. Drain the beans well and transfer them to a large bowl.

Prepare the vinaigrette:

Pour the vinegar into a small bowl. Gradually whisk in the oil, beating until it is well incorporated. Add the onion, parsley, salt and pepper, and blend well.

Pour the vinaigrette over the warm beans and gently toss. The beans may be served at room temperature or chilled. They will keep, covered, in the refrigerator up to 4 days.

Makes 8 side or 12 appetizer servings

Tip: It's handy and a comfort to keep a bag of frozen chopped onions in the freezer for those times when you're too frazzled to peel and chop them yourself. Ore-Ida freezes chopped sweet Spanish onions with no preservatives; ½ cup is equal to 1 medium-size onion. You'll find it in the supermarket's frozen vegetables case.

3

Light Bites for Brunch, Lunch, and Supper

La Bonne Soupe's light bites include the creamy omelets Francophiles order *baveuse,* soft and runny; the chef's savory Quiche Lorraine or his quiche of the day, filled with fresh green asparagus, broccoli, onions, and other pleasing partners; the classic Baked Ham and Cheese Sandwich; and the fun fondues—Cheese Fondue and Beef Fondue—with a cluster of zingy dipping sauces. These are the light bites enjoyed from lunchtime throughout the day until the late evening hours. Light bites are so adaptable to the time of day and to the diner's appetite. They're also super standbys for informal home entertaining. Guests especially enjoy the fun of fondues, and the boon for the host is once everything's been set in motion, he or she can close the kitchen door and join in the festivities. Easy entertaining. That's what La Bonne Soupe's Light Bites is all about.

Pipérade Basquaise

BASQUE-STYLE EGGS WITH PEPPERS, TOMATOES, AND HAM

This is often referred to as the Basque national omelet, although it's more like soft-scrambled eggs than an omelet. It's a dish Jean-Paul and Monique Picot are fond of preparing for Sunday brunch. "It really makes a flavorful brunch or lunch entrée, and even though the vegetables need to be cooked slowly until they're tender and browned, this part can be done ahead and reheated. Then all that's left to be done is to cook the eggs and add the ham," explains Jean-Paul.

The Picots like to add the garlic toward the end of the cooking time to give an authentic garlic spin—a strong jolt of flavor. But if you prefer your garlic a bit milder, add it as indicated here, at the same time as the onions at the start of the recipe. Or do a little of both. That's the fun of cooking, isn't it?

2 tablespoons extra-virgin olive oil

1 large onion, chopped

4 cloves garlic, finely minced

2 large green, red, or yellow bell peppers, cut into 2 x 1-inch strips

2 medium-size tomatoes, peeled, seeded and coarsely chopped

Salt and freshly ground pepper to taste

8 large eggs

4 thin slices Bayonne ham, or other air-dried, mild ham

Heat the oil in a heavy 12-inch skillet over medium heat until hot but not smoking. Add the onions and garlic (or half the garlic, if you're set on adding the remainder toward the end of the cooking) and cook over medium-low heat, stirring occasionally, until the onions are softened but not browned, 3 to 4 minutes. Add the bell peppers and cook over medium heat, stirring and turning so the pieces brown evenly, until lightly browned, 10 to 15 minutes. Add the tomatoes, salt and pepper and cook until soft, about 10 minutes.

Break the eggs in a medium-size bowl and, using a fork, stir them lightly but don't beat them up as you would for an omelet. Raise the heat under the skillet to medium-high and pour the lightly stirred eggs into the pan. Cook the eggs over medium-high heat, stirring to help them to set evenly. As soon as the eggs have set and are lightly browned on the bottom, take the skillet off heat, sprinkle with the remaining garlic, if you have chosen to deepen the garlic flavor, and spoon the *pipérade* onto warmed plates. Lay a slice of the ham alongside or on top and serve at once.

Makes 4 servings

Variation: Use a variety of colored bell peppers, if you like.

Bread: A thick-crusted sourdough bread and a crock of sweet country butter make this an irresistible meal.

Dinner: Hold the Basque mood and serve Chicken in the Pot (page 131) and a Savory White Bean Salad (page 47).

Dessert: Apple slices sprinkled with brown sugar and a little ground nutmeg, then baked until tender and glazed, are a wonderful windup.

Wine: A light red country wine such as Corbières from southwest France or a chilled Beaujolais makes fine sipping.

Low-Fat Plan: Sprinkle all the vegetables with ¼ cup of water and cook, covered, over low heat, stirring occasionally, until softened but not browned, 15 to 20 minutes. Use 8 to 10 egg whites and add 1 tablespoon of low-fat cottage cheese as you stir them. Continue with the recipe and, instead of the ham, substitute a thin slice of low-fat semihard cheese such as Alpine Lace Swiss cheese.

Omelette aux Fines Herbes

HERBED OMELET

"Since day one, omelets have been a mainstay of La Bonne Soupe," Jean-Paul Picot says, as he surveys the chattering throngs at lunchtime. "We use 150 dozen of the freshest grade-A eggs that are on the market every weekend and we usually serve them in the traditional French style—baveuse—slightly runny. Of course, increasingly health conscious diners want their omelet bien cuite, *and if that's their choice, they shall have it well done. Many of our patrons who are watching their*

cholesterol intake are asking for egg white–only omelets, which we're happy to whip up. It takes a bit of ingenuity to give these omelets the right texture and flavor, but with a little herbal alchemy, magical things can be accomplished."

1 tablespoon unsalted butter

2 large eggs

1 tablespoon finely minced fresh flat-leaf parsley

¼ teaspoon *each* dried chives, chervil, and tarragon

Salt and freshly ground white pepper to taste

¼ cup Tangy Tomato Sauce (page 148)

Heat the butter in a 6- or 8-inch omelet pan over low heat until it melts and becomes bubbly, about 1 minute. While the butter is heating, break the eggs into a small bowl and, using a wire whisk or a fork, beat vigorously until the eggs are light and frothy. Whisk in the parsley, herbs, salt and pepper. This should take about 30 seconds.

A guest scans the menu at a main dining room table.

Pour the eggs into the pan, tipping the pan so that the mixture adheres evenly. Raise the heat to medium-high and cook the eggs, pushing the sides to the center as they cook, while gently shaking and tilting the pan so that the uncooked parts flow to the bottom and are cooked.

When the bottom of the omelet is lightly browned and the top has set, remove the pan from the heat and loosen the edges of the omelet with a fork, shaking the pan gently. Tilt the pan and fold the omelet in half as you turn it onto a warmed plate. Spoon the Savory Tomato Sauce on top and serve at once.

Makes 1 serving

Bread: A warm, crusty baguette is a fine omelet partner.

Lunch: Add a salad of sliced ripe tomatoes flecked with chopped shallots and drizzled with a little extra-virgin olive oil.

Dinner: If you're serving omelets for dinner or late supper, add a hearty dish such as Scalloped Potatoes (page 140) and a salad of julienned cooked beets, chick peas, and chopped red onion with Jean-Paul's Zesty Vinaigrette (page 146).

Dessert: Top Dr. Vassaux's Rice Pudding (page 156) with a cloud of crème fraîche or lightly sweetened whipped cream and pour lots of hot double espresso. Or spoon plums cooked in red wine into pretty dishes and sprinkle with grated orange rind.

Wine: A fruity white, such as Chenin Blanc; a light-bodied red, such as Côtes du Ventoux (a Provençal wine); or another French country wine can be quaffed with pleasure with the omelet.

Low-Fat Plan: Omit the butter and use a nonstick pan. Add 1 teaspoon of water to the eggs while whisking them and continue with the recipe. See the Low-Fat Plan for the Scalloped Potatoes (page 141) to accompany this dish.

Egg Whites Omelet

The chefs at La Bonne Soupe work miracles with this unpromising but healthful proposition. A liberal lacing of herbs dramatically improves the flavor of the plain egg whites, and a dollop of low-fat cottage cheese lends texture while turmeric gives it a golden color.

6 large egg whites

1 tablespoon low-fat, small-curd cottage cheese

1 tablespoon each finely minced fresh chives, basil, and thyme or ¼ teaspoon *each* dried

1 tablespoon thinly sliced scallion

¼ teaspoon ground turmeric

Salt and freshly ground white pepper to taste

Dash of hot pepper sauce

½ cup Tangy Tomato Sauce (page 148)

1½ tablespoons peanut or corn oil

Break the egg whites into a mixing bowl and beat lightly with a wire whisk or fork until they start to foam up. Add the cottage cheese, whisking to blend well; then add all the remaining ingredients, except the Tangy Tomato Sauce and oil, whisking until the egg whites are a little fluffy and the herbs are well incorporated.

Heat the oil in a 9-or 10-inch omelet pan over medium heat until it is hot but not smoking. Add the egg mixture and raise the heat to moderately high. When the omelet starts to cook at the bottom, pull the cooked eggs from the sides to the center of the pan, tilting the pan so that the uncooked egg whites run to the bottom. When the eggs have set, after cooking for about 4 minutes, remove the pan from the heat. Tilting the pan, fold the omelet in half and slide it onto a warmed platter. Spoon Tangy Tomato Sauce over the omelet and serve at once.

Makes 2 servings

Bread: We think a crusty five-grain or other multigrain bread is a fine foil for this omelet.

Lunch and Supper: A big, mixed seasonal greens salad tossed with a favorite salad dressing is all that's needed as this light bite go-with.

Dessert: Pears Poached in White Wine (page 159) makes the perfect sweet ending.

Wine: Enjoy a glass of an inexpensive French Merlot.

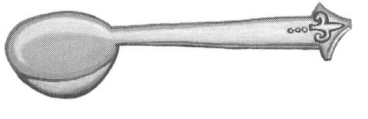

Omelette Paysanne Garniture

COUNTRY-STYLE OMELET

Andy Tseng, who has been a waiter at La Bonne Soupe for some 20 years, counts this omelet among his favorite dishes. "It's simple, tasty, and I really like the potatoes and onions as an integrated part of the omelet instead of as a side dish."

For the garnish

½ pound boiling potatoes, peeled and cut into ½-inch dice

2 tablespoons peanut or corn oil

1 medium-size onion, chopped

2 slices boiled ham, cut into ½-inch dice

For the omelet

4 large eggs, beaten to mix

Salt and freshly ground white pepper to taste

1 tablespoon peanut or corn oil

½ cup Mushroom Sauce (page 148) or Tangy Tomato Sauce (page 148)

Prepare the garnish:

Place the potatoes in a small saucepan, cover with water, and bring to a boil over high heat. Reduce the heat to medium-high, partially cover, and cook the potatoes until they are tender, 10 to 15 minutes. Drain well and reserve.

Heat the oil in a 9-inch skillet over medium-high heat until the oil is hot but not smoking. Add the onions and cook until they are softened but not browned, 3 to 4 minutes. Add the potatoes and cook, stirring occasionally, until they are lightly browned, 3 to 4 minutes. Add the ham and cook, stirring, just until the ham is heated through and the mixture is well blended, 2 to 3 minutes. Take off heat and reserve.

Prepare the eggs:

Break the eggs into a medium-size bowl and season with salt and pepper. Using a wire whisk or a fork, beat the eggs until they are light and frothy.

Heat the oil in a 9-inch omelet pan over medium-high heat and when it is hot but not smoking, add the eggs. Cook the eggs over medium-high heat, pushing the sides to the center as they cook, while gently shaking and tilting the pan so that the uncooked parts flow to the bottom of the pan.

When the bottom of the omelet is lightly browned and the top has set, remove the pan from the heat. Loosen the sides of the omelet with a fork, shaking the pan gently. Spoon the onion-potato-ham mixture onto one half of the omelet and fold the other half over. Slide the omelet onto a warmed platter and serve at once. Pass the Mushroom Sauce or Tangy Tomato Sauce separately or spoon over the omelet.

Makes 2 servings

Bread: Serve plenty of freshly baked baguettes with the omelet.

Lunch: The omelet makes a perfect brunch or lunch entrée with a basket of bread and a bowl of crisp red radishes for crunch.

Dinner: For a Sunday night dinner, augment the omelet with Jean-Paul's Pommes de Terre Savoyarde (page 143) and a big seasonal greens salad.

Dessert: Wedges of Apple Tart (page 163), topped with poufs of crème fraîche and lots of steaming cups of espresso are in order.

Wine: A French country wine such as Cahors or a nicely chilled Beaujolais makes companionable sipping.

Low-Fat Plan: Make the Egg Whites Omelet (page 52) and serve poached fruit for dessert.

Omelette aux Épinards

SPINACH OMELET

Fresh spinach may certainly be used for the filling. As a handy expedient, however, we've used frozen chopped spinach, which works very well.

For the filling

5 ounces frozen chopped spinach, thawed
1 tablespoon unsalted butter
¼ cup heavy cream
Salt and freshly ground pepper to taste
Pinch of ground nutmeg

For the eggs

4 large eggs
Salt and freshly ground pepper to taste
2 tablespoons unsalted butter
Mushroom Sauce (page 148) or Tangy Tomato Sauce (page 148)

Prepare the filling:

Cook the spinach, according to the package's directions. Drain and place in a strainer or colander. Using a large, wooden spoon or spatula, press out as much liquid as possible. (Save the liquid for a vegetable soup.)

Heat the butter in a small skillet over medium-low heat. Add the drained spinach and the cream and cook, stirring, until the mixture is well blended, about 3 minutes. Remove from the heat, season with salt, pepper, and nutmeg, and keep warm.

Prepare the eggs:

Beat the eggs in a medium-size bowl with salt and pepper until they are well blended. Heat the butter in a 9-inch omelet pan over medium-high heat and when it is hot but not smoking, add the eggs. Cook the eggs over medium-high heat, pushing the sides to the center as they cook, while gently shaking and tilting the pan so that the uncooked parts flow to the bottom of the pan.

When the bottom of the omelet is lightly browned and the top has set, remove the pan from the heat. Loosen the sides of the omelet with a fork, shaking the pan gently. Spoon the spinach mixture onto one half of the omelet and fold the other half over. Slide the omelet onto a warmed platter and serve at once with the Mushroom Sauce or Tangy Tomato Sauce.

Makes 2 servings

Quiche Lorraine

QUICHE LORRAINE WITH BACON AND HAM

This velvety, savory custard-filled pastry shell has been on the bistro's menu since day one, Jean-Paul Picot points out. "The name of this restaurant when I bought this place was La Quiche [it had formerly been La Crêpe]. They were featuring quiche, of course, so I kept the quiche on the menu, but we made them irresistibly delicious! Instead of the traditional bacon or ham filling, you can add so many flavorful things—onion, cheese, spinach, anything you like, even leftovers are great in a quiche—bits of cooked salmon, shrimp, lobster, and crabmeat."

When cut into bite-size morsels, quiche makes a superb hors d'oeuvre. Serve quiche hot, tiède *(room temperature) or cold.*

6 slices bacon, cut into 1-inch dice

4 large eggs

1 cup milk

1 cup heavy cream

Salt and freshly ground white pepper to taste

⅛ teaspoon ground nutmeg

One slice, about ¼-inch thick, boiled ham, cut into small dice

3 ounces Gruyère or other Swiss-type cheese, finely grated

One 9-inch Homemade Pastry Shell (page 56) or store-bought shell, partially baked

Preheat the oven to 375°F.

Cook the bacon in a skillet over medium-high heat until nicely crisp. Drain the crisped bacon on paper towels, crumble, and reserve.

Break the eggs into a medium-size mixing bowl and beat lightly with a fork. Stir in the milk and cream and add the salt, pepper, nutmeg, ham, and cheese. Beat until well blended.

Sprinkle the crumbled bacon over the bottom of the pastry shell. Pour the egg mixture into the shell and bake in the center of the oven until the custard has set and the top is puffed and golden, about 25 minutes. Cut into wedges and serve at once.

Makes 4 entrée or 6 appetizer servings

Bread: If you feel you must have bread on the table, even with a pastry shell, a thin-crusted ficelle (a skinny baguette) is probably your best bet.

Lunch: A small tossed green salad dressed simply with extra-virgin olive oil, red wine vinegar, and a hail of cracked pepper makes a pleasing accompaniment for the quiche.

Dinner: Cut the quiche into thin wedges and serve as a first course. Follow with halibut steaks broiled with lemon and butter. Garnish the plates with chopped steamed spinach and herb-scented rice.

Dessert: Individual peach melbas are an eye-catching, ambrosial finish to the meal: Place scoops of rich vanilla ice cream into dessert coupes, top with a poached or canned peach half, and spoon Rosy Raspberry Sauce (page 164) lavishly over the top. For a dash of panache, strew with slivered toasted almonds.

Wine: A young, fruity French country wine, such as Chinon or Bourgueil (both from the Loire Valley), is a convivial partner for a quiche. Or uncork a flowery Beaujolais, such as Fleurie or a California Gamay Beaujolais. These wines can take a light chilling. You can stay with the red wine for the halibut, which is a robust fish.

Homemade Pastry Shell

You can partially bake this pastry shell a day ahead and keep it, covered with foil, in the refrigerator. Bring it to room temperature before filling and baking.

1¼ cups sifted flour
Pinch of salt
¼ cup vegetable shortening
About 2 tablespoons ice water

Place the flour and salt in a mixing bowl. Using a pastry blender or two forks, cut in the shortening until the mixture resembles coarse meal. Sprinkle the water over the flour mixture and, using a fork, lightly and quickly mix until the pastry holds together. If it seems too dry, add another tablespoon of ice water. Form the pastry into a ball, wrap in plastic or waxed paper, and chill in the refrigerator for 20 minutes.

Preheat the oven to 425°F.

Roll out the dough on a floured board into a circle about 12 inches in diameter. Transfer the pastry to a 9-inch pie pan and press lightly to fit. Press the sides so that about 1 inch of the pastry hangs over. (If it hangs unevenly, trim it to an even 1 inch.) Using your thumb and forefinger, flute the edges. Using a fork, prick the bottom and sides at random to prevent shrinkage.

To partially bake the shell, cut a piece of aluminum foil or waxed paper to fit the bottom of the pastry shell and place it in the bottom of the pan. Add dried beans or rice to weight it down. Bake the shell in the center of the oven just until it turns light tan, about 10 minutes. Remove the shell from the oven, and cool before filling. Remove the foil and discard the beans. The shell is now ready to receive the quiche filling and finish baking.

Makes one 9-inch pastry shell

Tip: Frozen 9-inch deep-dish pie shells are available in most supermarkets. They make a fine pastry shell for quiche with a minimum of fuss, so you may want to keep a package or two in your freezer.

Quiche aux Asperges

ASPARAGUS QUICHE

Fresh asparagus spears are the best choice for this version. But if you can't find any around and you're determined to do an asparagus quiche, defrost frozen spears, pat them dry with paper towels and cut them into ½-inch pieces. They'll have a slightly different texture but the flavor should be true.

1½ tablespoons unsalted butter

8 spears asparagus, tough ends removed, spears peeled and cut into ½-inch pieces

4 large eggs

1 cup milk

¾ cup heavy cream

Salt and freshly ground white pepper to taste

Pinch of ground nutmeg

½ cup grated Gruyère or other Swiss-type cheese

One 9-inch Homemade Pastry Shell (page 56) or store-bought shell, partially baked

Preheat the oven to 375°F.

Melt the butter in a medium-size skillet over medium-high heat. Add the asparagus and cook, stirring, just until the pieces start to soften, 3 to 4 minutes. Remove from the heat and reserve.

Milk-to-Cream Ratio

La Bonne Soupe uses all cream for its quiches, which are indeed luxurious. However, you can adjust the proportions to your tastes and predilections. You can use half milk, half light cream. You can use 1 or 2 percent milk or even all skim milk. Unfortunately, La Bonne Soupe could not come up with a satisfactory egg whites quiche.

Quiche à l'Oignon

ONION QUICHE

Here's a personal favorite of Jean-Paul Picot. "If you're an onion lover like myself, be lavish with the onions and cook them gently until they're soft; you don't want them to brown."

2 tablespoons unsalted butter or margarine

2 large onions, thinly sliced

4 large eggs

1 cup milk

1 cup heavy cream

Salt and freshly ground white pepper to taste

One 9-inch Homemade Pastry Shell (page 56) or store-bought shell

½ cup Gruyère or other Swiss-type cheese, finely grated

Preheat the oven to 375°F.

Melt the butter in a large skillet over medium heat. Add the onions and cook, covered, stirring occasionally, until they have wilted and softened but not browned, about 20 minutes. Remove from the heat and reserve.

Break the eggs into a medium-size mixing bowl and beat lightly with a fork. Add the milk, cream, and salt and pepper and beat until well blended.

Strew the cooked onions over the bottom of the pastry shell. Pour the egg mixture on top of the onions and sprinkle the top of the filling with the cheese. Bake in the center of the oven until the custard has set and the top is puffed and golden, about 25 minutes. Cut into wedges and serve at once.

Makes 4 entrée or 6 appetizer servings

Quiche aux Épinards

SPINACH QUICHE

Although you can use fresh spinach, Chef Francis finds frozen chopped spinach a flavorful expedient, with the added plus of having a handy supply in the freezer, ready for spur-of-the-moment use.

One 10-ounce package frozen chopped spinach

4 large eggs

1 cup milk

¾ cup heavy cream

Salt and freshly ground pepper to taste

Pinch of ground nutmeg

One 9-inch Homemade Pastry Shell (page 56) or store-bought shell, partially baked

¾ cup grated Gruyère or other Swiss-type cheese

Preheat the oven to 375°F.

Cook the spinach according to the package's directions. Drain and place the spinach in a strainer or colander. Using a large wooden spoon or spatula, press out as much water as possible. (Save the liquid for a vegetable soup.)

Break the eggs into a medium-size bowl and beat lightly with a fork. Add the milk, cream, salt and pepper, and nutmeg and beat until well blended.

Strew the spinach over the bottom of the pastry shell. Pour the egg mixture on top of the spinach and sprinkle the top of the filling with the cheese. Bake in the center of the oven until the custard has set and the top is puffed and golden, about 25 minutes. Cut into wedges and serve at once.

Makes 4 entrée or 6 appetizer servings

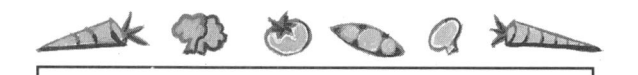

Some Saucy Thoughts on Making Béchamel Sauce

Béchamel is simply a basic white sauce, and the one possible caveat in cooking a flour-based sauce is to avoid lumps. After the melted butter and flour mixture (known as a *roux* in French cooking) is smoothly formed, the addition of the milk is best accomplished by using a wire whisk that can reach all around the pan. The mixture should become thick and smooth. If you do find it contains lumps, take the pan off heat and beat vigorously with the whisk or a rotary beater, until smooth.

Some *béchamel* sauces have the cheese incorporated into the mixture (these are often called Mornay sauces), but here, Jean-Paul likes to sprinkle the cheese on top.

The proportions in the recipe will make a medium-thick sauce. If you prefer a thinner sauce, add another ¼ cup of milk.

Never leave a white sauce or *béchamel* standing over direct heat without stirring. It is a very stick-and-scorch-prone mixture.

Croque Monsieur

BAKED HAM AND CHEESE SANDWICH

Here's a Parisian favorite at cafés for lunch or supper after an evening on the town. It's said to have been created at a little café on the Boulevard des Capucines shortly after the end of World War I. The sandwich is layered with slices of baked ham and Swiss cheese, and baked under a coverlet of Gruyère-flavored béchamel (white) sauce until golden and bubbly. The bread used in the original recipe may have been a brioche, but Jean-Paul Picot feels this makes the sandwich too rich, so he suggests half a baguette cut in half or, even more authentic, two slices of firm white bread.

For the sandwiches

- 4 thin slices baked ham, trimmed to fit the bread
- 4 slices firm-textured white bread, crusts removed, lightly toasted
- 4 thin slices Swiss cheese, trimmed to fit the bread

For the *béchamel* sauce

- 2 tablespoons unsalted butter
- 2 tablespoons all-purpose flour
- 1½ cups milk, whole or skim, heated until bubbles appear around the edge
- Salt and freshly ground pepper to taste
- ½ cup grated Gruyère or other Swiss-type cheese
- 6 cherry tomatoes
- 4 sprigs parsley

Preheat the oven to 375°F.

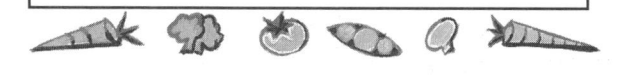

Prepare the sandwiches:

Have ready an ovenproof dish that will hold the two sandwiches. Lay 2 slices of ham on each of two slices of toast and top with two slices of cheese. Close the sandwiches with the second slice of toast and place in the ovenproof dish.

Prepare the sauce:

Melt the butter in a heavy 1-quart saucepan over low heat. Add the flour, stirring with a wire whisk or wooden spoon, until a smooth paste forms, about 1 minute. Don't allow the mixture to brown. Raise the heat to medium and slowly stir in the milk, whisking until the sauce boils. Continue to whisk or stir until the sauce is thick and smooth, about 2 minutes. Season with salt and pepper, remove from heat.

Spread half of the sauce on the top of each sandwich. Sprinkle with the cheese and bake in the center of the oven until the cheese has melted and the sauce is golden brown, 15 to 20 minutes. To serve, transfer the sandwiches to two warmed plates and garnish with tomatoes and parsley sprigs.

Makes 2 servings

Lunch or supper: Add a crunchy salad of mixed lettuces, shredded red cabbage, and matchstick strips of green pepper dressed with olive oil, red wine vinegar, and a little grated onion.

Dessert: Serve apple wedges poached in a light cinnamon syrup and crisp Lacy Tile Cookies (page 158).

Wine: A chilled rosé from Provence or a simple Beaujolais make a delightful sipping.

Low-Fat Plan: Make the sandwich with low-fat ham and a low-fat cheese. For the *béchamel* sauce, use 1 tablespoon canola oil, 1 tablespoon flour, and 1 cup hot skim milk. Season well with salt, pepper, and a dash or 2 of hot pepper sauce or ground hot pepper. Omit the final sprinkling of cheese.

Fondue au Fromage

CHEESE FONDUE

Fondues au fromage *(with melted cheese) and* à la Bourguignonne *(with beef) reflect Jean-Paul Picot's Swiss sojourn and the time he spent at the L'École Hôtelière in Lausanne as a chef trainee. It was there that he developed a passion for these fondues, which he lovingly recreates at La Bonne Soupe. Somehow, there always seems to be a* caquelon, *or fondue pot, simmering at one of the checkered-cloth-covered tables. Sometimes it's a twosome, relishing the morsels of melted-cheese-swathed bread. Often it's a large party, engaged in lively conversation between mouthfuls of fondue and sips of white wine. It's such a convivial dish! And, as Pierre Franey points out, anyone who loses his or her morsel of bread in the pot buys a round of drinks for the table.*

As with the Beef Fondue (page 62), long-handled forks for dipping the bread into the fondue pot are set at each place. But unlike the beef fondue, where a dinner fork is also set at each place, the long-handled fork does yeoman's job for the cheese dish. "The heat is not as intense, and the morsel can be cooled a bit before eating it," Jean-Paul Picot explains. "You can use the long-handled fork to impale the bread and then deposit the covered cube on the plate." The whole idea is to provide a happy ambiance for informal jollity and gustatory pleasure.

1 small clove garlic

About 1½ cups dry white wine, such as Swiss
    Fendant

1 pound Gruyère or other Swiss-type cheese,
    coarsely grated

Pinch of ground red pepper

Pinch of ground nutmeg

Pinch of baking soda

1 tablespoon kirsch or other cherry brandy

1 or 2 loaves French bread, cut into 1-inch cubes, each cube with crust on one side, untoasted

Use a 1½-quart cheese fondue pot or other heavy, enameled cast-iron pan with a handle. Rub the inside of the pot with the garlic clove, add the wine, and set the pot over medium heat. Cook the wine until bubbles form around the edge. Add the cheese gradually, stirring until the mixture is smooth. Don't allow the mixture to come to a boil. Add the ground red pepper, nutmeg, baking soda, and kirsch, stirring after each addition, and cook just until the mixture is hot but not boiling and the consistency of a medium-thick white sauce.

To serve, place the fondue pot over a gas or alcohol table burner. Regulate the heat so that the fondue barely simmers. Pile the bread cubes into a napkin-lined basket. Equip each diner with a long-handled fondue fork and a small plate. Each person spears a bread cube and swirls it about in the fondue until it's well coated.

Keep an eye on the fondue, and if the cheese becomes too thick, stir in ¼ cup of warmed wine. (Cold liquids will cause the cheese to separate.)

Makes 4 entrée or 12 snack servings

Lunch: Add a salad of peeled, diced cucumbers and matchstick strips of red and yellow bell peppers dressed with a little extra-virgin olive oil and red wine vinegar for pleasing color, textural contrast, and a refreshing tang.

Supper: As a supper or late-evening meal, add the cucumber and bell pepper salad mentioned in the lunch suggestion above and pile homemade cole slaw into a bowl. Set out another big bowl of cut up fresh fruits.

Dessert: Offer Lacy Tile Cookies (page 158) or a large platter of store-bought *petits fours*—individual decorously iced cakes—and pour copious cups of espresso.

Wine: The classic cheese fondue wine is a Neuchâtel from the Swiss region on the northern shore of Lake Neuchâtel. This is a dry light-bodied white wine with good acidity. However, a Mâcon-Villages Blanc, or California Chenin Blanc will do very nicely.

Wine Temperature

It is important that you avoid adding cold wine to the fondue pot once it has been made. The Swiss frown on drinking chilled wine with the hot cheese, based on their impression that the two elements can encourage stomach distress. However, we can report that we have indeed sipped chilled white wine with our hot cheese fondue—with no discomfort whatsoever.

Fondue Bourguignonne

BEEF FONDUE

Nello and Madame Santi often invite a group of friends for a Fondue Bourguinonne after a performance at the Metropolitan Opera. The renowned Italian conductor, who also conducts the Zurich Opera, shares the fun of cooking cubes of steak in the simmering pot of oil. "I like mine à point, rare," says the ebullient Santi, "with a nice glass of red wine, good, crusty bread, and lots of tasty, spicy relishes for dipping."

2 cups peanut or corn oil

2 pounds fillet of beef, tenderloin, or other very tender cut of beef, cut into bite-size cubes less than 1 inch

Tartar Sauce (page 63)

Sauce Aurore (page 63)

Curry-Sherry Sauce (page 63)

Heat the oil in a heavy enameled steel pot (see Note) over low heat on top of the stove until it is very hot but not smoking. To test the oil for readiness, add a small cube of bread to the pot. If it browns in just 1 minute the oil is ready. Cover the pot and transfer it to an alcohol burner stand at the table.

Set each place with a salad plate, long-handled fork, and regular dinner fork. Pile 4 dinner plates with about one-quarter of the beef cubes and place one in front of each guest. Place the sauces in small bowls for guests to help themselves.

Uncover the fondue pot and let guests cook their cubes of beef as they like: for rare, about 10 seconds should do it; for medium, about 15 seconds; for well done, about 20 seconds.

Makes 4 servings

Tip: Set out additional relishes to add more variety: A good tangy chutney, piccalilli, spicy and sweet mustards, and pickled mushrooms and onions.

Bread: A fresh sliced baguette is your best bet.

Lunch: Serve a smaller amount of meat and add a small tossed green salad.

Dinner: Add a bowl of oven-browned potatoes and a big salad of seasonal greens tossed with extra-virgin olive oil and red wine vinegar.

Dessert: Offer a big fresh-fruit salad macerated in kirsch (cherry brandy), and a platter of Lacy Tile Cookies (page 158).

Wine: Because of the mayonnaise sauces, we suggest a robust red such as Côte de Beaune.

Low-Fat Plan: Replace the oil with 2 cups of chicken or beef broth and replace the beef with chicken breasts cut into ½-inch cubes. Increase the cooking time for the chicken cubes to 1 minute. Check the hot broth from time to time with a morsel of bread to make sure it is kept hot enough. If the bread doesn't brown in 1 minute, add more boiling broth, or reheat the broth on the stove and return it to the alcohol burner.

Variations: Instead of the beef, try cooking small, peeled shrimp, bay scallops, or sea scallops cut into bite-size portions.

A word on fondue pots

The fondue pot ideally should be deep and wide to allow the twirling of several forks in the melted cheese. It should be weighty enough and solid enough so that the heat is diffused, thus enabling you to coddle the cheese mixture without letting it separate. An enameled cast-iron or enameled steel pan with a long handle is perfect. These come in 1- and 1 ½-quart sizes and they can be used for other prepping, such as making a *béchamel* sauce or cooking vegetables.

For the Bourguinonne you will need a heavy enameled steel pot that holds 3 cups of oil and is shaped wider at the bottom than the top. A cheese fondue pot is not suitable because of its wide, shallow shape. The utensil must be narrower at the top to prevent the oil from spattering, and it needs to be bottom-heavy for maximum stability.

Fondue bourguignonne pots and sets that come with burners may be found in specialty kitchenware shops and are really very nice to have. They're appropriately shaped with heavy bottoms and narrow tops, made of materials that will hold the heat well. Some come with spatter-shield covers with apertures for the long-handled forks for greater safety.

Tartar Sauce

This and the other two zingy sauces easily double as dips for crudités—carrot sticks, endive leaves, cauliflower, cherry tomatoes, celery, and fennel.

¾ cup mayonnaise
¼ cup chopped *cornichons* or drained pickle relish
¼ cup nonpareil capers (tiny capers), drained
¼ cup chopped fresh flat-leaf parsley
½ teaspoon Worcestershire sauce
¼ teaspoon freshly ground pepper

Blend all ingredients and refrigerate until ready to use.

Makes about 1 cup

Sauce Aurore

¾ cup mayonnaise
¼ cup ketchup
½ teaspoon hot pepper sauce
1 tablespoon brandy

Blend all ingredients and refrigerate until ready to use.

Makes about 1 cup

Curry-Sherry Sauce

¾ cup mayonnaise
2 tablespoons curry powder
1 tablespoon dry fino sherry

Blend all ingredients and refrigerate until ready to use.

Makes about ¾ cup

Les Hamburgers and Filet Mignon

"Everyone loves our French-American hamburgers," muses Jean-Paul Picot as he sits at a checkered-cloth–covered table during an afternoon lull. "We grind the steak ourselves. Normally we use about 10 pounds of meat daily, except when the kids are on vacation. Then it zooms up to 25 pounds. We get a lot of teenagers. In fact, after all these years we are now starting to have a second generation of hamburger eaters. They clamor for *steak haché* and *pommes frites* [a hamburger and French fries].

"Our hamburgers are a bit different from those most Americans see. The pure meat is grilled and then we add a little sauce—say *au poivre* [a peppery sauce]; *paysanne* [a zesty garlic-butter sauce]; or *sauce maison,* made with shallots, wine, and mushrooms. And the hamburger is served without a bun. But there are plentiful pommes frites and crusty French bread to sop up the sauces."

Steak Haché Pizzaiola

HAMBURGERS WITH ZESTY GARLIC SAUCE

This pizzaiola sauce is a nod to Jean-Paul Picot's stint at the Hotel Excelsior in Florence. "It was my first working experience," Jean-Paul Picot explains, "and I loved the zesty sauces, such as this, which is a basic tomato and garlic mélange. In Italy, the sauce is scented with wild marjoram or oregano, but here at our bistro, we like the tingle of fresh basil."

For the *pizzaiola* sauce

3 tablespoons extra-virgin olive oil

1 medium-size red or yellow onion, chopped

3 or 4 cloves garlic, minced

2 medium-size tomatoes, peeled, seeded and chopped

¾ cup fresh basil leaves, chopped

One 6-ounce can tomato paste

½ teaspoon hot pepper flakes

Salt and freshly ground pepper to taste

For the hamburgers

Four 8-ounce hamburger patties made from lean ground sirloin or ground round

4 slices mozzarella cheese

Prepare the pizzaiola sauce:

Heat the oil in a 1½-quart saucepan over medium heat. Add the onion and garlic and cook, stirring, until softened but not browned, 6 to 7 minutes. Add the tomatoes and cook until wilted and slightly softened, 3 to 4 minutes. Add the basil and cook, stirring, for another minute.

Add the tomato paste, pepper flakes, salt and pepper, and simmer for 5 minutes.

Cool the sauce slightly and place the tomato mixture in a food processor or blender and process until puréed. Return to the saucepan and keep warm.

Prepare the hamburgers:

Preheat the broiler. Broil the hamburgers 3 inches from the heat, 5 minutes per side for rare, 6 minutes for medium, and 8 minutes for well done. Transfer the hamburgers to a baking pan that will hold them in one layer. Spoon some of the sauce over each and place a slice of mozzarella on top. Broil 3 inches from the heat just until the cheese melts, about 1 minute. Serve at once.

Makes 4 servings

Lunch: Garnish the hamburger plates with mounds of thin French Fries (page 142) and a salad of tossed seasonal greens dressed with Shallot Vinaigrette (page 146).

Dinner: Double up on the French Fries (page 142) and serve an extra-large salad.

Dessert: A luscious Melting Chocolate Mousse (page 162) is an ideal finale.

Wine: Pour a robust red country wine such as a Corbières or Minervois from southwest France, or try a fruity, lightly chilled Beaujolais.

Low-Fat Plan: Omit the oil in the sauce. Place the onion and garlic in a nonstick skillet and sprinkle with 3 tablespoons water or white wine. Cover and cook over low heat until the vegetables are softened but not browned, 5 to 6 minutes. Proceed with the recipe. Use extra-lean meat and reduce the weight to 4 ounces for each person. When broiling the thinner patties, cut the cooking time by 2 minutes per side.

Steak Haché Sauce Paysanne

HAMBURGERS WITH PEASANT SAUCE

Jean-Paul calls this a peasant sauce because the simple components—garlic, shallots, lemon juice, salt, and pepper—are ingredients most working folks in rural France would have readily available. The butter log is Chef Francis's classic contribution. It adds a touch of elegance and fine flavor, which may seem like a contradiction for a peasant sauce, but so what? It's delectable!

The butter log may be stored in the freezer, but be sure to wrap it in freezer paper. You can still cut the slices when the log is frozen, but allow the cut slices to defrost a little before placing them atop the hamburgers.

For the butter log

¼ pound unsalted butter (1 stick), at room temperature (see Note)

4 shallots, finely chopped

1 or 2 cloves garlic, finely chopped

Juice of 1 small lemon

Salt and freshly ground pepper to taste

½ cup finely chopped fresh flat-leaf parsley

For the hamburgers

Eight 8-ounce hamburger patties made from lean ground sirloin or ground round

Prepare the butter log:

Using a spatula or wooden spoon, mash together all the ingredients. Tear off an 8 x 10-inch sheet of waxed paper or aluminum foil. Transfer the butter mixture to the center of the paper and, using your hands, shape the mixture into a cylinder, approximately 4 inches long and 1 inch wide. Wrap the log securely and store in the coldest part of the refrigerator. It will keep up to 1 week.

Prepare the hamburgers:

Preheat the broiler.

Broil the hamburgers 3 inches from the heat: 5 minutes per side for rare, 6 minutes for medium, and 8 minutes for well done. To serve, cut the butter log into 1-inch slices and place 1 slice on top of each cooked hamburger.

Makes 8 servings

Note: Depending on how cold the butter is and how warm your kitchen is, this can take from 5 minutes in a 70 to 80° kitchen to 15 minutes in a cooler room.

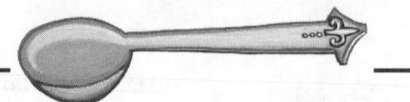

Growing Up with La Bonne Soupe

What is it like working at La Bonne Soupe when your parents own the place? François Picot tells his story.

Yves (left) and François in the fishing port of Honfleur, circa 1972.

"When my brother Yves and I were in our teens (my teens being 18 months ahead of Yves's), we worked at our parents' bistro during the summer to earn extra money. I was the first to work in the kitchen under the watchful eye and often tart tongue of Chef René. He was a Swiss and a very hot-tem-

pered guy. He also resented our working there. He felt we were taking jobs away from kids who really needed them. So he gave me all the hard jobs, like peeling onions and potatoes down in the basement; well, the kitchen was so small, there really wasn't room to do these chores there. Finally, when I was 16, I was promoted to *sous-chef*. I made the hamburgers and the soups and the salad dressings and even some of the desserts, one of which got me in trouble. It was the *mousse au chocolat*, which I kept tasting and tasting—only to make sure it was absolutely perfect, right?"

Trouble in Paradise

"Well, Chef René and I were always a little bit edgy with each other and he really tried to make my life miserable. So one hot summer day René said to me, 'François, you're fired.' To which I replied, 'You can't fire me because I quit.'"

"But it was fun working at the bistro and good experience. I learned a little bit about the restaurant business; plus La Bonne Soupe is a very homey place. I really got to know the staff, and we had great rapport. I'd always bring my dates there, not because we got a free meal but because the food was so good (and so reasonable). I'd never tell my date that my father owned the restaurant until afterward. All my dates loved La Bonne Soupe."

François was also bartender for a week, filling in for the indisposed regular. "I didn't know much about mixing drinks, but I knew how to open a bottle of wine, and that was a start. The wait staff came behind the bar and mixed the drinks until I did some research and began to get the hang of it. The really big sellers were frozen daiquiris and margaritas, which, I must say, we do very well. They're still very popular with a certain young crowd. It was fun working behind that tiny bar.

"It amazes me that with that small kitchen such a diversity and abundance of dishes can be prepared. What this taught me is that in order to get things done in life you have to be really organized.

"The pivotal force behind the bistro, of course, is my father and the key thing about him is he's so very kind to people, including the staff and everyone working with him. And his graciousness to his friends is legendary. Then there's my mother, who has done so much for the bistro. She definitely gave

it its really French ambiance, setting the tone of the decor and adding big charm to everything. She is still the *éminence grise* behind it, always giving it style and class and helpful menu suggestions.

"I think La Bonne Soupe has done so well for these more than 20 years because it is so diverse. Sure, there will always be the classic *plats du jour*, but people are becoming so health conscious and are not eating the way they used to and so there must be adjustments for this. My father recognizes this and he sent our chef down to Florida to Yves's restaurant to observe the light and trendy dishes that are prepared there. I think this is being pretty much with it."

Birthday Party at La Bonne Soupe

"The best moment of my life at La Bonne Soupe was the big surprise party there on my 21st birthday. My father closes the restaurant three days a year: on Thanksgiving, Christmas, and New Year's. Well, on my birthday I was with my girlfriend, planning to go out to celebrate. She said we were going out, but that we first had to meet my parents at La Bonne Soupe. I wasn't so thrilled at that. But when we arrived at the bistro it was filled with flowers, friends, and family; and there was this really great surprise party just for me. It was wonderful!"

Steak Haché Sauce Maison

HAMBURGERS WITH THE HOUSE SAUCE

Here's a deep-flavored sauce enhanced with mushrooms and red wine that gives a sophisticated lagniappe to hamburgers. You could also use it to dress up a plain omelet or spoon over broiled salmon or swordfish.

For the sauce

1 tablespoon vegetable oil

1 large shallot, finely minced

¼ pound mushrooms, stems removed (see Note), sliced

1 cup dry red wine

1 cup Homemade Beef Broth (page 3) or low-sodium canned broth

Salt and freshly ground pepper to taste

1 tablespoon unsalted butter

For the hamburgers

Four 8-ounce hamburger patties made from lean ground sirloin or ground round

Prepare the sauce:

Heat the oil in a medium-size skillet over medium heat until hot but not smoking. Add the shallot and cook over medium heat until softened but not browned, 3 to 4 minutes. Add the mushrooms and cook over medium heat just until they darken and exude their juices, 3 to 4 minutes. Add the wine and broth and bring to a boil over high heat. Reduce the heat to medium-high and cook until the liquid has reduced to half, about 8 minutes. Season with salt and pepper and swirl in the butter, stirring to blend well. (The sauce may be made ahead and stored, covered in the refrigerator for up to 3 days.)

Prepare the hamburgers:

Preheat the broiler.

Broil the hamburgers 3 inches from the heat: 5 minutes per side for rare, 6 minutes for medium, and 8 minutes for well done. To serve, spoon the sauce over the hamburgers.

Makes 4 servings

Note: Save the mushroom stems to add flavor to soups and stews.

Filet Mignon au Poivre

PEPPERED FILET MIGNON

Steak au poive, *here made with filet mignon—the choice boneless cut of beef from he narrow end of the tenderloin—is rubbed generously with cracked black pepper, is pan cooked, and is usually served with a velvety wine or mushroom sauce. It has been a Paris bistro favorite through the years.*

When Jean-Paul and Monique Picot were first planning La Bonne Soupe's menu, back in the early 1970s, they were keen on including a pepper steak in their à la carte listings. But was the timing right? Did it fit in with the economy of the times? In the end, they decided to put the filet on hold, but from the moment it did appear—a decade later—it became an in-demand special. Jean-Paul buys only prime beef, and the filets are sinfully tender and voluptuously sauced with red wine, Dijon mustard, and Cognac.

Four 8-ounce filet mignon steaks (see Note)

2 tablespoons cracked black peppercorns

1 tablespoon peanut or corn oil

2 tablespoons Cognac

1 cup dry red wine

1 cup Homemade Beef Broth (page 3) or low-sodium canned broth

Salt to taste

1 tablespoon Dijon mustard

1/2 teaspoon Worcestershire sauce

1/3 cup heavy cream

1 tablespoon unsalted butter

Sprinkle the steaks on both sides with half the black pepper and press in well with the heel of your hand. Heat the oil in a large heavy skillet over medium heat. When the oil is hot but not smoking, add the steaks and cook to the desired doneness: 3 minutes on each side for rare, 4 to 5 minutes for medium, and 5 to 7 minutes for well done. Transfer the steaks to a warm platter and keep warm.

Add the Cognac, wine, and broth to the skillet and bring to a boil over medium heat. Cook until the liquid is reduced to about 1/2 cup, 8 to 10 minutes. Add all the remaining ingredients except the butter and cook over medium heat until the sauce thickens a bit, 3 to 4 minutes. Swirl in the butter until it blends smoothly.

To serve, place the filet mignons on warmed dinner plates, and spoon some of the sauce on top.

Makes 4 servings

Note: *If the filet mignons are too pricey, you can substitute boneless sirloin or other steak that happens to be a* bon marché *(good deal) at your supermarket or butcher shop.*

Bread: Any fresh, crusty French loaf makes an ideal companion to the steak and its savory sauce.

Lunch: Do a La Bonne Soupe lunch: Serve big bowls of Peasant-Style Mushroom and Barley Soup (page 5), a basket of chunky peasant bread, and a salad of thinly sliced endive and julienned beets dressed with a little extra-virgin olive oil, freshly squeezed lemon juice, and a sprinkling of chopped shallots.

Dinner: French Fries (page 142) are a natural with the filet mignon or you could serve Monique's Garlicky Mashed Potatoes (page 137). Follow with a salad of tossed arugula, curly chicory, and sliced raw mushrooms in a mustardy vinaigrette.

Dessert: Scoop melon balls into individual dessert dishes and sprinkle with a medium-rich, gold Verdelho Madeira. Pass a plate of thin, crisp store-bought ginger cookies.

Wine: Uncork a mature red Bordeaux or California Cabernet Sauvignon.

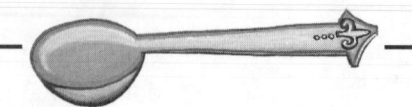

A Son Remembers

Being the owner's son doesn't necessarily mean receiving kid-glove treatment. Yves Picot talks about working his way up at La Bonne Soupe.

"I started as a dishwasher at La Bonne Soupe when I was about 12. My brother and I had to become a team very quickly, because lunch would get so busy that we often found ourselves 'in the weeds.'

"At the beginning, we could not keep up with the mountains of dishes and silverware atop the stainless-steel prep tables. Considering the size of the kitchen, which we called *le sous-marin*, or 'the submarine,' this was something that you wanted to keep control of. It took about a week to figure out the system, after which no more foreign objects were hurled at us by Chef René."

Yves and dessert pastries in Paris, circa 1968.

Into the Dungeon

"When the pace slowed at about 2:30 P.M., René would relegate one of us to the 'dungeon'—the basement—to peel vegetables or separate what seemed to be a million eggs. While my brother preferred to stay in the kitchen, I would jump at the opportunity for a quiet time in the dungeon.

"Toward the end of high school, I started working upstairs in the office with Pat Thieffry, the manager. It didn't hurt that she was blond and beautiful as well as a good teacher of the administrative duties in a restaurant.

"I enjoyed this tremendously, because it was my first experience in a position of responsibility. I learned about restaurant labor laws, payroll, taxes, accounts payable, and many other tasks."

Quality Time

"As new and interesting as all this was, the 3:00 P.M. walk to the bank with my father was what I enjoyed the most. We developed a real friendship on these daily journeys. My father had worked so hard all his life that I, as a child growing up, did not see him very often. On Sunday mornings, we had to be very quiet so as not to wake him. Sunday was the only time that we all spent together. My father would take us to the same restaurant every week, first Luchow's, then La Rotisserie, and then Victor's Cafe. Now, as we went to the bank and back, for the first time we talked to each other about what was on our minds.

"These trips were never without interruption; since my father often was referred to as 'the mayor of Fifty-fifth Street,' we always would be stopped by a shop owner, friend, customer, or acquaintance. This really gave me the feeling of being in a small town, despite living in one of the busiest cities in the world.

"It is my father's gentle and personable manner, I believe, that has brought him to his level of success and of respect, which he returns in full measure. For example, when he would arrive at the restaurant every morning, he would always go out of his way to say hello to all the employees, often shaking their hands.

"At the end of every working day we would gather at the bar. Pat [the bartender], my father, and I were the permanent fixtures, and we were joined by various friends, usually French, who worked in the area. It would be easy talk and gossip about friends and the trade and all the occurrences of the day. There never seemed to be a dull moment."

5

Fish

Fish is as expensive as meat these days, both in this country and in France, especially since the health-awareness groups have touted its low-cholesterol, low-fat attributes. In France, fish has always had a starring role in any menu. In *haute cuisine,* the "noble" fish—sole, turbot, salmon—dominate the menu, accompanied by an infinite array of lavish sauces. In French country cooking, more humble fish—skate, eel, rockfish, mackerel—are cooked in a seemingly endless variety of ways.

At La Bonne Soupe, Jean-Paul Picot's own special version *Bouillabaisse de Bonne Soupe* (page 123) is featured once a week—usually on Friday, and it is one of the bistro's sought-after dishes, with its delicately seasoned broth and enticing chunks of the freshest fish and shellfish. And Chef Francis Freund sees to it that there's at least one fish dish daily on the special *plats du jour* menu. Jean-Paul procures the fish for the restaurant from his longtime prime purveyor on Long Island, and he is exceedingly particular in choosing only fresh, catch-of-the-day seafood, which is then treated with expertise and imagination by Chef Francis.

"I try to create exciting fish dishes," Chef Francis explains, with typical enthusiasm. "We at the bistro like to mix classic fish recipes, such as Salt Cod Puréed with Garlic, Olive Oil, and Cream;

Grilled Salmon with Watercress Sauce; and other fish of the day, simply grilled and sauced." Diners eagerly await the daily special when it's Monkfish in Red Wine Sauce, with its meaty texture, smooth, savory sauce, and subtle seasoning of spices.

On the following pages are some captivating recipes the Picots prepare at their homes in New York City and in the Hamptons. They're not only great tasting and healthful, they're easy to prepare and make superb company dishes. Guests can't get enough of Jean-Paul's Mussels Steamed in White Wine and his quickly made appetizer named Jean-Paul's Delightful Mussels on the Half Shell—definitely no-fuss, no-muss recipes. What's more, you can purchase ready-to-use mussels, which will eliminate the debearding and save you from scrubbing so hard!

Jean-Paul's Grilled Tuna by the Sea is enticing and exciting, with its Asian condiments to zip up the piquant marinade. And you'll love the Baked Haddock with Chive Sauce, which is baked briefly in the oven, then elegantly served with a creamy chive-accented sauce.

Do zero in on the wonderful Leslie Revsin's Halibut with Provinçal Herbs and Lemon Oil, one of the recipes so generously contributed to this book. The fish is baked; it's simple and succulent, and its lemon oil garnish is sheer magic. And Leslie Revsin's Swordfish with Caper Vinaigrette, Watercress, and Avocado makes a most intriguing entrée.

Turn the pages and treat yourselves to these irresistible fish dishes.

Salmon Grillé, Sauce Cresson

GRILLED SALMON WITH
WATERCRESS SAUCE

The French are fond of tart green sauces with their fish, as they believe these sauces balance any fatty flavor. Shad is often teamed with agreeably acidic sorrel, haddock with spinach, mackerel with tart gooseberries, and cold poached trout with an herbed mayonnaise. Chef Francis Freund has found diners at the bistro clamor for his eye- and taste-appealing recipe of grilled or broiled fresh salmon, sauced with a blend of puckery watercress, broth, lemon juice, and just enough cream to give it a touch of creaminess. The plate of lovely pink salmon and deep green sauce makes a visually gratifying presentation.

Chef Francis Freund and one of the day's specialties in La Bonne Soupe's kitchen.

For the sauce

1 bunch watercress, stems removed, washed and drained

⅔ cups Homemade Chicken Broth (page 4) or low-sodium canned broth

½ cup heavy cream

3 tablespoons unsalted butter, cut into ½-inch pieces

Salt and freshly ground pepper to taste

For the fish

Four 6- to 7-ounce salmon steaks

1 tablespoon extra-virgin olive oil

2 tablespoons freshly squeezed lemon juice

Salt and freshly ground pepper to taste

Prepare the sauce:

Place the watercress in a blender or food processor and process until finely chopped. Pour the broth and cream into a 1½-quart saucepan, bring to a boil over medium-high heat, and cook until the liquid has reduced by half, about 8 minutes. Reduce the heat to low. Using a wire whisk, add the butter, piece by piece, whisking in between until the butter is incorporated. Add the watercress, stirring to blend, and season with the salt and pepper. Set the sauce aside and keep warm.

Prepare the fish:

Prepare a hot grill or preheat the broiler. Rub the salmon on each side with oil and lemon juice and season with salt and pepper. Grill or broil on a rack or in a shallow pan 4 inches from the heat for 5 minutes on one side and 4 to 5 minutes on the second side. Serve the salmon on warmed dinner plates and spoon some of the sauce along one side.

Makes 4 servings

Bread: Warm a ficelle (a skinny baguette) in the oven and cut it into manageable chunks.

Lunch: A salad of thinly sliced cucumber seasoned with salt, pepper, and a pinch of sugar and then marinated in a little white wine vinegar makes a pleasing crunch with the salmon.

Dinner: Start off an elegant dinner with steamed leeks marinated in a vinaigrette and garnish the salmon with steamed red creamer (little new) potatoes under a coverlet of butter and lemon juice.

Dessert: Melting Chocolate Mousse (page 162) mounded in dessert coupes is an ambrosial windup. For a light dessert, arrange sliced, peeled peaches or pears in store-bought meringue shells and spoon currant jelly melted with a little red wine over the fruit.

Wine: For the salmon and its creamy sauce, a full-bodied white Burgundy, such as a Meursault, or a full-bodied California Chardonnay will match well.

Low-Fat Plan: Obviously, it is necessary to omit the cream and butter from the sauce. Add ½ cup white wine to the broth and reduce the liquid as directed; add the watercress and season. Omit the oil for the salmon, but use plenty of lemon juice and seasonings before broiling.

Brandade de Morue

SALT COD PURÉED WITH GARLIC, OLIVE OIL, AND CREAM

"A superlative brandade," *is how food writer Bryan Miller describes the fragrant Provençal dish he admires so at La Bonne Soupe. "It's an unusual dish to find in New York," Miller adds. "But from the moment I first tasted it back in the 1980s, when I was food critic for* The New York Times, *I've been hooked, and return for my* brandade *fix as frequently as I can."*

Jean-Paul Picot blends the cod with a potato, which, along with the garlic, cream, and olive oil, lends a pleasingly fluffy texture. The brandade *is served with the traditional toasted rounds of bread.*

1 pound dried salt cod

½ cup extra-virgin olive oil

1½ pounds Idaho potatoes, peeled and cut in half

5 cloves garlic, finely minced

1 cup heavy cream

1 cup milk

Freshly ground white pepper to taste

12 thin slices of baguette, toasted

Start soaking the cod the day before you plan to serve *brandade*. Rinse the fish under cold, running water; place in a shallow, nonreactive dish; cover with cold water; and soak overnight, changing the water occasionally.

Drain the cod, place in a 2-quart saucepan, and add water to cover the fish by 1 inch. Bring the water to just below a boil over medium-high heat, then reduce the heat to low, cover, and cook until barely tender, 8 to 10 minutes. Drain and cool slightly. Carefully discard the skin and bones and place the fish in a food processor.

Meanwhile, cook the potatoes in a small saucepan with water to cover until tender, 15 to 20 minutes. Drain the potatoes and add to the fish in the food processor.

In a small saucepan, heat the oil until hot but not smoking. Add the garlic and then remove the pan from the heat. In another small saucepan, heat the cream and milk just until bubbles start to form around the edge. Remove from the heat.

With the machine running, add the hot oil-garlic mixture very slowly to the cod and potato mixture in the food processor until well incorporated. Use the same procedure with the cream and process just until the mixture is smooth and fluffy. Add pepper and taste to correct the seasoning. Since the salt cod is salty, you may not want additional salt, but you might like more pepper or garlic.

Mound the *brandade* in the center of 4 warmed dinner plates and garnish each with 3 slices of baguette.

Makes 4 entrée or 8 appetizer servings

Bread: Jean-Paul always garnishes the *brandade* with toast points (here we call for rounds of toasted breads, but there's always a fresh baguette on the table in reserve.

Lunch: A crisp salad of red-leaf lettuce, sliced red radishes, and thin curls of red onion dressed with extra-virgin olive oil and red wine vinegar complements the purée in color, taste, and texture.

Dinner: Start with vibrant Carrot Soup (page 20). The *brandade*, served in more generous portions,

can be complemented with a side dish of marinated green beans or stir-fried leaf spinach.

Dessert: Thin-crusted Apple Tart (page 163) glazed with raspberry jam and served warm, with tiny glasses of framboise (raspberry *eau-de-vie*) makes a charming finale.

Wine: Pour a Sancerre, the steely, crisp white wine from the upper Loire Valley, or a smoky Pouilly-Fumé with the *brandade*.

Aiglefin, Sauce Ciboulette

BAKED HADDOCK WITH CHIVE SAUCE

"I like haddock, a smaller member of the cod family, because it cooks up quickly and lends itself to a nice variety of sauces," explains Chef Francis Freund, as he stirs several simmering pots on his stove in La Bonne Soupe's small kitchen. "Since it's a lean fish, I feel that a rich sauce sets it off beautifully. Of course, for diners who are avoiding butter and cream, we either serve the sauce on the side or broil the fish for them with lemon juice, parsley, and chives. But I must say that there are occasions for a bit of indulgence, and I hope this elegant chive sauce will be one of them."

For the fish

Four 7- to 8-ounce skinned haddock fillets

Juice of 1 lemon

4 teaspoons unsalted butter

½ teaspoon sweet paprika

¼ teaspoon salt

1 tablespoon finely chopped fresh flat-leaf parsley

For the sauce

1 cup Homemade Chicken Broth (page 4) or low-sodium canned broth

1 cup fish broth or bottled clam juice (see Note)

1 cup heavy cream

Salt and freshly ground white pepper to taste (see Note)

¼ cup unsalted butter (½ stick)

⅓ cup finely chopped fresh chives or 1 tablespoon dried

Prepare the fish:

Preheat the oven to 400°F.

Place the fillets on a lightly oiled or non-stick baking sheet. Pour the lemon juice over the fish; place 1 teaspoon of the butter in the center of each fillet and sprinkle with the paprika, salt, and parsley. Bake the fish in the center of the oven until lightly browned, 8 to 10 minutes. Haddock tends to be soft textured, so you don't want to overcook it. Transfer the fillets to a warmed platter and keep warm.

Prepare the sauce:

In a 1- or 1½-quart saucepan, heat the chicken and fish broths over medium-high heat and cook until the liquid has reduced to one-third. Add the cream, salt and pepper and bring to a boil over medium heat, stirring with a small wire whisk. Remove from the heat. Whisk in the butter bit by bit, until it is well blended and the sauce is smooth. Add the chives, stirring to blend well. Place the saucepan back on low heat and reheat just until warmed through. Arrange the fish on warmed dinner plates and spoon some of the sauce alongside or on top.

Makes 4 servings

Note: Bottled clam juice is rather salty and, for some tastes, a bit on the strong side. For a less assertive flavor, use ¾ cup clam juice and ¼ cup water, and adjust the salt in the recipe.

Bread: Slices of ficelle (a skinny baguette) make an elegant accompaniment.

Lunch: If you plan to serve the haddock for lunch, reduce the size of the fillets to 5 or 6 ounces and garnish the plates with a tossed seasonal-greens salad.

Dinner: Fluffy rice and steamed whole green beans are colorful and satisfying plate mates for the fish. Follow with a salad of seasonal greens tossed with Jean-Paul's Zesty Vinaigrette (page 146).

Dessert: Combine strawberries and raspberries and top with a small puff of crème fraîche.

Wine: Try a crisp, elegant dry white such as a Chablis, a young Meursault, or a California Chardonnay.

Low-Fat Plan: Skip the sauce and bake the fish with lemon juice and the seasonings.

Lotte au Vin Rouge

MONKFISH IN RED WINE SAUCE

Another of Chef Francis Freund's quick fish dishes, this one stars firm-fleshed monkfish with an enrobement of spicy red wine sauce. The fish is cut into medallions, quickly pan cooked on top of the stove, and served with the tangy sauce. In France, lotte *is also a prime ingredient of* bouillabaisse *and other fish stews. Its popularity as a solo entrée owes in part to its leanness. Also there's very little waste, and it lends itself well to seasoned sauces.*

For the fish

1¾ pounds monkfish fillets, cut into 2-inch slices or medallions

Salt and freshly ground pepper to taste

2 tablespoons extra-virgin olive oil

For the sauce

1½ cups fruity red wine, such as Merlot or Beaujolais

½ teaspoon freshly ground pepper

Pinch *each* of ground cloves, ground ginger, and ground cinnamon

½ teaspoon sugar

2 tablespoons unsalted butter

⅓ cup chopped fresh flat-leaf parsley

Prepare the fish:

Season the fillets with salt and pepper. In a heavy skillet large enough to hold the fish in one layer, heat the oil over medium-high heat until hot but not smoking. Reduce the heat to medium, add the fish and cook until lightly browned on the bottom, about 4 minutes. Using a spatula, turn the fillets and cook until they are opaque and lightly browned on the other side, about 4 minutes. Transfer the fish to a warmed platter and keep warm.

Prepare the sauce:

In a heavy 1-quart saucepan, add the wine, spices, sugar, and pepper and cook over high heat until reduced to about ⅓ cup, 6 to 8 minutes. Reduce the heat to low and add the butter in small bits, whisking after each addition, until the butter has blended into the sauce. Keep the sauce warm. Spoon the sauce over the monkfish on the serving platter and sprinkle with the chopped parsley.

Makes 4 servings

Bread: A fresh, crusty baguette is just the ticket.

Lunch: For lunch this recipe will stretch to serve six. Add a salad of romaine lettuce and sliced mushrooms in a grainy mustard–tinged vinaigrette.

Dinner: Steamed Brussels sprouts flecked with toasted almond slivers and Monique's Garlicky Mashed Potatoes (page 137) complete a flavorful entrée.

Dessert: Black currant sherbet and vanilla ice cream sprinkled with crème de cassis (black currant liqueur) and cups of double espresso wind up the meal splendidly.

Wine: A French or American Merlot will match the spicy overtones of the sauce and complement the fish very well.

Low-Fat Plan: Omit the oil and cook the fish with a little lemon juice. For the sauce, omit the butter.

Pinch Me!

I've always wondered, when reading a recipe, what a pinch of something really means. I surmise it's the quantity of whatever dry stuff you are pinching that can be held between your thumb and forefinger. Whether you happen to have capacious or very petite digits is probably a moot point. But I did read in a food lexicon that although no cook worth his or her salt would ever think of measuring a pinch, it is approximately ⅛ of a teaspoon.

—Doris Tobias

Moules Marinière

MUSSELS STEAMED IN WHITE WINE

"In the 1960s, Monique and I had a little apartment in Deauville, along the coast of Normandy, where the boats returned from the day's fishing brimming with beautiful fresh fish and shellfish," says Jean-Paul Picot. "It was a sight to behold; an embarrassment of piscatory riches! We'd pick dozens of tiny mussels, called moules de bouchot *[bouchots are the telephone pole–like posts that cultivated mussels grow on], and they were so sweet smelling and plump. I cooked them with love and a little white wine, and* Moules Marinière *became my specialty. Even Monique says this is the best dish I prepare.*

"But here in the States we have excellent mussels," Jean-Paul adds. "Many are now farmed; are clean, fresh, and sweet; and are sold in supermarkets' fish departments. Or if you live near a port, you can find mussels fresh from the fishing boats. In either case, enjoy this ambrosial dish."

¼ cup unsalted butter (½ stick)
1 cup finely chopped shallots (about ¼ pound)
3½ pounds mussels, well scrubbed, beards removed
3 cups dry white wine
Freshly ground pepper to taste
½ cup finely chopped fresh flat-leaf parsley

In a heavy, 6-quart saucepan, melt the butter over medium heat. Add the shallots and cook, stirring occasionally, until they are softened but not browned, 3 to 4 minutes. Add the mussels and wine, raise the heat to medium high, and bring the liquid to a boil. Cover the pan tightly and cook the mussels, shaking the pan from time to time, until they open, about 4 minutes. Lift the lid, and if some of the mussels have not yet opened, replace the lid and cook for another 2 to 3 minutes.

Have ready 4 warmed oversize soup bowls. Using a slotted spoon, transfer the mussels to the bowls, discarding any that have not opened. Spoon the sauce on top and sprinkle with the pepper and the parsley.

Makes 4 entrée or 8 appetizer servings

Bread: A warm-from-the-oven crisp-crusted baguette is in order here.

Lunch: The mussels and bread can be followed by a salad of arugula and endive leaves topped with julienned cooked beets and tossed with a mustardy vinaigrette.

Dinner: If you're serving the mussels as an entrée, start with Creamy Tomato Soup (page 7); and with the mussels, offer a big platter of French Fries (page 142). A salad of seasonal greens dressed with a red wine vinaigrette can be topped with chunks of tangy chèvre.

Dessert: Offer Caramel Custard (page 154) and a platter of thin ginger cookies.

Wine: If your predilection is for crisp, bone-dry wine, try a Muscadet de Sèvre-et-Maine.

Low-Fat Plan: Omit the butter. Sprinkle the shallots with 3 tablespoons white wine or water, cover, and cook over low heat, stirring occasionally, until softened but not browned, 3 to 4 minutes. Proceed with the recipe.

A Little Test for Freshness

When handling mussels, you may come upon one or two whose shells have started to open. This can happen with changes in temperature and does not necessarily mean the mussel is dead. To test a mussel, hold it between your thumb and forefinger and gently try to move the top and bottom shells sideways. If the mussel remains firm and rigid, it's still alive. If the shell slides laterally, discard the mussel.

Thon Cru sur Mer de Jean-Paul

JEAN-PAUL'S TUNA SASHIMI BY THE SEA

"Monique and I are very fond of Asian cuisine. We learned to love sashimi by frequenting many fine Japanese restaurants in New York," explains Jean-Paul, who prepares his own version. *"Actually, I find the Japanese treatment of sashimi too bland, so I turn to the more aggressively spicy flavors of hot pepper and Worcestershire sauces and a touch of lemon juice for a pleasing acidic tang."*

1 pound skinless tuna fillet, the freshest available (see Note)

6 shallots, finely minced

2 tablespoons finely grated fresh ginger

¼ cup light soy sauce

2 tablespoons freshly squeezed lemon juice

2 tablespoons Pickapeppa sauce or other Louisiana-style hot pepper sauce

5 or 6 dashes of Worcestershire sauce

⅓ cup extra-virgin olive oil

½ cup chopped cilantro

4 to 6 crisp curly lettuce leaves

Place the tuna on a clean cutting board and, using a very sharp knife, cut razor-thin slices, about 2 x 1 inches overall, following the grain of the fish. Place the slices in a shallow glass, china, or other nonreactive dish.

In a small bowl, blend together all the remaining ingredients, except the lettuce, and pour over the tuna. Cover the dish and refrigerate for 2 hours.

Serve as an appetizer on chilled salad plates, garnished with the lettuce on the side.

Makes 4 entrée or 6 appetizer servings

Note: With sashimi, everything hinges on the freshness of the fish. If you have any doubts about the fish's freshness, choose another fish or wait until guaranteed-fresh fish arrives at the market. You can prepare the sashimi with any firm-fleshed fresh fish such as swordfish or halibut, but tuna has a very special synergism with the condiments in this dish.

Bread: Have plenty of sliced baguette on hand to mop up the last drops of zesty sauce.

Lunch: Follow the sashimi with a salad of seasonal greens.

Dinner: The sashimi can be the start of a summer meal starring broiled salmon steaks basted with lemon butter and a salad of spinach leaves, crunchy radicchio, and chèvre dressed with a red wine vinaigrette.

Dessert: Offer raspberry sherbet, scooped into pretty dessert coupes and topped with curls of shaved dark chocolate.

Wine: A semidry white wine, such as a Vouvray from the Loire Valley or a California Chenin Blanc, would be a good choice for the tangy sashimi. Or serve saké or beer.

Low-Fat Plan: Omit the oil in the sashimi and increase the lemon juice to 3 tablespoons. Broil the salmon with freshly squeezed lemon or lime juice and freshly ground pepper. Use defatted chicken broth in place of the olive oil in the salad dressing.

Thon Grillé sur Mer de Jean-Paul

JEAN-PAUL'S GRILLED TUNA BY THE SEA

In the garden near the big, open country kitchen of the Picot's nineteenth-century country house in the Hamptons on New York's Long Island stands the big iron grill on which Jean-Paul cooks the fresh fish he buys at the local market. On summer weekends, Jean-Paul and Monique often plan a meal starring whatever fish looks the most attractive in the market that day—tuna, swordfish, or mahi mahi steaks or perhaps some opalescent scallops. When he buys the fish steaks, Jean-Paul is apt to buy a little extra for one of their favorite appetizers, Jean-Paul's Tuna Sashimi by the Sea (page 84), "but only when the fish has just been brought in from the boats," Jean-Paul is quick to add.

he Picots' country home in the Hamptons.

For his grilled tuna steaks, Jean-Paul first marinates the fish in olive oil, garlic, light soy sauce, and chopped cilantro, then he sears them on a very hot grill, cooking them so that they're still a little pink inside. "At least, that's the way we like them," le patron says. The reserved marinade is quickly turned into a tasty little sauce to accompany the grilled fish.

Four 7- to 8-ounce fresh tuna steaks
⅓ cup chopped shallots (2 to 3 large)
2 cloves garlic, finely chopped
⅓ cup extra-virgin olive oil
2 tablespoons finely chopped cilantro
Salt and freshly ground pepper to taste
1 teaspoon Kosher salt
½ cup dry white wine

Place the tuna in a large bowl. Add the shallots, garlic, oil, cilantro, and salt and pepper, and turn the steaks in the bowl so that they're covered evenly. Cover the bowl and let the tuna marinate in the refrigerator for 1 hour.

Prepare a hot grill or preheat the broiler. Remove the fish from the marinade. Scrape the marinade that clings to the tuna back into the bowl and sprinkle the tuna with kosher salt. Grill or broil the tuna 4 inches from the heat for 4 minutes on each side if you want them a little pink inside. Give them another 2 minutes on each side for well done. Transfer the steaks to a warmed platter.

Meanwhile prepare the sauce. Pour the marinade into a small saucepan and add the white wine. Bring the mixture to a boil over medium-high heat, then reduce the heat to medium and cook until the wine has reduced just a little, 3 to 4 minutes. Taste to correct seasoning and pour over the tuna. Or pour the sauce into a small sauceboat and pass separately at the table.

Makes 4 servings

Bread: The Picots like a crisp-crusted baguette with the tuna.

Lunch: Plenty of good bread and a tossed mesclun (mixed baby greens) salad is all that's needed for a super little lunch.

Dinner: Try Monique's Little Roasted Potatoes with Rosemary (page 142) and Golden Brown Zucchini with Basil (page 136) followed by a tossed seasonal green salad.

Dessert: A refreshing and deep-flavored mélange of sliced ripe peaches and mangoes tossed with a *soupçon* of crème de cacao is just right.

Wine: Jean-Paul likes a red wine with his tuna; in fact, he doesn't hesitate to pull out a good vintage grand *cru* from his cellar for his guests to enjoy.

Low-Fat Plan: Substitute ⅓ cup freshly squeezed lemon or lime juice for the olive oil and proceed with the recipe.

Leslie Revsin's Halibut with Provençal Herbs and Lemon Oil

This recipe comes from Leslie Revsin, the innovative chef, TV personality, and food consultant who is a devotee of La Bonne Soupe and is particularly fond of its fish specialties. She finds the light and fragrant combination of herbs and fresh lemon "just the right note for the meaty halibut, which is baked with herbs, mushrooms, and a little white wine, and served on a bed of steamed spinach. The lemon oil is drizzled over the fish just before serving, lending gloss and flavor. The lemon oil can be made and kept refrigerated up to 2 weeks."

For the lemon oil

2 tablespoons freshly squeezed lemon juice

¼ cup extra-virgin olive oil

1 small clove garlic, crushed

Three ½ x 2-inch strips lemon zest

Salt and freshly ground pepper to taste

For the halibut

Four 7-ounce halibut steaks, cut ½-inch thick, skin removed

Salt and freshly ground pepper to taste

1 teaspoon dried *herbes de Provence*, or ½ teaspoon finely chopped fresh rosemary

1 teaspoon finely chopped fresh thyme

½ teaspoon chopped fresh sage

4 teaspoons chopped fresh flat-leaf parsley

2 teaspoons unsalted butter or extra-virgin olive oil, divided

2 cups sliced white mushrooms

¼ cup dry white wine

Salt and freshly ground pepper to taste

For the garnish

1 pound fresh spinach, stemmed and washed

Salt and freshly ground pepper to taste

Prepare the lemon oil:

Make the oil at least 1 day before using. Put the lemon juice in a non-aluminum bowl and gradually whisk in the olive oil. Add the garlic. Stir in the lemon zest, season with salt and pepper, and refrigerate, covered, until ready to use.

When you are ready to make the fish, take the lemon oil out of the refrigerator and allow it to come to room temperature while you are preparing the fish.

Prepare the halibut:

Season the fish with salt and pepper. Sprinkle each steak with the dried herbs and press the parsley onto the fish; or, if you are using fresh herbs, mix them together and press them onto the fish. If possible, let the fish absorb the flavors of the herbs by placing it, covered, in the refrigerator for a good hour or longer.

Preheat the oven to 425°F.

Using 1 teaspoon of the butter, coat the bottom of a shallow, heatproof baking dish large enough to hold the steaks in one layer. Scatter the mushrooms over the bottom of the dish, pour in the wine, and place the halibut on top in a single layer. Pinch the remaining teaspoon of butter into a few pieces and scatter over the fish or drizzle the remaining oil over all.

Place the baking dish directly over high heat for 30 seconds to hasten the cooking.

Cover the dish, put it into the center of the oven, and bake until just cooked through, about 12 to 15 minutes, until the fish is opaque throughout.

Prepare the garnish:

Meanwhile, place the spinach with the water still clinging to the leaves in a large saucepan and set over medium heat. Cover and cook, stirring occasionally, just until the spinach wilts, about 2 to 3 minutes. Season with salt and pepper.

To serve, remove the cooked fish to a warmed platter and keep warm. Place the baking dish over high heat and boil the cooking juices until they are reduced and a little syrupy. (If there are 2 tablespoons of juices or less, do not boil.) Place a bed of the steamed spinach on each dinner plate. Place a fish steak on top, drizzle the syrupy juices over top, and scatter the mushrooms around. Drizzle the lemon oil over the fish and around the plate and serve immediately.

Makes 4 servings

Bread: Chef Revsin serves small dinner rolls with the halibut.

Lunch: You might want to serve smaller portions of the fish—5 or 6 ounces make pleasing portions—unless, of course, you're planning a main meal of the day, in which case stay with the recipe as is. Add a salad of tossed seasonal lettuces.

Dinner: Chef Revsin adds grilled, small red potatoes with skins on (lightly brushed with oil) along with the steamed spinach, and follows with a salad of sliced endive, thinly sliced red onion, and capers in a light vinaigrette.

Dessert: Try poached pears in vanilla syrup topped with vanilla ice cream and slathered with warm Chocolate Sauce (page 152).

Wine: A light, herbal Sauvignon Blanc, served well chilled, teams very well with the fish and its herbal essences.

Low-Fat Plan: Omit the oil from the lemon oil and blend the lemon juice and garlic with ¼ cup defatted chicken broth. Omit the butter or oil when baking the halibut and increase the wine to ½ cup. Don't place the fish pan over direct heat; put the fish directly in the oven. Proceed with the recipe.

Moules Amuse-Gueules de Jean-Paul

JEAN-PAUL'S DELIGHTFUL MUSSELS ON THE HALF SHELL

"I do love to cook," Jean-Paul Picot admits, as he deftly dices fat shallots in his airy, open country kitchen, with its charming array of French porcelain bowls and platters and pots of freshly picked herbs from the garden. "Here, we like to dine informally when we can and have our guests sit around our center wooden table sipping wine while dinner is being prepared. This may not be the most sophisticated way of entertaining, but it works in the country and everyone has a good time.

"In the city, things tend to get a bit more formal. But we're always looking for little nibbles to have with the wine. Sometimes it's as simple as fresh raw clams on the half shell nestling in crushed ice and garnished with lemon wedges. We always have a canister of homemade croutons for pâté and spreads. And when I find fresh, shiny mussels in the fish market, we'll offer these delightful mussels on the half shell."

16 mussels, well scrubbed and beards removed

3 shallots, finely chopped

3 slices bacon, cooked until crisp, drained, and crumbled

2 tablespoons chopped fresh flat-leaf parsley

Salt and freshly ground pepper to taste

3 tablespoons unsalted butter

Open the mussels, either by steaming them, covered, over simmering water for 2 minutes, or by using a paring knife to pry them open. Place the shell halves containing the mussels in a shallow ovenproof dish. Remove and discard the empty shells.

In a small bowl, combine the shallots, bacon, parsley, and salt and pepper, stirring to blend well. Strew a little of this mixture over each of the mussels and top with bits of butter.

Preheat the boiler. Broil the mussels about 4 inches from the heat just until the tops are lightly browned, 2 to 3 minutes.

Makes 4 appetizer servings

Bread: A just-baked ficelle (a skinny baguette) is great with these dainties.

Lunch: Double the recipe and offer a big basket of bread and plenty of sweet country butter. Follow with a *Salade Niçoise* (page 44).

Dinner: Make these an elegant first course to be followed by Jean-Paul's Grilled Tuna by the Sea (page 85).

Dessert: Lemon Tart (page 160) garnished with clusters of red raspberries and a streak of Rosy Raspberry Sauce (page 164) is simply scrumptious.

Wine: With the mussels, a chilled, crisp Muscadet de Sèvre-et-Maine; with the tuna, try a medium-bodied Merlot from France or California.

Low-Fat Plan: It sounds too simple to be true, but you can squeeze lemon juice over the opened mussels, season them with plenty of pepper, add drops of olive oil, and sprinkle with parsley; then broil them for no longer than 1 minute. They'll be succulent and sweet!

Leslie Revsin's Swordfish with Caper Vinaigrette, Watercress, and Avocado

From Chef Leslie Revsin, a regular at La Bonne Soupe, here's another fish specialty, which she describes as delicious, light, and easy to prepare. Chef Revsin cooks the swordfish on top of the stove before baking it briefly in a hot oven, which results in a nicely browned, juicy fish. The caper vinaigrette works very well with rich fish, such as swordfish and salmon, and equally well with more delicate fish, such as halibut and sole.

For the vinaigrette

1 teaspoon grainy mustard, such as Pommery

1 teaspoon Dijon mustard

1 tablespoon capers, drained

1 tablespoon caper brine

1 tablespoon freshly squeezed lemon juice

½ small clove garlic, chopped

⅓ cup extra-virgin olive oil

Salt and freshly ground pepper to taste

For the fish

Four 7-ounce swordfish steaks, ¾ inch thick

Salt and freshly ground pepper to taste

1 tablespoon olive oil

For the garnish

1 bunch watercress, 2 inches of stems trimmed, washed and dried

1 ripe avocado, halved, pitted, peeled, and cut into ½-inch dice (see Note)

2 teaspoons capers, drained

Prepare the vinaigrette:

Place all the ingredients except the olive oil and salt and pepper in a blender or food processor and blend or pulse until a smooth paste is formed. Gradually add the olive oil in a steady stream, with the machine on low, or, if you are using a food processor, pulse on and off until the oil is well incorporated. Season with salt and pepper and set aside or refrigerate for another day. (It will keep up to 1 week.)

When you are ready to prepare the fish, take the vinaigrette from the refrigerator and allow it to come to room temperature.

Prepare the fish:

Preheat the oven to 425°F.

Season the fish with salt and pepper. Place the oil in a large, ovenproof skillet or dish large enough to hold the steaks in one layer and heat over medium heat until the oil is hot but not smoking. Place the fish in the pan and cook until browned, 3 to 4 minutes. Using a spatula, carefully turn the steaks over, transfer the skillet or dish to the center of the oven, and bake until the fish is cooked through, 5 to 6 minutes, or just until the fish is opaque throughout.

To serve, have ready 4 warmed dinner plates. Arrange the watercress on the plates and place a swordfish steak in the center. Scatter the avocado around the fish. Drizzle the vinaigrette over all and garnish with the remaining capers.

Makes 4 servings

Note: If you dice the avocado in advance, squeeze the juice of half a lemon over the pieces and cover with plastic wrap or aluminum foil to prevent darkening.

Bread: Chef Revsin suggests a *petit parisien,* the shorter, fatter, softer-in-the-center version of a baguette.

Lunch: Smaller-size portions of fish, 5 to 6 ounces, make a most satisfying midday meal. Add a side dish of sliced tomatoes dressed with a touch of extra-virgin olive oil and a hail of chopped shallots.

Dinner: Start the meal with Chilled Green Pea Soup (page 27) and serve a warm vegetable with the fish—steamed asparagus or green beans perked up with a bit of grated red onion.

Dessert: Creamy, smooth Caramel Custard (page 154) is the dessert of choice to end the meal on a high note.

Wine: A spicy-fruity Gewürztraminer from Alsace matches well with the zippiness of the sauce.

Low-Fat Plan: Substitute ⅓ cup defatted chicken broth for the oil in the vinaigrette and bake the fish in a nonstick pan without first searing it on top of the stove.

Filets de Flet et Écrevisses en Papillotte

FILLETS OF FLOUNDER AND SHRIMP IN PAPER

Charles Morris Mount, a direct descendent of the great American genre artist William Sydney Mount, is himself an artist and a brilliant designer of restaurants and other public edifices. He's also a longtime friend of the Picots and admirer of La Bonne Soupe, where he often dips in for a bowl of Peasant-Style Mushroom and Barley Soup (page 5), a glass of good red wine, and lots of lively conversation. His talents include a fine hand at the stove.

"I do like to cook," Charles says, "especially in our weekend house, Frog Hollow Hall, which is where we relax after the urban crunch. For Friday evenings, this quick, satisfying, low-fat dish is always welcome. Extra portions can be made and served cold or at room temperature for Sunday lunch. Variations on this theme are limited only to what's fresh at the market, such as bay scallops, small shelled lobsters, or even oysters paired with the catch of the day."

Parchment paper and 1 teaspoon softened butter

4 flounder fillets, 6 to 8 ounces each

16 medium-size shrimp, peeled and deveined

For the vegetables

2 cups cooked, steamed, chopped spinach, seasoned with salt and freshly ground pepper

2 medium sweet bell peppers, red and yellow, cored, seeded and cut into confetti dice

8 thin strips of lemon zest

2 knobs of fresh ginger, each about 1 inch long, peeled and cut into thin, julienne strips

For the vinaigrette

4 tablespoons sherry vinegar

4 cloves garlic, finely chopped

1 small onion, cut in quarters

4 tablespoons lime juice

¼ cup extra-virgin olive oil

Salt and freshly ground pepper to taste

Preheat the oven to 350°F.

Place the vinegar, garlic, onion, and lime juice in a small bowl. Slowly add the oil, whisking until well blended. Season with salt and pepper.

Cut a piece of parchment paper into 4 rectangles twice the length of a fish fillet and fold each rectangle in half crosswise. Unfold the rectangles and lightly butter one side.

Make a layer of cooked spinach on one half of each buttered rectangle. Lay a fish fillet on top of the spinach. Spoon 3 tablespoons of the vinaigrette over each fillet and arrange 4 shrimp on top. Strew the bell peppers, lemon zest, and ginger over all. Add salt and pepper. Fold the parchment over the fish package and fold the edges of the package several times to make a tight seal.

Place the packets on a baking sheet and bake in the center of the oven for 15 minutes. Serve on warm dinner plates in the paper case and let guests open them at the table.

Makes 4 servings

Tip: If you plan to make the fish packets to store in the refrigerator for up to 2 days, open the packets and transfer the contents to a chillable covered dish. Store in the coldest part of the refrigerator until ready to serve.

Bread: A crusty multigrain bread goes very well with the fish.

Lunch: As Charles Mount suggests, make extra packets and serve them for lunch the next day. Add a salad of sliced tomatoes and chopped scallions dressed with a little extra-virgin olive oil and a squeeze of lemon juice.

Dinner: At Frog Hollow Hall, the fillets are accompanied by baked or boiled sweet potatoes and followed with a fresh green salad.

Dessert: Fresh seasonal fruit and wedges of Roquefort cheese make a simple and elegant finish.

Wine: A French or California Sauvignon Blanc is a pleasing companion to the briny fish.

Low-Fat Plan: Use heavy aluminum foil for the packages and you won't need to butter them. Replace the oil in the vinaigrette with ¼ cup defatted chicken broth, and serve the fruit with a low-fat cheese.

Paper Talk

In France, cooking food *en papillotte* (in a paper or foil case) is a popular way of serving fish or veal chops. The paper is cut to surround the fish or chop, which is placed in the center and then sealed by folding the edges of the parchment so that no steam or aromas can escape until the packet is opened at the dinner table. If you can't find parchment paper at a housewares or kitchen specialty store, use heavy aluminum foil but cut the baking time to 10 minutes, as the foil conducts heat faster than paper.

Poultry and Rabbit

Jean-Paul Picot thinks the state-of-the art supermarkets in France and America are getting better and better. But as a restaurateur admits he still prefers to buy his chickens and rabbits directly from a poultry dealer. "I appreciate the freshness, quality, and variety that the specialist offers. There are grain-fed chickens and corn-fed chickens, young hens and old roosters, capons and all manner of small birds such as quail and ortolons."

Jean-Paul comes from a country where every region has its own breed of chicken, goose, and duck and its local poultry specialties. "Every region of France has a favorite method for cooking chicken. In Franche-Comté and Bresse [a region in Burgundy], a hen is stuffed with rice and crayfish. In Normandy, cream and Calvados team up with the bird, like Madame Davenet's Chicken with Salsify. In Provence, garlic, tomatoes, and peppers are pot mates with chicken. And there's the classic Chicken in White Wine Sauce from Alsace that incorporates the region's famous Riesling.

"Probably the most famous chickens in France are the *poulets de Bresse,* which have especially large breasts. They're so special that poultry sellers tie a little metal tag on each bird to validate its breed.

"Here in the States I buy only free-range chickens that are grain or corn fed and rely on my poultry purveyor for La Bonne Soupe's first-class chicken supply. It really makes a big difference in the flavor and texture of the bird," *le patron* (the owner) explains. "No *poulets de batteries*—assembly-line chickens—for La Bonne Soupe!"

The recipes collected here are from La Bonne Soupe's daily specials plus some wonderful recipes the Picots prepare at home with pleasure, including a couple of great favorites of Jean-Paul from Monique's mother—Madame Davenet's Chicken with Salsify and Madame Davenet's Casseroled Rabbit. And once you taste Monique's Roast Chicken Stuffed with Goat Cheese Croutons, you'll place it high on your list of best dishes to make for company.

Poulet Chasseur

HUNTER'S CHICKEN

One of François Picot's favorite plats du jour, this succulent chicken dish incorporates sweet bell peppers, mushrooms, white wine, and garlic, and is a popular meal in France in the autumn. If the hunters have brought back wild birds, they would be used instead of chicken. But the chicken makes a very tasty dish, especially if it's a free-range bird, which is the type Jean-Paul prefers.

In this version, fresh tomatoes are replaced by tomato paste, since by the time the fall hunting season sets in, garden tomatoes are generally long past their peak.

- 2 tablespoons peanut or other vegetable oil
- One 3½-pound chicken, cut into 8 serving pieces
- 2 cloves garlic, finely minced
- ½ pound white mushroom caps, sliced
- 1 medium-size red bell pepper, cored, seeded, and chopped
- 1 large onion, thinly sliced
- 1 cup dry white wine
- 2 cups Homemade Chicken Broth (page 4) or low-sodium canned broth
- 2 tablespoons tomato paste mixed with 2 tablespoons water
- 1 teaspoon chopped fresh thyme or ½ teaspoon dried
- 1½ teaspoons chopped fresh rosemary or ½ teaspoon dried
- 2 small bay leaves
- Salt and freshly ground pepper to taste

Heat the oil in a large heavy Dutch oven or skillet with a lid over medium heat until hot but not smoking. Add the chicken pieces and brown over medium-high heat, turning the pieces so they brown evenly. Transfer the chicken to a warmed dish and reserve.

Add the garlic, mushrooms, and bell pepper to the pot, cover, and cook over medium heat until the vegetables are softened but not browned, 5 to 6 minutes. Add all the remaining ingredients, raise the heat to high, and bring just to the boil. Reduce the heat to medium-low and return the chicken pieces to the pot. Cover and cook over medium-low heat until the chicken is tender, about 1 hour.

Transfer the chicken pieces to a warmed platter. Bring the liquid in the pot to a boil over high heat and cook until slightly thickened, 5 to 6 minutes. Remove and discard the bay leaves and pour the sauce over the chicken.

Makes 4 servings

Bread: Individual petits pains (dinner rolls) are a nice choice with this dish.

Lunch: Add a small salad of seasonal greens dressed with Jean-Paul's Zesty Vinaigrette (see page 146) and you have a tasty lunch.

Dinner: Accompany the chicken with a big bowl of mashed potatoes or couscous and follow with a salad of pungent arugula and sliced endive in a mustard-tinged vinaigrette.

Dessert: Here's a simple but appealing dinner finale: Place thinly sliced peeled blood or other oranges into dessert coupes, sprinkle with shredded, sweetened coconut, and moisten with a little Curaçao or other orange-flavored liqueur.

Wine: A robust, full-bodied red wine, such as a Côtes du Rhône pairs very well with this Provençal dish.

Low-Fat Plan: Remove the skin from the chickens and cut away the fat. Brown the chicken parts in a nonstick pan and proceed with the recipe.

Coq au Vin

CHICKEN SIMMERED IN RED WINE

"In olden days on the farm," Monique Picot says, "when the roosters had passed their useful days, they were first marinated to tenderize them and then cooked in wine for quite a long time." Monique is talking about the farm in Normandy where she grew up. "Today, of course, coq au vin is made with grain-fed chickens that are flavorful and much more tender, so my mother didn't find it necessary even to marinate them. And, although each region in France has its own special way with coq au vin, the one we liked best was simple and traditional: chicken cooked in a good red wine, with herbs, onions, and mushrooms."

The Davenet's home in Saint-Saëns, Normandy.

⅛ pound lean salt pork or 2 slices bacon, cut into ¼-inch dice

One 3½-pound chicken, cut into 8 serving pieces

12 white pearl onions, blanched in boiling water for 2 minutes, then drained and peeled

12 medium-size white mushroom caps, cut into quarters

2 tablespoons extra-virgin olive oil

1 medium-size yellow onion, chopped

2 garlic cloves, crushed, then minced

1 medium-size carrot, peeled and thinly sliced

3 cups dry red wine, such as a Beaujolais

1 cup Homemade Chicken Broth (page 4) or low-sodium canned broth

1 teaspoon fresh thyme or ½ teaspoon dried

1 teaspoon fresh rosemary, chopped, or ¼ teaspoon dried

Salt and freshly ground pepper to taste

Place the salt pork in a heavy 3-quart Dutch oven or lidded saucepan and cook over medium heat, stirring occasionally, until lightly browned, 3 to 4 minutes.

Using a slotted spoon, take out the pork and reserve. Add the chicken pieces and cook over medium-high heat until lightly browned, turning the pieces so that they brown evenly, 6 to 8 minutes.

Transfer the chicken to a large plate and reserve. Add the pearl onions and cook, stirring, until lightly browned, 4 to 5 minutes. Remove the onions and reserve. Add the mushrooms to the pan and cook just until they turn dark and start to exude their juices, 3 to 4 minutes. Remove the mushrooms and reserve.

Heat the oil in the same pan, add the yellow onions and garlic and cook over medium heat until softened but not browned, 3 to 4 minutes. Add the carrots and cook over medium heat just until they start to soften, 3 to 4 minutes.

Return the chicken and the pork to the pan. Add the wine, broth, thyme, rosemary, and salt and pepper. Bring nearly to a boil over medium heat, then reduce the heat to medium-low, cover, and cook until the chicken is tender, 45 minutes to 1 hour. Add the reserved pearl onions and mushrooms and cook over low heat just until everything is nicely hot. Taste the sauce to correct the seasoning.

Makes 4 servings

Bread: A country-style crusty loaf cut into fairly thick slices is just fine for catching the last, winey drops of sauce.

Lunch: A modest portion of chicken can be followed by a crunchy salad of sliced endive and julienned beets, dressed with extra-virgin olive oil, freshly squeezed lemon juice, and just a tiny tot of Dijon mustard.

Dinner: Mashed potatoes are a very pleasing foil for the stew. You might want to add a dish of green peas cooked, French style, that is, with a lettuce leaf. Offer a salad of sliced endive and julienned beets, topped with a wedge of chèvre.

Dessert: Individual store-bought meringue shells filled with pecan ice cream and topped with caramel sauce are a deserved indulgence! Or try this light dessert: Scoop out raspberry sherbet and drizzle with a little framboise (raspberry eau-de-vie).

Wine: "Do use a sound red wine," advises Jean-Paul. "Oh, certainly you needn't uncork a Clos de Vougeot, but a sturdy Côte de Beaune-Villages or a hearty Beaujolais would make a delicious stew at a bon prix [gentle price]."

Low-Fat Plan: Omit the salt pork or bacon and oil. Skin the chicken, if you like, and brown it by roasting it in a 350°F oven for 10 minutes. Cook all the vegetables, covered, with ¾ cup of water (or wine) over low heat until softened but not browned, 5 to 6 minutes. Proceed with the recipe.

Poulet à l'Estragon

CHICKEN TARRAGON

Certainly, this is a famous classic French chicken dish. The pairing of tarragon and chicken is a flavor marriage made in heaven; and the mushrooms, shallots, tomatoes, and white wine cook down to a velvety sauce. Chicken Tarragon is a frequent daily special at La Bonne Soupe.

If you can find fresh tarragon, the flavor will be sweetly anise, but dried tarragon will also lend a similar tang, so don't hesitate to use it. French chefs from mountain regions like the Jura in eastern France would doubtless throw in a couple of handfuls of crayfish, culled from local mountain streams.

2 tablespoons extra-virgin olive oil

One 3½-pound chicken, cut into 4 serving pieces

3 shallots, finely chopped

½ pound white mushrooms, thinly sliced

1 cup dry white wine

1 cup chopped canned plum tomatoes, drained

2 tablespoons finely chopped fresh tarragon or 1 teaspoon dried

1 cup Homemade Chicken Broth (page 4) or low-sodium canned broth

Salt and freshly ground pepper to taste

Heat the oil in a large heavy skillet over medium-high heat until hot but not smoking. Add the chicken and cook, turning, until browned on all sides. Transfer the chicken to a large plate and reserve.

Add the shallots and mushrooms and cook over medium heat, stirring occasionally, until the mushrooms turn dark and exude their juices, about 5 minutes. Add the white wine, raise the heat to high, and boil just until it reduces a little, 3 to 4 minutes. Reduce the heat to medium and add all the remaining ingredients, including the reserved chicken. Cover the skillet and cook over medium-low heat until the chicken is tender, about 45 minutes. Taste the sauce to correct the seasoning.

Makes 4 servings

Bread: Pile a napkin-lined basket with individual petits pains (dinner rolls).

Lunch: A portion of this chicken along with a couple of crusty outside, tender inside petits pains makes a satisfying lunch. For a refreshing crunch, you might add a side dish of thinly sliced cucumbers sprinkled with a pinch of sugar and splashed with cider vinegar.

Dinner: The chicken may be spooned over a bed of steamed rice or couscous. Offer a platter of halved zucchini, oven-baked with extra-virgin olive oil, freshly ground pepper, and a shake of dried oregano.

Dessert: Spoon drained Pears Poached in White Wine (page 159) into dessert coupes and pass a sauceboat of Rosy Raspberry Sauce (page 164) spiked with a dash of Grand Marnier or other orange-flavored liqueur.

Wine: A light-bodied, fruity white wine, a Sauvignon Blanc from the Loire Valley or California makes agreeable sipping and is a pleasing counterpoint to the tarragon overtones of the dish.

Low-Fat Plan: Skin the chicken pieces, omit the oil, and brown them in a 350°F oven for 10 minutes. Cook the vegetables, covered, with 3 tablespoons of water or wine over low heat until softened but not browned. Proceed with the recipe. For the zucchini, sprinkle with freshly squeezed lemon juice before baking.

Poulet au Vin Blanc

CHICKEN IN WHITE WINE SAUCE

Here's a variation on coq au riesling, *Alsace's version of the ubiquitous* coq au vin *made with the local wine. Chef Francis Freund adds this speedy interpretation to his* plats du jour *frequently. He uses skinless, boneless chicken breasts (instead of bone-in chicken pieces), which cook up quickly; he adds the classic Riesling wine, together with white pearl onions, mushrooms, and fresh chervil. It's an elegant, no-fuss dish you can put together for family or company with ease.*

¼ cup vegetable oil

2 skinless, boneless chicken breasts (about 2 pounds total), cut in half

12 white pearl onions, blanched for 2 minutes in boiling water, then drained and peeled

½ pound white mushrooms, thinly sliced

1 cup dry white wine, such as Riesling

Salt and freshly ground pepper to taste

1 teaspoon chopped fresh chervil or ½ teaspoon dried

½ cup heavy cream

Heat the oil over medium heat in a heavy skillet large enough to hold the chicken in one layer. When the oil is hot but not smoking, add the chicken and cook until lightly browned on both sides, 4 to 5 minutes total. Using tongs, transfer the chicken to a warmed plate and reserve.

Add the onions to the skillet and cook, stirring, over medium heat until lightly browned, about 5 minutes. Add the mushrooms and cook, stirring just until they turn dark and exude their juices, 2 to 3 minutes. Add the wine to the skillet and bring to a boil over medium heat. Reduce the heat to medium-low. Return the chicken to the pan and add the salt and pepper, and chervil. Cover and cook until the chicken is tender, 15 to 20 minutes. Stir in the cream and cook until the sauce is smooth, 1 to 2 minutes.

Makes 4 servings

Bread: Thin rounds of Garlic Toast (this page) make good munching with the chicken.

Lunch: This chicken, along with warmed goat cheese slices set atop mixed lettuces (tossed with vinaigrette), makes a tasty light lunch. Pass warmed individual brioches with the salad.

Dinner: Buttered noodles are typically Alsatian, and they marry mellifluously with the chicken. Steamed green beans peppered with crisp bacon bits add color and flavor contrast.

Dessert: Maintain the Alsatian accent with really great store-bought individual *babas au rhum*—rum-soaked little yeast cakes—if you can find them. Or mound raspberry sherbet in dessert coupes and garnish with store-bought almond macaroons

Wine: A soft, fruity Riesling from Alsace is perfect.

Low-Fat Plan: Omit the oil and cook the chicken breasts in a little chicken broth, then proceed with the recipe, omitting the cream.

Garlic Toast

Cut a baguette or ficelle into slices about ¼-inch thick. Lay the slices on an ungreased cookie sheet and toast in a 400°F oven until lightly browned, 3 to 4 minutes. (You might check after 3 minutes, as ovens vary and you don't want the bread too dark.)

Remove from the oven and, when the toast has cooled off a bit, rub each slice lightly on one side with a clove of garlic. Pile the slices into a napkin-lined basket or other bread container.

Macaroon Memories

A little bit of history: Both *babas au rhum* and macaroons are specialties of Alsace. The original source of the *babas* is said to be an eighteenth century Polish king, exiled to Lorraine, who improved the local yeast cake with a liberal soaking of rum.

Macaroons, on the other hand, were a specialty of the Carmelite nuns in Nancy, the capital of Lorraine. At the time of the Revolution, the nuns were evicted from their home and two of them set up a bakery specializing in macaroons on the street known now as the *Rue des Soeurs Macarons.*

Poulet aux Salsifis de Madame Davenet

MADAME DAVENET'S CHICKEN WITH SALSIFY

Jean-Paul Picot admired his mother-in-law's cooking so much that even today he longs for many of her farm-fresh Normandy specialties. Among these was her chicken cooked with salsify, the intriguing root vegetable also known as the oyster plant. Despite the marine associations of its name, salsify's taste is reminiscent of artichoke hearts. In any case, Madame Davenet cooked the chicken with shallots and aromatic herbs, then added the salsify and finished the dish in true Normandy style: with an egg yolk–cream enrichment and Calvados.

Augustine Davenet feeding the chickens on the Davenets' Normandy farm, circa 1965.

1½ pounds salsify, peeled and cut into 1-inch chunks (see Note and "Sizing up Salsify," page 101)

1 quart water

3 tablespoons vinegar or freshly squeezed lemon juice

¼ cup vegetable oil

12 shallots, peeled but left whole

One 3½-pound chicken, cut into 8 serving pieces

2 cups Homemade Chicken Broth (page 4) or low-sodium canned broth

2 bay leaves

Pinch of dried thyme

Salt and freshly ground pepper to taste

1 cup heavy cream

Yolk of 1 large egg

1 tablespoon Calvados or other apple brandy

Prepare the salsify:

Using gloves, trim and peel the salsify. Cut it into 1-inch pieces and immerse the pieces in the water; add the vinegar. Drain the salsify before using it.

Prepare the chicken:

Heat the oil in a 4-quart Dutch oven or lidded skillet over medium heat until hot but not smoking. Add the shallots and cook, stirring occasionally, until they are lightly golden, 5 to 6 minutes.

Raise the heat to medium-high, add the chicken and cook, turning, until browned on all sides. Add the broth, herbs, and salt and pepper and bring the liquid to a boil over high heat. Reduce the heat to medium-low and add the drained salsify. Cover and simmer until the chicken and salsify are tender, about 50 minutes. Test for doneness with the tines of a fork.

Reduce the heat to very low. In a small bowl, beat the cream and egg yolk until well blended. Add 1 tablespoon of the cooking liquid from the chicken dish and Calvados, whisk to blend. Then, very slowly, stirring as you pour, add the egg yolk–cream enrichment. Allow the dish to warm briefly over the very low heat just until the enrichment is blended into the sauce. Serve either from the cooking dish or arrange the chicken and salsify on a heated platter and pour the sauce over all.

Makes 4 servings

Note: If you can't find fresh salsify, substitute a can of sliced salsify. Drain well and add during the last 15 minutes of cooking. If you can't find salsify in any form, substitute parsnips, which don't need the acidulated (vinegar or lemon juice) water treatment. Don't overcook the parsnips or they will turn mushy. Add them during the last 10 minutes of cooking.

Bread: A plain baguette is the best bet to catch the last drops of the rich sauce.

Lunch: Small portions and a crunchy seasonal green salad make a super repast.

Dinner: Monique serves the chicken with either mashed potatoes or a rice pilaf and follows it with a salad of romaine and cos lettuce dressed with Jean-Paul's Zesty Vinaigrette (page 146).

Dessert: Crêpes with Chocolate Sauce (page 151) are a delightful way to bring the meal to a close.

Wine: With the rich creamy sauce, a white Burgundy, such as an elegant French Pouilly-Fuissé or Saint Véran, or a California Chardonnay is an elegant partner.

Low-Fat Plan: If you simply skip the egg yolk–cream enrichment, you will have a satisfying succulent dish.

Sizing Up Salsify

Salsify is a long, thinnish root vegetable that resembles a black parsnip. The root has a brownish or black skin, and often there are numerous baby rootlets attached, making peeling a little arduous. Use a vegetable peeler and run it from the top of the root downward. If a few rootlets are sacrificed in the process, it's no big deal.

Once peeled, the ivory-hued flesh quickly turns dark, and handling it will stain your hands. So here's the best way to tackle the salsify: Wear rubber or plastic gloves to keep your hands clean. Trim the tops and ends of the salsify, then peel and cut into 1-inch pieces. Immediately drop the pieces into a bowl of acidulated water. When ready to use, drain the salsify and add to the recipe as indicated.

Is it worth all this bother, you may well ask? It is. Madame Davenet's Chicken with Salsify is bound to become one of your favorite savory chicken recipes.

Poulet Rôti Farci aux Croûtons de Chèvre de Monique

MONIQUE'S ROAST CHICKEN STUFFED WITH GOAT CHEESE CROUTONS

"Actually," Monique Picot muses, as she surveys a plump bird on her country kitchen work table, "this is a recipe from cousins who lived in Limoges, in France's center, famous for its chinaware, and I don't recall ever seeing it in a cookbook. The beauty of the stuffing is that the flavorful garlic–goat cheese–olive oil croutons retain their texture and don't get soggy as some stuffings do. In fact, in our family, everyone asks plaintively for 'more stuffing, please.'"

The chicken is given a strong spine of garlic by placing cloves of garlic underneath the skin, then the chicken is roasted until golden, perfuming the kitchen and beyond with beguiling aromas.

"When my mother roasted her chicken in our Normandy kitchen, she liked to make a little garnish to serve with it," Monique adds. "It was a very simple one, made from the chicken's innards, which she chopped very fine and cooked on top of the stove with shallots, chopped parsley, and bread crumbs. We all loved it."

For the chicken

One 3½- to 4-pound roasting chicken
Salt and freshly ground pepper to taste
8 small cloves garlic, peeled and left whole
6 sprigs rosemary
Two 8 x 5-inch slices sourdough or peasant bread, about 1½ inches thick, toasted lightly and cut into sixteen 1½-inch cubes

1½ tablespoons olive oil
⅛ pound soft mild goat cheese or Neufchâtel cheese
Coarsely ground black pepper
½ cup dry white wine or freshly squeezed lemon juice

For the garnish

1 tablespoon olive oil
Giblets from chicken, including the liver, rinsed, patted dry, and ground in a meat grinder or finely chopped by hand
5 to 6 shallots, chopped
½ cup fine fresh bread crumbs
⅓ cup water
⅓ cup chopped fresh flat-leaf parsley
Salt and freshly ground pepper to taste

Prepare the chicken:

Preheat the oven to 350°F.

Rub the chicken inside and out with salt and pepper. Loosen the skin around the chicken breast and thighs by wiggling your fingers between the skin and flesh. Tuck 7 cloves garlic between the skin and flesh, placing some on the breast side and some on the thighs near the back. Tuck 3 rosemary sprigs underneath the skin at random. Crush the remaining clove garlic lightly and rub over the croutons. Brush the croutons with oil and spread the goat cheese on one side of each, season with coarsely ground pepper.

Stuff the chicken cavity with the remaining rosemary sprigs and the cheese croutons. Truss the chicken for roasting: skewer the cavity with steel trussing skewers; tie a piece of kitchen string around the breast, pinning the wings against the breast; and tie the legs together with a second piece of string.

Place the chicken in a roasting pan. Roast the chicken in the center of the oven until golden brown and the juices run yellow when an inner thigh is pierced with a knife, about 1¼ hours. Transfer the chicken to a warmed platter and keep warm.

Add the wine to the pan juices and bring to a brisk boil over heat, scraping up the brown bits, until the sauce is reduced by one-third, about 4 minutes. Strain the sauce through a fine sieve into a sauceboat.

Prepare the garnish:

While the chicken is roasting, heat the oil in a small heavy skillet over medium heat. Add the giblets and cook, stirring, until they lose their color and begin to brown, about 10 minutes. Add all the remaining ingredients and cook, covered, over low heat until the giblets mixture is tender. Stir occasionally so the mixture cooks evenly and does not burn. Taste for seasoning. Transfer to a warmed serving bowl.

Carve the chicken at the table and spoon out equal amounts of stuffing. Pass the garnish and sauce separately. Or, if you prefer, carve the chicken in the kitchen and arrange on warmed dinner plates with the garnish alongside the meat. Pass the sauce separately.

Makes 4 servings

Bread: Here the croutons are the delicious bread!

Lunch: Offer an hors d'oeuvre selection: Bowls of flavorful *Ratatouille* (page 138), sliced ripe tomatoes flecked with chopped basil, and a platter of thinly sliced country ham and salami.

Dinner: With the chicken, Monique serves mashed potatoes and a big salad of young lettuces and chervil dressed with 1 tablespoon balsamic vinegar, 3 tablespoons extra-virgin olive oil, and salt and pepper to taste.

Dessert: Pile mounds of frozen coffee-flavored yogurt into dessert dishes and top with sliced strawberries, raspberries, and blueberries.

Wine: A fine red Bordeaux, especially one from Margaux or Saint-Émilion (or the best you can afford), matches felicitously with the richness of the chicken and its opulent stuffing.

Low-Fat Plan: Use low-fat or fat-free cream cheese instead of the goat cheese and bake the chicken on a rack to catch the drippings. Omit the garnish and the sauce and serve with lemon wedges.

Poulet Rôti au Citron et Madère

CHICKEN ROASTED WITH LEMON AND MADEIRA

Jean-Paul Picot gives this roast chicken a tangy citrusy spin by sliding thin slices of lemon underneath the skin, which serve to baste the bird. The lemon, plus a touch of dry Madeira, gives the bird a stunningly burnished finish. "Of course," Jean-Paul adds, with his droll humor, "if you don't happen to have lemons handy, you can always substitute black truffles!"

One 3½-pound roasting chicken

Salt and freshly ground pepper to taste

3 large lemons, ends trimmed, seeded, and thinly sliced

8 shallots, peeled and left whole

8 sprigs thyme or ½ teaspoon dried

6 sprigs flat-leaf parsley

½ cup dry Madeira, preferably Sercial

Preheat the oven to 350°F.

Rub the chicken inside and out with salt and pepper. Loosen the skin around the chicken breast and thighs by wiggling your fingers between the skin and flesh. Gently insert the lemon slices between the skin and flesh, making sure the slices are flat against the bird. Don't crowd the slices; leave about 1 inch between them. Place the lemon slices on top of the breast and in the back areas. For the legs and thighs, make small slits to insert a slice or two on each leg and thigh.

Stuff the cavity of the bird with the remaining lemon slices, the shallots, thyme, and parsley and truss the bird for roasting: skewer the cavity with steel trussing skewers; tie a piece of kitchen string around the breast, pinning the wings against the breast; and tie the legs together with a second piece of string.

Place the bird on a rack in a roasting pan breast side up and roast in the center of the oven, basting with the Madeira after ½ hour, until the skin is golden brown and the juices run clear yellow when the inner leg is pricked with the tines of a fork, about 1 hour. Transfer the chicken to a heated platter and carve at the table.

This bird is so moist it really doesn't need any sauce. However, if you feel a sauce is necessary, add 1 cup of dry white wine or chicken broth to the roasting pan, scraping up any bits of pan drippings from the bottom, and cook over high heat until the liquid has reduced by half, about 10 minutes. Strain the sauce and pour into a sauceboat to be passed at table.

Makes 4 servings

Roasting a Chicken

One of the greatest compliments one chef can pay to another is to say, "You know how to roast a chicken perfectly!" A good chicken is easy to cook well; but to roast a chicken perfectly? Well, that takes expertise!

Bread: Small, oval petits pains (dinner rolls) are a pleasing accompaniment.

Lunch: Leftover cold roast chicken makes superb sandwiches. Slice a baguette in half lengthwise, then crosswise into sandwich-size pieces. Layer the bread with sliced chicken, an herbed mayonnaise, sliced tomatoes, and tangy watercress leaves. Garnish with radish roses and carrot curls.

Dinner: Steamed little potatoes (tossed with a little butter and chopped parsley) and a cluster of cooked broccoli florets look attractive on the plate.

Dessert: Scoop rich vanilla ice cream into dessert coupes and top with warmed caramel sauce.

Wine: A light, fruity red, such as a Brouilly from Beaujolais served lightly chilled, makes a pleasing consort with the roast chicken.

Low-Fat Plan: Most of the fat drips off into the roasting pan, but if you want to roast the bird without the skin, stuff the cavity with the lemon slices, shallots, and herbs and roast under a tent of aluminum foil, basting with the Madeira and more lemon juice, if necessary. About 20 minutes before the end of the roasting time, carefully pull back some of the top of the foil so that the bird can brown a bit.

Lapin Lardé de Madame Davenet

MADAME DAVENET'S CASSEROLED RABBIT

"My father, Léopold, was a hunter," explains Monique Picot, "and in the fall he'd bring home a variety of small feathered creatures, as well as hare or rabbit, which my mother cooked in a simple but absolutely tender way." As she prepares her mother's recipe in her own country kitchen, Monique says, "My mother layered the cut-up rabbit parts with fragrant fresh thyme, bay leaves, and slices of pork belly to enrich and further flavor the lean meat, and she baked it in an earthenware casserole.

Monique Picot's parents, Augustine and Léopold Davenet, in Normandy, circa 1925.

"This was one of Jean-Paul's favorite dishes, and he always asked for it whenever we went to Normandy to visit my family. Madame Davenet would always ask him, 'What can I cook for you today, Jean-Paul?' And the answer would usually turn out to be: 'Lapin lardé, s'il vous plaît [Your casseroled rabbit, please].'"

¼ pound fresh pork belly, cut into ½-inch cubes (see Note 1)

One 2½- to 3-pound ready-to-cook rabbit, cut into 8 serving pieces

Salt and freshly ground pepper to taste

8 to 10 sprigs thyme or 1 teaspoon dried

6 sprigs fresh rosemary or 1 teaspoon dried rosemary

6 to 8 bay leaves

1 cup water

Preheat the oven to 375°F.

Place half of the salt pork in a heavy 2-quart casserole, add the rabbit legs and thighs in one layer, and sprinkle with salt, pepper, and half of the thyme, rosemary, and bay leaves. Top with the remaining salt pork and arrange the remaining rabbit pieces, herbs, salt, and pepper on top. Pour the water into the casserole and cover it tightly. If you're in doubt about the seal, wrap a double thickness of heavy aluminum foil around the casserole where the lid meets the bottom part (see Note 2).

Bake in the center of the oven until the rabbit is tender, about 50 to 60 minutes. Serve directly from the casserole or transfer the rabbit to a warmed platter.

Makes 4 servings

Note 1: *Fresh pork belly is available from butcher shops and some supermarket meat departments. If you cannot find any, use the* same amount of Canadian bacon, cut into ½-inch cubes.

Note 2: *Madame Davenet used a flour-and-water paste to seal her earthenware casserole, but a heavy or tight-fitting lid will also do the trick.*

Variation: For a touch of vinous vibrancy, substitute ½ cup dry white wine for the water.

Bread: The Davenets enjoyed a crusty country loaf, fresh from the village bakery, with the rabbit.

Lunch: A robust soup, such as Split Pea Soup (page 13), and a salad of sliced ripe tomatoes dressed with Shallot Vinaigrette (page 146) makes a satisfying midday meal. The rabbit also makes a superb cold dish, if you have any left over. The sauce transmogrifies into a burnished aspic and the rabbit is succulent. In fact, you can serve it as a cold buffet dish.

Dinner: With the rabbit, the Davenets offered Monique's Little Roasted Potatoes with Rosemary (page 142) and a big seasonal salad.

Dessert: Since the rabbit is a Normandy specialty, serve an Apple Tart (page 163) sprinkled with Calvados—apple brandy—for a fitting windup.

Wine: A deep-flavored, fruity Beaujolais, such as Moulin-à-Vent, served lightly chilled or a medium-bodied red Bordeaux marries well with the rabbit.

Low-Fat Plan: Omit the pork belly, and increase the liquid, preferably white wine, to ¾ cup. Make certain you have a good seal so that the rabbit will be moist.

7

Meat

The French have always eaten small portions of meat, both because meat is expensive and because they feel such a rich food can only be absorbed by the body in small quantities. Thus, a steak that would feed one hearty eater in the United States would probably serve at least two people in France. Because meat is so expensive, great care is lavished on its preparation and it is garnished artfully. Conversely, many vegetable dishes are garnished with meat. An omelet might be stuffed with ham and cheese; a dish of potatoes au gratin might be garnished with ham; endives might be braised with a coverlet of ham; cooked cubes of beef are often cooked with chopped onions and served almost like a sauce atop mashed potatoes.

Americans, on the whole, take a larger overview of beef. And, despite the inroads of cholesterol watchers, there are still beef-eaters galore out there, relishing their commodious portions of steak, roast beef, hamburgers and all manner of barbecue treats. At La Bonne Soupe, Jean-Paul zeroed in on the luscious, 8-ounce *steaks hachés*, with their delectable sauces, and on three steak choices. Flank steak is grilled to the diner's preference and served *au naturel*. The tender filet mignon is offered *au naturel*, or as *Filet Mignon au Poivre*, served with a suave wine and Cognaclaced sauce. Jean-Paul buys only prime meat from his specialty butcher and the *steaks hachés* are ground to order by the chef. On the *plats du jour*, diners may find a delicately cooked calf's liver, or a succulent stew. And there's *Fondue Bourguinonne* for those who enjoy cooking their own morsels of prime beef at the table.

Also included are some of the Picot family's savory stews: *Monique's Veal Stew*, which is a standout favorite company dish, and the earthy *Tripe Cooked with Apple Cider and Calvados*, based on her mother's Normandy recipe.

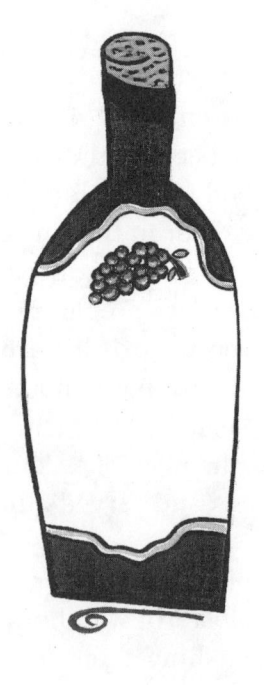

Blanquette de Veau de Monique

MONIQUE'S VEAL STEW

When Monique Picot cooks dinner for guests chez Picot she often relies on an elegant veal stew as the centerpiece. "I like to simmer the delicate veal in a light broth," she says, "with herbs and aromatic vegetables. I always add plenty of mushrooms and lots of fresh pepper." As for that fresh pepper, Monique smiles as she recalls that the illustrious Claude Monet so adored copiously applied pepper that he had to serve his guests a separate, mild dressing for their salads.

2 pounds boneless veal shoulder, cut into 1½-inch chunks

1 medium-size yellow onion

1 large leek, white part only, rinsed well and chopped

1 medium-size carrot, peeled and left whole

1 *bouquet garni*: 2 sprigs thyme, 1 sprig rosemary, and 3 bay leaves tied in a cheesecloth square

About 3 cups Homemade Chicken Broth (page 4) or low-sodium canned broth

½ cup dry white wine

2 tablespoons unsalted butter

2 tablespoons all-purpose flour

2 large egg yolks, lightly beaten

1 cup heavy cream

1 pound small white mushrooms, trimmed and cut into quarters

16 white pearl onions, blanched in boiling water for 2 minutes, then drained and peeled

Salt and freshly ground pepper to taste

Place the veal in a large saucepan, cover with cold water, and bring to a boil over high heat. Reduce the heat to medium-low, and simmer for 2 minutes. Drain the veal in a colander and rinse with cold water. Rinse and dry the saucepan.

Return the veal to the clean saucepan and add the yellow onion, leek, carrot, *bouquet garni,* broth, and wine. If there is not enough liquid to cover the solid ingredients, add more broth. Bring to a boil over high heat, reduce the heat to medium-low and simmer, covered, until the veal is tender, 1 to 1¼ hours.

Using a slotted spoon, transfer the veal to a bowl. Strain the broth and discard the vegetables. Rinse and dry the saucepan. Return the broth to the saucepan and over high heat, cook until reduced to 1 cup. Set aside.

Melt the butter in 1-quart saucepan over low heat and sprinkle in the flour, whisking to make a smooth paste. Slowly add the hot broth, whisking to blend well, then stirring with a wooden spoon until the mixture has thickened. Keep over low heat.

Blend the egg yolks with the cream in a bowl and add 1 tablespoon of the hot broth. Very slowly add this mixture back to the saucepan, stirring to blend. Add the mushrooms and cook, stirring, over low heat for 2 to 3 minutes. Don't let the mixture boil or it will curdle. Add the pearl onions and the reserved veal, stirring gently to blend. Season with salt and pepper. Cook over low heat just until the veal is warmed through, 2 to 3 minutes.

Makes 4 servings

Bread: Fill a basket with slices of *petit parisien,* a shorter, fatter version of the baguette that usually has a softer center.

Lunch: The stew makes a somewhat hearty lunch and is best followed by a crisp salad of mesclun or other seasonal greens dressed with light olive oil and white wine vinegar.

Dinner: Monique serves hot, steamed rice with the stew. The salad course she particularly likes afterward consists of romaine, mâche, and crunchy endive leaves tossed in a mustard-tinged vinaigrette (try Jean-Paul's Zesty Vinaigrette, page 146). With the salad she likes thin wedges of properly runny Brie.

Dessert: The thin-crusted Apple Tart (page 163), garnished with tiny scoops of vanilla ice cream, is an elegant ending to the meal. Or serve apple slices simmered until tender in cider and a pinch of cinnamon. The apple slices are delicious warm or chilled. Offer steaming cups of double espresso for a beverage.

Wine: Uncork an elegant white Burgundy, such as a full-bodied, flavorful Meursault.

Low-Fat Plan: Omit the egg and cream enrichment. After the broth has been reduced, return the veal and broth to the saucepan, add the onions and the mushrooms and cook over low heat, stirring, until the mushrooms turn dark and exude their juices, 3 to 4 minutes. Serve the stew with the rice, and dress the salad with equal parts of white wine vinegar and chicken broth.

Scum Chaser

When veal is cooked without first having been browned, as in this stew, it throws off a good deal of scum. To avoid this, the veal is first parboiled, then rinsed in cold water, as is the saucepan, before proceeding with the recipe.

Boeuf Bourguignon

BURGUNDIAN BEEF STEW

"A very typical bistro dish," Jean-Paul Picot says of the famed Burgundian beef stew. *"This is a favorite in our family, and I do recommend using a good red Burgundy wine. Oh, certainly don't cook with a Grands Échézeaux, but a fruity Beaujolais is fine. And I like plenty of aromatic vegetables to simmer with the beef and a small veal bone that adds gelatin and acts as a natural thickener. The pearl onions and mushrooms are added last to preserve their texture and flavor."*

1 small veal bone, optional

2 tablespoons extra-virgin olive oil

3 pounds boneless beef, chuck or rump, cut into 2½-inch cubes

1 large yellow onion, chopped

2 cloves garlic, finely minced

3 cups Beaujolais or other red Burgundy wine

1 cup Homemade Beef Broth (page 3) or low-sodium canned broth

2 large carrots, peeled and cut in half

2 ribs celery, cut in half

4 sprigs flat-leaf parsley

1 bay leaf

2 tablespoons tomato paste mixed with 2 tablespoons water

Salt and freshly ground pepper to taste

2 slices bacon, cut into ¼-inch dice

18 white pearl onions, blanched in boiling water for 2 minutes, then drained and peeled (see Note)

½ pound small mushrooms, stems removed, cut into quarters

If you are using the veal bone, you will need to first parboil it or it will release scum into the stew. Place the bone in a small saucepan and add cold water to cover by 1 inch. Bring to a boil over high heat and simmer, uncovered, until the scum rises to the top, about 6 to 8 minutes. Drain the veal bone and rinse it under cold, running water. Reserve.

Heat the oil in a heavy 4- or 5-quart Dutch oven or lidded casserole over medium heat until hot but not smoking. Add the beef and brown the pieces on all sides, about 8 minutes. Add the yellow onion and garlic and cook, stirring occasionally, until softened but not browned, 3 to 4 minutes. Pour in the wine and broth, raise the heat to high, and bring the liquid just to a boil, then reduce the heat to medium-low. If using, add the reserved veal bone, then add the carrots, celery, parsley, bay leaf, tomato paste mixture, and salt and pepper. Cover and simmer over medium-low heat until the beef is fork tender, 1½ to 2 hours.

Meanwhile, in a medium-size skillet, cook the bacon pieces over medium-high heat, stirring, until they exude their fat and become crisp. Add the pearl onions and cook over medium heat until they are lightly browned on all sides, 6 to 8 minutes. Turn the pearl onions from time to time so they brown evenly. Transfer to a dish and reserve.

Add the mushrooms to the skillet and cook over medium heat until they turn dark and exude their juices, 5 to 6 minutes. Add to the pearl onions and bacon.

When the beef is tender, remove and discard the veal bone, carrots, celery, parsley, and bay leaf. Add the reserved onions and mushrooms, together with the bacon bits and cook over low heat until heated through. At this point the stew may be cooled and refrigerated, covered, for up to 2 days. The flavor improves on reheating.

Makes 6 servings

Note: To peel pearl onions, drop them into a saucepan of rapidly boiling water for 2 minutes. Drain the onions and rinse them under cold, running water briefly. The skins will slip right off.

Bread: You will certainly want a crusty country loaf with plenty of crumb to catch the last of the savory sauce.

Lunch: Serve modest portions of the stew with a small salad of sliced tomatoes.

Dinner: Jean-Paul loves buttered broad noodles under his Boeuf Bourguignon, but you could also opt for steamed rice, if you prefer. Follow with a refreshing salad of cooked artichoke hearts stuffed with chopped red radishes and drizzled with Shallot Vinaigrette (page 146).

Dessert: Place a poached pear in each of 6 dessert coupes. Spoon Rosy Raspberry Sauce (page 164) liberally on top and sprinkle with a few slivered toasted almonds.

Wine: A full-bodied, fruity Beaujolais, such as a Moulin-à-Vent or Brouilly, makes fine sipping with this stew.

Low-Fat Plan: Preheat the oven to 400°F. Omit the veal bone, oil, and bacon from the recipe. Place the beef cubes in a baking pan that will hold them in one layer and bake, uncovered, until the cubes are browned, 8 to 10 minutes. Transfer the beef to the Dutch oven and add all the ingredients except the pearl onions and mushrooms. Bring the liquid to a boil, reduce the heat, and cook as directed.

In a separate nonstick skillet, brown the pearl onions: Sprinkle them with 3 tablespoons of red wine or water and cook over medium-high heat until they begin to color a little, 5 to 6 minutes. Transfer them to a dish and reserve. Repeat the process with the mushrooms, cooking them over medium heat just until they turn dark and exude their juices. Finish the recipe as directed.

Tripes à la Mode de Caen

TRIPE COOKED WITH APPLE CIDER AND CALVADOS

"My mother, Augustine Davenet," says Monique Picot, "was a charming woman and a talented cook, who did marvelous things with the apples and apple products of our family's farm in Normandy." Monique sits with a glass of herbal tea and recalls her happy childhood in the lush Varenne Valley and the dishes her mother prepared with a lavish and loving hand.

*M*onique Picot's mother, Augustine Davenet, circa 1942.

"I am still trying to re-create some of her dishes for Jean-Paul, who remembers them fondly, but they don't taste the way they did in Normandy," Monique adds with a tiny sigh. But her tripe simmered in apple cider, apples, Calvados, (the famed apple brandy of the region), and aromatic herbs has that marvelous Norman touch.

"Each year in Caen there was a chefs' competition for the best tripe recipe, but Maman Davenet's outshone them all. She baked the tripe in a big, earthenware casserole with its lid sealed with a flour-and-water paste. She would let the tripe simmer slowly for many hours to tenderize the meat and coalesce all the heady flavors. She liked to serve it hot from the casserole, but it's also delicious tiède—at room temperature. And, should there be any left over, the rich sauce turns into a deep-flavored aspic in the refrigerator. It makes a great lunch."

3 pounds beef tripe, trimmed of any fat, cut into 3-inch squares

1 calf's foot or oxtail (about 2 pounds; see Note 1)

6 tablespoons vegetable oil

1 large onion, thinly sliced

4 cloves garlic, crushed

2 ribs celery, thinly sliced

2 carrots, peeled and cut into ¼-inch dice

1 Granny Smith apple, peeled, cored, and cut into ¼-inch dice

¼ cup Calvados or other apple brandy

2 cups apple cider

1 quart Homemade Beef Broth (page 3) or low-sodium canned broth

1 teaspoon dried thyme

1 teaspoon dried rosemary

3 small bay leaves

Salt and freshly ground pepper to taste

4 medium-size boiling potatoes, peeled and quartered

Rinse the tripe and calf's foot or oxtail in a colander under cold water and drain well. Pat the tripe and calf's foot or oxtails dry between paper towels.

Heat 1 tablespoon of the oil in a 6-quart Dutch oven or other heavy lidded casserole over medium-high heat until hot but not smoking. Working in batches without crowding, brown the meats on both sides, transferring the pieces to a bowl as they are browned. Add ¼ cup of remaining oil as necessary to the casserole.

Add the remaining 1 tablespoon oil, the onion, garlic, celery, and carrots to the casserole and cook over medium heat, stirring occasionally, until the vegetables begin to soften, about 6 minutes. Add the apple, Calvados, cider, and broth and bring the mixture to a boil. Add the herbs and salt and pepper and simmer, covered, over medium heat or in a preheated oven (see Note 2) until the meats are tender, about 3 hours. Lift the lid and test the meats for doneness. If the meats are still not tender, cover and simmer for 45 to 60 minutes.

When the meats are fork tender, transfer the calf's foot or oxtail to a work surface and pick off the meat, discarding the bones. Stir the meat into the casserole. At this point, the casserole may be cooled and refrigerated, covered, for 2 days. Before reheating, skim off and discard any fat on surface.

Meanwhile, place the potatoes in a medium-size saucepan and cover with water by 2 inches. Bring to a boil over high heat, reduce the heat to medium and cook until the potatoes are tender, about 10 minutes. Add the potatoes to the casserole and heat over medium heat, stirring occasionally, until the stew is hot. Ladle the stew into warmed deep soup bowls.

Makes 6 to 8 servings

Note 1: *The calf's foot is generally split; the oxtail is usually cut into pieces by the butcher.*

Note 2: *Monique finds it easier to control the cooking process on the top of the stove, but you can also bake the casserole in a preheated 350°F oven for the same amount of time, checking for doneness after 3 hours.*

Bread: In Normandy, a rich white bread called *gâche* would be enjoyed with the tripe, but you can choose any fresh, crisp-crusted white loaf with a nice, firm inner crumb.

Lunch: Left over tripe, with its concentrated jellied sauce, makes a superb lunch, with plenty of good, crusty bread and a salad of watercress and Bibb lettuce tossed with a Shallot Vinaigrette (page 146).

Dinner: Serve the tripe in large, deep soup bowls and follow with a salad of tossed seasonal greens dressed with Jean-Paul's Zesty Vinaigrette (page 146) and add thin wedges of Camembert cheese to each plate.

Dessert: Stay with the Norman theme with wedges of thin-crusted Apple Tart (page 163).

Wine: A hearty, full-bodied Rhône red such as Châteauneuf-du-Pape or Gigondas will counterpoint the flavors and texture of the tripe felicitously.

Low-**F**at **P**lan: Omit the browning process. Bring a large pot of water to boil, add the tripe and calf's foot or oxtail and blanch the meats. Using a slotted spoon, transfer them to a bowl. Add 4 tablespoons of water, white wine, or broth to the casserole and cook the onion, garlic, celery and carrots over medium-high heat until they start to soften, about 6 minutes. Continue with the recipe. For a low-fat dessert, baked or poached apples with a spoonful of Calvados or other apple brandy would be delightful.

Foie de Veau à la Pommery

CALF'S LIVER WITH POMMERY MUSTARD SAUCE

A popular bistro dish, calf's liver is tender and flavorful, and it comes as no surprise that French cooks adorn their grilled, broiled, or sautéed liver with myriad sauces. There's calf's liver à la bourguignonne, in a rich, red wine sauce; à l'anglaise, in which the liver is cut into thin slices, cooked in butter, and garnished with crisp bacon and a few squirts of lemon juice; à la bordelaise, rich with bone marrow, shallots, and red Bordeaux wine; and many more.

For Chef Francis Freund's own favorite, he naps the quickly cooked liver with a savory blend of grainy mustard and balsamic vinegar mellowed with a touch of honey.

For the liver

2 tablespoons olive oil

8 slices calf's liver (about 1¼ pounds total), ⅓-inch thick

Salt and freshly ground pepper to taste

For the sauce

1 cup Homemade Beef Broth (page 3) or low-sodium canned broth

1 cup dry red wine

⅓ cup grainy mustard, such as Pommery

⅓ cup honey

Salt and freshly ground pepper to taste

1 tablespoon balsamic vinegar

1 tablespoon unsalted butter

Prepare the liver:

Heat the oil in a heavy skillet large enough to hold all the liver over medium-high heat until hot but not smoking. Season the liver on both sides with salt and pepper and cook until lightly browned on one side, about 3 minutes. Turn and brown on the other side, another 3 minutes. Transfer the liver to a warmed platter, cover, and keep warm.

Prepare the sauce:

Pour off and discard any oil in the skillet. Add the broth and wine, bring to a boil over high heat and cook until the liquid is reduced by half, 8 to 10 minutes. Reduce the heat to medium, add the mustard, honey, and salt and pepper, stirring to blend well. Add the balsamic vinegar and swirl in the butter, stirring until it is well incorporated into the sauce and makes it nicely shiny.

To serve, place 2 slices of liver on each of 4 warmed dinner plates and spoon the sauce on top or alongside.

Makes 4 servings

Bread: A thinly sliced bâtard, or short, fat baguette, is the premium choice.

Lunch: The calf's liver is a beguiling lunch or brunch dish, with lots of good crusty bâtard and a small leafy green salad.

Dinner: Glazed Carrots (page 139) and Monique's Garlicky Mashed Potatoes (page 137) are delightfully rewarding go-withs.

Dessert: Serve *Poires Belle Hélène* (page 157) for an elegant dessert. Add a plate of assorted small cookies, especially if you're pouring espresso.

Wine: A fruity red, such as a *cru* Beaujolais (Brouilly or Morgon, for example) or a Bordeaux Petit Château (a moderately priced château-bottled wine from Bordeaux) is agreeably appropriate.

Low-Fat Plan: Omit the oil and cook the liver in ⅓ cup of defatted beef broth. For the sauce, omit the butter; it will still be full of flavor.

Gigot Rôti à l'Ail et Romarin

ROAST LEG OF LAMB WITH ROSEMARY AND GARLIC

Thin slices of tender lamb roasted with the fragrant, flavorful duo of garlic and rosemary make a beguiling meal. Diners at the bistro love the lamb at Easter and when it's on the list of daily specials. We've adapted the recipe for home cooks so its preparation is no fuss. The lamb turns out so moist and tender, even a sauce is superfluous. It's a great company dish.

One 6- to 7-pound oven-ready leg of lamb
3 cloves garlic, cut into thin slivers
Salt and freshly ground pepper to taste
3 tablespoons chopped fresh rosemary
1¼ cups dry red wine

Preheat oven to 375°F.

Make certain the fell (the thin membrane) that covers the leg of lamb has been removed; if not, use a sharp knife to peel it off yourself. Trim away as much fat as possible.

Place the lamb on a rack set into a roasting pan that holds it comfortably. Using the point of a small sharp knife, make slits of about ¼ inch over the surface of the lamb, spaced about 2 inches apart. Insert the garlic slivers into the slits. Do this on both sides of the leg. In a small dish blend the salt and pepper, and rosemary. Rub half the mixture on both sides of the lamb.

Roast the lamb in the center of the oven until it is lightly browned, about 15 minutes. Reduce the oven temperature to 350°F and at this point, insert a meat thermometer into the thickest part of the meat. Continue to roast, basting with the wine at 20 minute intervals until the thermometer reads 150°F for rare and medium-rare, about 1 hour. If you like your lamb well done, wait until the thermometer registers 160 to 165°F, another 10 minutes or so.

Remove the lamb from the oven and transfer to a warmed platter. Allow the meat to rest for 5 minutes to absorb the juices. Cut thin slices and arrange them on the platter; allow guests to help themselves.

Makes 8 servings

Bread: A freshly baked baguette is the best choice here.

Lunch: Serve modest portions and accompany with Purée of Turnips (page 136).

Dinner: Accompany the lamb with Monique's Savory White Bean Salad (page 47) and her Tomatoes with Garlic and Herbs (page 139).

Dessert: Splurge with Poached Pears with Ice Cream and Chocolate Sauce (page 157).

Wine: A mature Bordeaux is the classic partner with lamb, but you could also uncork an American Cabernet Sauvignon.

Low-Fat Plan: There's no need for any special low-fat arrangement—there's no fat in the recipe since the lamb is trimmed of all fat.

What's Crushed Garlic?

To crush garlic, lay an unpeeled clove on a cutting board and place a heavy, broad-handled knife over it. Pound several times on the broad side of the knife, and you will have crushed garlic. Peel the clove before using. Rub the cutting board with the cut side of a lemon to erase the garlic odor.

8

One-Dish Meals

Here's a chapter of recipes, each of which is a meal in itself. The rewarding part of preparing one-dish meals is they can be done well in advance. By their very names, they connote festivity and are best enjoyed with a group of congenial diners. The dishes that follow all relate to different French regions. Each has its own personality and features the specialties of the area.

Among the traditional dishes is the *Cassoulet* from southwest France, in which pork, goose, or duck and sausages are simmered with white beans. A famed sauerkraut dish of Alsace combines ham, pork, and sausages with tangy sauerkraut; and there are other countless regional stews in which meats and poultry, even innards, are amalgamated advantageously. The great Mediterranean fish stew—*bouillabaisse*—is indeed a fabulous one-dish meal, with its beguiling array of varied seafood and shellfish and aromatic broth.

Meat, poultry, and fish simmered with aromatic vegetables and herbs are traditionally served in oversize soup bowls. And the last ambrosial drops can certainly be mopped up with some good French bread.

Choucroute Garnie Alsacienne

ALSATIAN SAUERKRAUT WITH SAUSAGES AND MEATS

The ultimate glorification of sauerkraut and sausages is the only way to describe this dish from Alsace, where the sauerkraut is embellished with a plethora of local sausages— knockwurst, pork, blood, cervelat *(fine-textured pork sausage)—some heady, some bland, some properly garlicky. It's a sausage lover's paradise! The sauerkraut is simmered in a fine Alsace Riesling, which also makes a felicitous drinking companion for the dish.*

Don't miss this stew when it appears on La Bonne Soupe's special plats du jour *menu. On a cold, gray day in winter, sit at one of the checkered-cloth-covered tables and enjoy a plate of steaming, fragrant sauerkraut and its garnishes. Or prepare it at home, following La Bonne Soupe's recipe.*

½ pound slab bacon, cut into ¼-inch dice

2 large onions, thinly sliced

2 Granny Smith apples, peeled, cored, and thinly sliced

2 cups thinly sliced white cabbage

2 cups dry white wine

Four ¼-inch-thick slices smoked ham (about ½ pound)

1 pound smoked pork loin

1 pound sauerkraut, rinsed and drained

1 *bouquet garni:* 1 teaspoon *each* coriander seeds, juniper berries, and cumin seed; 1 whole clove, 2 unpeeled cloves garlic, 4 small bay leaves, and 12 black peppercorns tied in a cheesecloth square

Salt and freshly ground pepper to taste

4 medium-size red potatoes (about 1½ pounds total)

4 fresh garlic-sausage links (about 1 pound total)

4 mild Polish-style sausage links (about ½ pound total)

Imported Dijon mustard

Cook the bacon in a 6-quart Dutch oven or heavy lidded casserole over medium-low heat, stirring occasionally, until the fat is rendered, but the bacon is not brown. Add the onions and cook over medium heat until they start to wilt, about 3 minutes. Add the apples and cabbage and cook, stirring, just until the cabbage starts to wilt, about 5 minutes.

Add the wine, ham, pork, sauerkraut, *bouquet garni,* and salt and pepper, stirring to blend. Reduce the heat to medium-low and cook, covered, until the cabbage is soft, about 1 hour.

While the cabbage mixture is cooking, place the potatoes in a 1½-quart saucepan and add enough water to cover by 1 inch. Bring to a boil over high heat and cook over medium heat, partially covered, until tender, 10 to 15 minutes. Drain the potatoes and reserve.

Prick the garlic and Polish sausages all around with the tines of a fork. Half fill a 2-quart saucepan with cold water and bring to a boil; add the sausages, and boil gently just until they are cooked through, about 20 minutes. Drain well in a colander.

To serve, discard the *bouquet garni.* Transfer the pork loin to a cutting board and cut into four slices. Return the meat to the casserole along with the potatoes and sausages and cook over medium heat, stirring occasionally, just until hot.

Have 4 warmed dinner plates ready. Mound the cabbage-sauerkraut mixture in the centers of each and top with a ham slice, a pork loin slice, and 1 of each type of sausage, and a helping of potatoes. Pass the mustard separately.

Makes 4 servings

Bread: "You don't really need bread with all those wonderful sausages and potatoes," Jean-Paul Picot comments, adding, "But a good, fresh baguette is never amiss!"

Lunch: This stew is such rich fare that it is really better suited for dinner than lunch. If you are planning to have the stew for diner, it is best to have a light lunch such as a Spinach Omelet (page 54).

Dinner: We find that even a salad is too much after this dish.

Dessert: Serve Peaches Poached in Red Wine (page 159) for a light and refreshing conclusion.

Wine: The first choice, of course, is a superb dry Riesling from Alsace or a mug of beer, but you could also opt for a light and fruity Beaujolais, if you prefer red wine.

Low-Fat Plan: For a mock choucroute, skip the bacon, pork loin, and sausages. Use instead ¾ lb. sliced low-fat ham and 1 lb. low-fat chicken sausages. Place the onions in the casserole, sprinkle with 4 tablespoons water or chicken broth and continue with the recipe, omitting the fatty meats. Boil the chicken sausages in water for 15 minutes, drain, and cut into chunks. Add the sliced low-fat ham to the cabbage and cook until heated through.

Too Much Crumb?

Some years back, when Jean-Paul Picot's French Bakery was in operation a couple of doors south of the bistro, it supplied many restaurants in Manhattan with freshly baked baguettes, petits pains, and other specialties. Jean-Paul Picot likes to tell this story: "One day the owner of one of the restaurants we supply called me and said, 'Your bread is not good.'

"'What is wrong with it?' I asked.

"'Too much crumb [the doughy inside],' was the reply.

"'Too much crumb? What do you expect from fresh bread? Our bread is delivered hot from the ovens. So maybe you tasted the bread when it was still too hot?'

"Some people are never happy," said Jean-Paul with a sigh.

Cassoulet

SAVORY FRENCH BEAN STEW

This great French bean-and-meat casserole is a winter specialty of the towns of Carcassone and Castelnaudary in southwest France. It's a savory combination of dried white beans baked in a casserole with duck or goose, sausages, and aromatic vegetables.

There was a time when French housewives assembled all the ingredients, including lots of poultry fat or lard, together in a big casserole and baked it for many hours in the bread oven. Many people in smaller French towns didn't have ovens, so the casseroles were taken to the baker's, where they simmered all night in the big wood-burning oven. Needless to say, there are many regional variations of the dish, but whatever the origin, the end result is a luscious stew.

Chef Francis Freund's adaptation is a lighter, quicker version than the traditional, and he cooks the stew on top of the stove. "It's easier to check the liquid and the cooking time," he says, adding, "This stew is really great."

1 pound dried white northern beans

4 duck legs (see Note) or one 1½-pound piece boneless pork loin

Salt and freshly ground pepper to taste

4 sweet Italian sausage links (about 1 pound total)

2 fresh garlic Italian or other sausage links (about ½ pound total)

2 tablespoons vegetable oil

1 large onion, thinly sliced

3 or 4 cloves garlic, finely minced

2 medium-size carrots, peeled and thinly sliced

2 ribs celery, thinly sliced

2 large tomatoes, peeled, seeded, and cut into rough dice

1 cup dry white wine

3 to 4 cups Homemade Chicken Broth (page 4), Homemade Beef Broth (page 3), or low-sodium canned broth

¼ teaspoon dried thyme

¼ teaspoon dried rosemary

2 bay leaves

2 tablespoons tomato paste mixed with 2 tablespoons water

½ cup finely chopped fresh flat-leaf parsley

⅔ cup fresh white bread crumbs

Soak the beans overnight in a 1½-quart saucepan in cold water to cover by 2 inches, or use the quick soaking method (page 13).

Drain the beans in a colander and return to the saucepan. Add water to cover by 1 inch and bring to a boil over high heat. Reduce the heat to medium and simmer the beans, partially covered, until tender but not mushy, about 45 minutes. Drain the beans in a colander and reserve.

Preheat the oven to 400°F.

If using duck legs, prick the skin all around. Rub the duck legs or pork loin with salt and pepper and roast in a baking pan in the center of the oven, uncovered, until lightly browned but not cooked through, 15 to 20 minutes. Reserve the meat.

Prick the sweet and garlic sausages all around with the tines of a fork. Half fill a 2-quart saucepan with cold water and bring to a boil over high heat; add the sausages, and boil gently just long enough for them to exude their fat, 5 to 6 minutes. Drain the sausages, cut them into ⅛-inch slices, and reserve.

Heat the oil in a 6-quart saucepan or Dutch oven over medium heat until hot but not smoking. Add the onions and garlic and cook until softened but not browned, 3 to 4 minutes. Add the carrots and celery and cook until wilted, 5 to 6 minutes. Add the tomatoes and cook until wilted, 2 to 3 minutes. Add the wine and cook over high heat until it is reduced by one-third.

Add the reserved beans and duck legs or pork loin and the broth, herbs, tomato paste mixture, and salt and pepper and bring to a boil over high heat. Reduce the heat to medium-low and simmer, covered partially, until the pork loin or duck legs are tender, about 1 hour. Check occasionally to see if there is enough liquid. The beans should be soupy but not drowning in liquid. Add the reserved sausages and simmer, covered, until they are heated through, 2 to 3 minutes. The cassoulet may be made up to this point, cooled completely and refrigerated, covered. Reheat the Cassoulet to proceed with the recipe.

Preheat the broiler. Sprinkle the parsley and bread crumbs over the Cassoulet and broil about 4 inches from the heat until the bread crumbs are lightly browned, 2 to 3 minutes—watch so they don't burn. Spoon the Cassoulet onto warmed bowls or dinner plates, making sure each has a serving of duck legs or pork loin, beans, and sausages.

Makes 4 to 6 servings

Note: *Duck legs may be found at your local butcher or supermarket, or may have to be ordered from them. Another choice is to order directly from D'Artagnan, the New Jersey purveyor of duck legs and specialty poultry. To order direct via catalog or telephone, call (800) D-a-r-t-a-g-n.*

Bread: A fresh sourdough loaf is a perfect foil for the Cassoulet.

Lunch: This stew is too hearty for most luncheons. If you're planning the stew for dinner, think light for lunch. A big Chef's Salad (page 42) and a bit of bread should do it.

Dinner: Toss together a large salad of red-tipped lettuce, mâche, curly endive, and sliced radishes, dressed with Jean-Paul's Zesty Vinaigrette (page 146) to enjoy after the stew.

Dessert: Scoop little balls of cantaloupe and honeydew melon into dessert coupes and spoon a little Rosy Raspberry Sauce (page 164) over them. Pass a plate of thin, crisp Lacy Tile Cookies (page 158).

Wine: This hearty stew calls for a sturdy red country wine. A Cahors, which used to be called the black wine of Cahors, because the Malbec grape gives it such a deep, dark red color, is today an agreeably fruity, soft-scented, and easy-to-drink wine that would be a superb choice. Or choose Bandol, Corbières, or other country red.

Second-Chance Bread

To freshen stale baguettes, sprinkle them with water and place in a 350°F oven for 2 to 3 minutes.

Some French Breads

Baguette: The star *pain ordinaire* or every-day Parisian bread, the baguette is a thin-crusted, crackly, long loaf, usually about 2 feet long and 2 inches wide, with a tender, light crumb and a fair amount of air holes. The texture is grainy, and it's generally at its peak when eaten as close to baking time as possible.

Bâtard: A shorter, fatter baguette, the bâtard measures about 1 foot long, with tapered ends.

Ficelle: Literally meaning "string," the ficelle is a string-bean version of a baguette, about 18 inches long and 1½ inches wide, with a slightly denser crumb.

Petit parisien: A shorter, squatter version of the baguette.

Pain de campagne: This is your basic French country bread, usually round with a thick crust and chewy crumb. Country breads in France made with *levain* (sourdough) are called *pains au levain.*

Boule: Another name for the thick-crusted round country bread that is often made with a sourdough starter.

Pain de seigle: This earthy, rye bread *à la française* is made with dough that has fermented over a period of days. It has a chewy texture and a sour rye tang to the taste. It will stay fresh for several days wrapped, and at room temperature. It contains no caraway seeds. It is the favorite bread, served with butter, for a raw seafood platter.

Pain épis: Literally "wheat shaft," this is a 12-inch baguette that has been shaped like a shaft of wheat, with small, roll-size clusters to pull off.

Petits pains: These are French dinner rolls, either oval or round.

Brioche: These round, egg- and butter-rich loaves come in various sizes and shapes, some with little doughy knobs on the top, all with a delicate crust and rich, soft crumb. Brioche is a bit sweet and is wonderful at breakfast or tea time with confiture (jam). Large braided brioches called *nanterres* and *parisiennes* are pulled apart rather than cut. *Brioche de tête*, an 8-inch-wide version, often is hollowed out and filled with chicken, meat, or seafood.

Croissants: These crescent-shaped rolls are made of buttery flaky layers of dough and are generally enjoyed at breakfast but are sometimes cut in half and used for sandwiches.

Fougasse: This is a specialty of southern France and is made from baguette or brioche dough and shaped like a ladder. Often Mediterranean ingredients—such as Niçoise olives, *herbes de Provence*, anchovies, and nuts—are baked into the breads.

Bouillabaisse de La Bonne Soupe

LA BONNE SOUPE'S MEDITERRANEAN FISH STEW

The kitchen is filled with the enticing aromas of sweet, fresh fish; aromatic herbs; and seductive saffron. It's Friday and Chef Francis Freund is simmering the broth for the bistro's version of the great bouillabaisse, *the renowned fish stew of Marseilles. "We put our* bouillabaisse *on the menu in 1977," Jean-Paul Picot says, tasting a sip of the heady broth and nodding his approval. "It was an instant succès fou [smash hit]. Since then we include it on our* plats du jour *at least once a week. It's always a sellout.*

"Of course, there are so many versions of bouillabaisse, *and always endless discussions over which fish to include and whether to add tomatoes or not. How about lobster? The fun of* bouillabaisse *is to add whatever fish or shellfish makes you happy," adds* le patron *(the owner). We use the freshest catch-of-the-day fish and shellfish, and we like to bring a big tureen to the table and let diners help themselves. It's a festive presentation."*

For the broth (see Note 1)

½ cup extra-virgin olive oil

2 medium-size onions, chopped

2 cloves garlic, crushed

3 ribs celery, chopped

2 leeks, white parts only, washed well, halved lengthwise, chopped, and drained

1 fennel bulb (½ to ¾ pound), chopped

Head, bones, and trimmings from the whole fish used for stew

Shells from the shrimp used for the stew

1 cup dry white wine

2 quarts water

½ cup tomato paste

2 tablespoons fennel seeds

Pinch of saffron

2 tablespoons chopped fresh tarragon

Salt and freshly ground pepper to taste

For the *rouille*

⅔ cup mayonnaise

½ teaspoon anchovy paste or to taste

1 teaspoon minced garlic mashed to a paste with a pinch of salt

Pinch of hot or sweet paprika

Ground red pepper to taste

Croûtons (page 9)

For the fish

4½ pounds whole white fish, such as snapper, whiting, or flounder, skinned, gutted, and filleted (head, bones, and trimmings reserved for the broth)

½ pound firm white fish fillet, such as cod, halibut, or hake

2 dozen mussels, preferably cultivated, scrubbed well and beards removed (see Note 2)

½ pound medium-size shrimp—about 1 dozen—peeled and deveined (shells reserved for the broth)

Salt and freshly ground pepper to taste

Prepare the broth:

Heat the oil in a 10-quart stockpot or kettle over medium-high heat until hot but not smoking. Add the onions, garlic, celery, leeks, and fennel and cook, stirring occasionally, until the vegetables have softened but not browned, about 5 minutes. Add the fish head, bones, and trimmings; shrimp shells; and wine and bring to a boil over high heat. Cook until the wine has reduced slightly, about 2 minutes. In a bowl, whisk 1 cup of the water into the tomato paste. Add the tomato paste mixture and all the remaining ingredients to the pot and simmer over medium-low heat, partially covered, 45 minutes. Strain the fish broth through a large sieve lined with several layers of cheesecloth set over a large bowl. The fish broth may be made 1 day ahead, cooled completely, and refrigerated, covered.

Prepare the *rouille:*

In a bowl, whisk together all the ingredients and then whisk in about 1½ tablespoons fish broth or enough to thin the mixture slightly. The *rouille* may be made 1 day ahead and kept refrigerated, covered.

Prepare the Croûtons:

Preheat the oven to 400°F. Rub the bread slices with the garlic halves and brush with oil on both sides. Toast the croutons on a large baking sheet in the center of the oven until golden, about 10 minutes. The croutons may be made 1 day ahead and kept in airtight containers.

Prepare the fish:

Cut both types of fish into 2-inch-wide pieces. If the fish broth has been refrigerated, place the broth in a kettle and bring to a boil over high heat, stirring occasionally. Add the mussels and cook, covered, until the shells open, about 3 minutes. Discard any unopened shells and transfer the mussels to a bowl.

Reduce the heat to medium and add the fish and the shrimp to the kettle. Simmer, uncovered, just until cooked through, about 3 minutes. Return the mussels to the kettle and season with salt and pepper if necessary.

To serve, divide among 8 deep, oversized soup plates. Spread 8 croutons with some of the *rouille* and center a crouton in each bowl. Serve the remaining croutons and rouille separately.

Makes 8 servings

Note 1: Some farmed mussels are available in 2-pound bags that contain about 56 mussels. In this case, use 24 of the mussels for the stew and freeze the remainder.

Note 2: Bottled clam juice can be substituted for the fish broth. After the vegetables have been cooked in the olive oil, add six 8-ounce bottles of clam juice and 2 ½ cups of dry white wine and proceed with the recipe. One caveat: Bottled clam juice is quite salty, so add salt with discretion.

Bread: The classic accompaniment is a crusty baguette or peasant loaf to catch the last drops of the soup.

Lunch and Dinner: A salad of seasonal greens is all that's needed with this hearty dish.

Dessert: Scoop lemon sherbet into balloon wineglasses and spoon a little vodka over the top. Pass a platter of crisp sugar cookies.

Wine: The heady fragrances and pungent flavors of the stew will wipe out most wines. It's wise to stay with a simple Rosé from Provence or an herbaceous white, such as a French or California Sauvignon Blanc. For red wine buffs, a light-bodied country red, such as Côte de Provence, served lightly chilled, is most agreeable.

Low-Fat Plan: Omit the oil and sprinkle the onions, celery, leeks, and fennel with ¼ cup of water; cover and cook over medium heat until the vegetables are softened but not browned, about 5 minutes. Proceed with the recipe. Use low-fat mayonnaise for the *rouille.* For the croutons, omit the oil and rub well with garlic.

The Rise and Fall of the House of Carts

During the time Jean-Paul's French Bakery was humming right along—a *succès fou* (smash hit)—Jean-Paul and Monique had the brilliant idea to market the wonderfully crusty baguettes as lunchtime sandwiches, along with a selection of *les bonnes soupes*. A very neat idea, everyone thought. So Jean-Paul went to the city commissioner's office and procured a license to operate a rolling cart. "It was back in the early 1980s and everyone at the bistro agreed the idea was terrific. After all, there were carts all over town selling everything from frankfurters to souvlaki, from shish kebab to Chinese stir-fries. Why not load up our cart with foods agreeable to the stomach and appealing to the eyes of the throngs of people who buy their lunch and snacks at these stands regularly?

"The staff all pitched in to make absolutely delicious sandwiches—ham, cheese, chicken, turkey, crunchy vegetables, the works—all attractively nestling between ample chunks of fresh baguette. We added some of our soups, both hot and cold, and frequently offered one of our quiches, pâte de campagne, and zesty saucisson. The cart sported a colorful red awning and La Bonne Soupe's logo was emblazoned on the sides. It looked pretty nifty.

"We picked a great spot—Grand Army Plaza, at Fifty-ninth Street, facing the elegant Plaza Hotel and close to Central Park—and rolled our cart there every day. For several months we did a brisk business and everyone was happy. But our rolling cart bonanza was abruptly terminated one day, when a tough-looking guy who owned most of the neighboring carts came up to me and said: 'I understand you have a very nice restaurant.'

"'Thank you,' I replied, wondering what this was all about.

"'You want to stay in the restaurant business?' the guy continued. 'Then get your cart out of here. Otherwise you may have no La Bonne Soupe to go back to.'

"Yes, New York is a very tough place to do business!"

Couscous à l'Algérienne

ALGERIAN COUSCOUS

Jean-Paul Picot tells us about his introduction to couscous. "I was a 21-year-old soldier in the French Army sent to Algeria to protect the French farmers. We were billeted on a French farm, and naturally, they had to feed us. The dish we were served most frequently was Algerian couscous, versions of which are legion all across North Africa. The word couscous *refers both to the grainlike pasta of wheat (usually semolina) that is steamed and often eaten solo, and to the dish in which the pasta serves as a base for meat, poultry, vegetables, and even fish, depending on the region, all bathed in a sharply peppery sauce.*

"The Algerian couscous we were served had both lamb and chicken, and at first taste I found it too spicy. However, in time I learned to enjoy it immensely. So, when we opened La Bonne Soupe and our chef offered to make a couscous for us, we said, 'Do it!' His was a wonderful dish—and still is—and we certainly were in the vanguard of French bistros with couscous on the menu."

5 tablespoons extra-virgin olive oil

1½ pounds boneless lamb stew meat, cut into 2-inch cubes

One 3- to 3½-pound chicken, cut into serving pieces, giblets reserved for another use

1 medium-size onion, chopped (about 1 cup)

1 small red bell pepper, diced (about 1 cup)

1 tablespoon chopped garlic

1 tablespoon ground cumin

1 tablespoon sweet paprika

1 teaspoon ground coriander

½ teaspoon ground red pepper

½ teaspoon ground turmeric

¼ teaspoon ground nutmeg

¼ teaspoon ground ginger

Pinch of saffron

Salt to taste

1 quart Homemade Chicken Broth (page 4) or low-sodium canned broth

2 medium-size zucchini, cut into ¾-inch dice (about 2 cups)

1 small rutabaga or 3 turnips, peeled and cut into ¾-inch dice (about 2½ cups)

1 small eggplant, trimmed and cut into ¾-inch dice (about 2 cups)

One 16-ounce can whole tomatoes, drained and cut into ¾-inch dice (about 1 cup)

1 cup drained cooked chick peas

4½ cups water

½ cup dark raisins

Two 10-ounce boxes quick-cooking couscous, or 6 cups if buying in bulk

Harissa sauce or other bottled hot pepper sauce (see Note)

Heat 3 tablespoons of the oil in a large heavy skillet over moderately high heat until hot but not smoking. Pat the lamb dry and brown in batches, transferring it with tongs to an 8-quart heavy casserole as browned. Pat the chicken dry and brown in the same manner, transferring to the casserole.

In the fat remaining in the skillet, cook the onion, bell pepper, and garlic over medium heat, stirring occasionally, until the vegetables have softened but not browned, 2 to 3 minutes. Add the spices, stirring to blend well. Stir in about 2 cups of the broth and pour the mixture over the meats in the casserole. Add the remaining broth and the vegetables and cook, covered, over medium heat until the chicken is nearly tender, 45 to 60 minutes. Remove the chicken, placing the pieces in a large bowl. Cover and place the bowl in a corner of the stove to keep warm. Continue to cook the lamb until fork tender, another 30 to 45 minutes. Return the chicken to the casserole along with the chick peas, cover and keep warm over very low heat while you prepare the couscous.

Bring the water, the rest of the oil, 1 teaspoon salt, and the raisins to a boil in a 3-quart heavy saucepan. Stir in the couscous and cover the pan. Remove the pan from the heat and let it stand 5 minutes. Fluff the couscous lightly with a fork.

To serve, place a mound of couscous in each warmed bowl. Add a few pieces of the lamb, and a piece of the chicken. Ladle the vegetable mixture over all and serve with the harissa sauce.

Makes 8 servings

Note: Harissa sauce is a sharply peppery North African condiment used to season stews and as a separate sauce to bolster the fieriness of a dish such as couscous. The prime ingredients are hot chili peppers, roasted red peppers, olive oil, garlic, and spices such as cumin and caraway seeds, all ground to a fine paste. Harissa is available at Middle Eastern markets and supermarkets with specialty foods departments, usually in cans or jars. (Be sure to warn your guests to add the condiment sparingly.)

Bread: A fresh-from-the-oven baguette makes a fine match for this flavorful dish.

Lunch: Since this dish is complete in itself, it may be too much for lunch. However, if you're planning the couscous for the evening meal, do a French version of a club sandwich. Slice a baguette in half lengthwise, then cut it into sandwich-size pieces. Spread one side of the bread with a lemon-infused mayonnaise, then add a slice of cold, poached chicken, a slice of crisp bacon, and a slice of tomato. Cover the sandwich with the top slice of bread, and garnish the plate with tiny ebony Niçoise olives.

Dinner: This meal-in-a-bowl really doesn't require even a salad, but if you feel the need for a greens fix, go right ahead.

Dessert: Something light and cooling is in order here. Mound a scoop of raspberry or lemon sherbet in dessert coupes and encircle with honeydew melon balls. Drizzle a soupçon of framboise (raspberry *eau-de-vie*) over all.

Wine: Jean-Paul Picot's wine of choice is a chilled bottle of dry rosé. "But you can also enjoy a chilled bottle of Beaujolais. A nice, flowery Fleurie suits the dish well."

Low-Fat Plan: Omit the oil. Brown the meat and chicken by placing them in a shallow roasting pan and baking them in a preheated 400°F oven just until lightly browned, 10 to 15 minutes. For the vegetables, sprinkle the onion, pepper, and garlic with ¼ cup of water; cover the skillet and cook until they have softened but not browned, 3 to 4 minutes. Continue with the recipe. For the couscous, omit the oil and sprinkle with 1 tablespoon of vinegar after it has cooked.

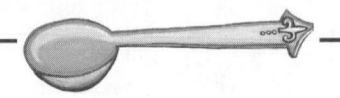

French Breads

"It's tough to do business in New York," Jean-Paul says with a rueful smile. "Monique and I, with sugar plums dancing in our heads, had been talking abut opening a bakery so that we'd have really top-quality, authentic French breads for our bistro. Well, in the building nearby that we'd bought, there was a street-level delicatessen that obviously was not doing very well. I knew the owner, Willie, pretty well, so I approached him and told him of my bakery plans. 'I think it's a fine idea,' said Willie, 'but I have a lease with seven years to go.' I offered to buy the lease. Then Willie asked, 'If I sell to you, will you consider keeping me in your new business?' 'Of course,' I replied."

Jean-Paul's French Bakery

"Willie became manager of Jean-Paul's French Bakery when we opened it in early 1980 and stayed with us for 10 years.

Jean-Paul's French Bakery's front window.

"At that time there really wasn't any source of good French bread in the city and we wanted to have as close an approximation to the wonderful Parisian baguettes and other specialties as possible. I contacted some of the big bread-oven manufacturers in France, and they came over here and looked at the place and made elaborate plans. In turn, I went to France to see the ovens in operation there. I decided to go ahead and buy them. Expensive? A gargantuan project? The actual implementation was a nightmare! We returned to the premises, took more measurements, talked, drank more coffee, and finally set the wheels in motion.

"One fine morning I looked out the window and there was this 18-wheeler standing in front of the bakery and creating a humungous traffic jam on Fifty-fifth Street. Out comes the driver, who announces: 'Okay, these are your bakery ovens.' Well, there was no way that we were going to be able to unload those gigantic, heavyweight ovens on Fifty-fifth Street. So, after figuring out the logistics as quickly as possible, we had to send the truck to New Jersey to a warehouse we had access to, where the ovens were unloaded onto smaller vehicles.

"The ovens finally were installed by company workmen from France. Then came the problem of getting enough electricity for them from the city. City officials claimed this was like having a plant in the city, with which we naturally disagreed. We haggled. We nearly gave up the whole idea of the bakery. In the end, we received permission.

"The next problem was the baker we hired from France. His name was Jacques and, whoof, what a temperamental guy. What a disagreeable character! He really made us all suffer. He was hardworking, to be sure. I almost decided to make the bread myself. At one point I thought of closing the bakery and going fishing! But Jacques—a surly, extremely competent, cigarette-dangling-from-the-lip kind of guy—had his own excellent formula for making the most delicious crisp baguettes, ficelles, *pains de campagne*, croissants, brioche—the works. They were extraordinary."

Jean-Paul did try his fine French hand at baking bread but found it too exacting and time-consuming. "You must know the exact amount of yeast to add and how to knead the dough. You've got to watch it constantly because the dough is alive and it can go sour if not properly attended. Then there were the croissants. The butter here is full of water, and they weren't

continues

turning out ideally flaky. So Jacques stamped his feet and resorted to importing French butter for them.

"Well, *finalement,* we opened. We had the right flour, the right butter, the right bread. We also had a teacher from Paris come to the bakery to teach the entire staff the art of French bread baking. The bakery became a success. We had bread for La Bonne Soupe, and we sold to other restaurants, and we did a lively retail business. The window was always chockablock with charmingly shaped baked loaves, and the shop was redolent of freshly baked bread. Then one day Jacques stalked off in high dudgeon, which was okay by the staff, who had learned all the *trucs* [tricks] they needed.

"But there were always other headaches. The ovens would break down from time to time and repair was expensive. The delivery boys had a penchant for not showing up, and the stress of running a bistro and a bakery became too much."

The day came when Jean-Paul Picot sighed and admitted: "A bakery is really not my business. I am a restaurateur, not a baker. I sold Jean-Paul's French Bakery in 1987 to a very nice capable bakery firm, and it seems to be doing nicely. They even sell sandwiches, which gives La Bonne Soupe a bit of delicate competition," Jean-Paul says.

The Best Baguette

What does Jean-Paul look for in a French baguette? "A good, honest, crisp loaf. The crust should not be too thin and not too thick. If the crust is not exactly right, the bread hardens too quickly. There must be the proper ratio of crust to crumb—the inside of the bread.

"The crumb should be airy or dense, according to the type of bread. You need a lot of humidity to get this, and these French ovens do the trick."

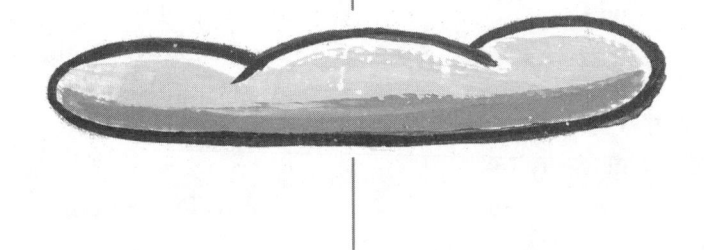

Poule au Pot à la Béarnaise

CHICKEN IN THE POT

There are many versions of Chicken in the Pot, and Jean-Paul Picot points out it is one of Béarn's great specialties. "Whether or not the legend is true that King Henry IV made a dedicated promise to the French people of a chicken in the pot every Sunday, our family in Lagor, Béarn, looked forward to that bird and its intensely flavored broth as our Sunday dinner treat. My grandmère, Marguerite Forsans, a fabulous cook, bought chickens from a neighboring farmhouse. She cooked them in a big pot with garden-fresh vegetables and pungent herbs and set it on the stove to simmer slowly. Some cooks add meat or meat bones to the pot, but Grandmère Marguerite was a purist. Only chicken, and the freshest chicken, she would insist. And the broth had to be rich and golden as the noonday sun. And no one would suggest otherwise."

Chef Francis serves a little pot of peppy horseradish sauce as a piquant foil for the chicken.

The Picot family home in Lagor in the Pyrenees.

For the chicken

2 quarts Homemade Chicken Broth (page 4) or low-sodium canned broth

One 3½-pound chicken, cut into quarters

2 large carrots, peeled and cut into large dice

1 large white turnip, peeled and cut into large dice

2 ribs celery, cut crosswise into ¼-inch slices

4 medium-size boiling potatoes (about 1½ pounds), peeled and cut into large dice

1 *bouquet garni*: 1 small bay leaf, 5 sprigs parsley, and ½ teaspoon *each* dried thyme and rosemary tied in a cheesecloth square

Salt and freshly ground pepper to taste

For the horseradish sauce

1 cup sour cream

¼ cup bottled white horseradish, drained

Dash of Worcestershire sauce

Prepare the chicken:

Place the broth in a 6-quart saucepan and bring to a boil. Reduce the heat to medium, add the chicken, and simmer partially covered, 20 minutes, skimming the surface from time to time. Add all the remaining ingredients. Cover partially and cook over medium heat until the vegetables are tender but not soggy, 15 to 20 minutes. Remove and discard the *bouquet garni*.

Prepare the horseradish sauce:

Blend the sour cream, horseradish, and Worcestershire sauce in a small bowl or sauceboat.

To serve, place one-quarter of the chicken in each of 4 large, deep soup bowls. Add a ladleful of broth and some of the vegetables. Pass the horseradish sauce separately.

Makes 4 servings

Bread: Jean-Paul Picot likes the very long, thin ficelle with this stew, but any member of the baguette family will do very well.

Lunch or Dinner: Since this dish is a meal in itself, you could follow it with a small salad of endive leaves and watercress tossed with Herbed Vinaigrette (page 147), but this is really optional.

Wine: An opulent Meursault from Burgundy or a big, buttery California Chardonnay makes a fine companion.

Dessert: Serve Pears Poached in White Wine (page 159).

Low-Fat Plan: Skin the chicken completely and remove all fat. Be sure to use defatted broth. For the sauce, use nonfat or low-fat sour cream.

9

Vegetables

Vegetables at La Bonne Soupe are treated with great respect. Jean-Paul Picot and Chef Francis Freund recognize the key role vegetables play in fine menu planning, adding vibrant color, varied textural nuances, and of course, flavor to a wide swath of entrées and side dishes. In selecting top-quality vegetables, Jean-Paul relies on his purveyors to send the daily selections. "We get the most gorgeous, vine-ripened tomatoes from a woman in Pennsylvania, who provides us with perfect, lush tomatoes the year round," Jean-Paul explains. "That's why when a diner orders sliced tomatoes we can happily present a plate of these beauties dressed just with a touch of extra-virgin olive oil and chopped shallots."

All of the vegetables served at the bistro—from carrots to greens for salads—must be crisp, tender, bruise free, and perfect to ensure flavor to the max and preserve vitamin content.

And when Jean-Paul and Monique cook *chez* Picot, they always include at least two vegetables with their lunch or dinner entrées.

"My mother's lush vegetable garden in Normandy was her pride and joy," says Monique Picot. "And I grew up with a passion for fresh-grown garden vegetables that has always influenced the meals

133

I prepare at home." She regards fish, poultry, or meat "as a comple-ment to the vegetables." She especially enjoys the summers at their home on Long Island when she visits "the legendary Green Thumb farm market, with its colorful array of fresh produce. I serve their organic mesclun at almost every meal—fresh, tender lettuce and mustard greens, or my favorite chervil, dressed with balsamic vin-egar and olive oil."

Here's a succulent sampling of vegetable dishes from the bistro and the Picots at home. And we're not forgetting La Bonne Soupe's famed French Fried Potatoes!

Haricots Verts à la Vapeur

STEAMED GREEN BEANS

These crisp green beans are first given a steam bath to preserve their bright color, then cooked briefly in a little olive oil with some red onion and garlic until slightly softened but still firm. Their bright color and fresh flavor make them ideal garnishes for Monique's Roast Chicken Stuffed with Goat Cheese Croutons (page 102) or broiled fish.

1½ pounds green beans, trimmed and, if large, cut in half (see Note)

⅓ cup extra-virgin olive oil

1 medium-size red onion, chopped

2 cloves garlic, pressed

½ cup water used for steaming

Salt and freshly ground pepper to taste

⅓ cup chopped fresh flat-leaf parsley for garnish

Place the beans in a steamer basket set over simmering water and steam, covered, over medium heat just until crisp-tender, 8 to 10 minutes. Remove from the heat and shake the basket to rid the beans of excess water.

Heat the oil in a large skillet over medium heat until hot but not smoking. Add the onions and cook until they are softened but not browned, 3 to 4 minutes. Add the garlic and cook until softened but not browned, about 1 minute. Add the steamed green beans and the water and cook, stirring, until the beans are well coated and glistening, 2 to 3 minutes. Season with salt and pepper and garnish with the parsley. Serve hot or *tiède*—at room temperature.

Makes 6 to 8 servings

Note: Yellow wax beans may be given the same treatment, with equally rewarding results.

Chou Braisé

BRAISED CABBAGE

"Everyone in our family is crazy about my braised cabbage. I guess they love the flavor of cilantro, which gives plain cabbage a new dimension," says Monique, who serves the dish hot from the skillet or at room temperature. It's great with roast chicken, and it's a sensational accompaniment to a Sunday night supper of grilled frankfurters.

1 small cabbage (about 1½ pounds)

¼ cup extra-virgin olive oil

Salt and freshly ground pepper to taste

⅓ cup chopped cilantro or 1 teaspoon dried coriander

Core the cabbage and discard any tough outer leaves. Cut into ½-inch slices and place in the basket of a steamer set over simmering water. Steam, covered, over medium heat until the cabbage is wilted, about 10 minutes. Remove from the heat and shake the basket to remove excess water.

Heat the oil in a large skillet over medium heat until hot but not smoking. Add the cabbage and cook over medium heat, stirring occasionally, until it turns translucent and golden, about 15 minutes. Season with salt and pepper and sprinkle with the cilantro. Serve hot or at room temperature.

Makes 4 to 6 servings

Courgettes Dorées

GOLDEN BROWN ZUCCHINI WITH BASIL

Summer's tender-from-the-field zucchini are sliced by Monique, who likes to cook them quickly in olive oil, then bake them until crisp-tender. She strews chopped basil over the slices and serves them with a cheese omelet at lunch or at dinner to accompany pepper steak or broiled fish.

⅓ cup extra-virgin olive oil

4 medium-size zucchini (about 2 ½ pounds), trimmed and cut into ½-inch slices

3 cloves garlic, pressed

10 fresh basil leaves, chopped or 1 teaspoon dried

Salt and freshly ground pepper to taste

Preheat the oven to 325°F.

Heat half of the oil in a large, preferably nonstick skillet over medium heat until hot but not smoking. Add the zucchini and cook over medium-high heat until browned on each side, 2 to 3 minutes. The zucchini should be lightly browned but still firm. Don't overcook.

Transfer the zucchini to a shallow, ovenproof baking dish spreading it evenly over the bottom, strew with the garlic and one-quarter of the basil, and drizzle the remaining oil over the top. Bake in the center of the oven until the zucchini is tender, about 10 minutes. Remove from the oven and strew with the remaining basil, salt and pepper. Serve hot or *tiède*—at room temperature.

Makes 4 servings

Variation: Monique prepares eggplant in the same manner. She cuts the eggplant into ½-inch-thick slices, then strews the slices with kosher (coarse) salt and lets them stand for 10 to 15 minutes to rid them of any bitter juices. She then wipes off the salt with paper towels and proceeds with the recipe.

Purée de Navets

PURÉE OF TURNIPS

Some people shy away when turnips are on the menu. But when these earthy roots are tenderly steamed, then puréed or mashed with a liaison of heavy cream, their earthiness mellows and gentles. They're an attractive accompaniment to roast Leg of Lamb with Rosemary and Garlic (page 115) as well as with veal, pork, and turkey.

2 pounds turnips or rutabagas

½ cup heavy cream

Salt and freshly ground white pepper to taste

Peel the turnips, cut off the root ends, and cut into quarters. Place in a steamer basket set over simmering water and steam over medium heat until tender, 10 to 15 minutes. (Alternatively, cover with water and boil until tender.) Shake off any excess water and transfer to a medium-size saucepan.

Mash the turnips with a fork, potato masher, or electric hand mixer. Turn the heat to medium and slowly add the cream, beating until smooth and creamy. Season with salt and pepper and serve hot.

Makes 4 servings

Low-Fat Plan: Substitute ½ cup defatted chicken broth for the cream.

Variations: Monique also purées celery root and cauliflower in the same fashion.

Monique's Purée de Pommes de Terre à l'Ail

MONIQUE'S GARLICKY MASHED POTATOES

Whether in their country or city kitchen, family, friends, and admirers request one dish more than others. It's Monique's Garlicky Mashed Potatoes. Ask anyone who's tasted them why, and the answer is likely to be, "because they taste so good!" They also dress up a galaxy of entrées, from roast chicken to calf's liver and roast turkey.

2 pounds boiling potatoes, peeled and cut into quarters

6 cloves garlic, finely chopped or put through a press

¼ cup unsalted butter (½ stick)

Salt and freshly ground white pepper to taste

About ⅓ cup hot milk or cream

Place the potatoes and garlic in a 3-quart heavy saucepan, cover with water, and bring to a boil over high heat. Reduce the heat to medium, cover, and cook until the potatoes are tender, about 20 minutes. Drain off any water left in the pan and shake the pan over low heat for about a minute to dry them off.

Off the heat, mash the potatoes, using a hand mixer or potato masher. Add the butter and salt and pepper and blend well. Place the saucepan back over low heat and slowly beat in the hot milk. If the mixture seems too thick, heat an additional ¼ cup of milk or cream and beat into the potatoes. Serve at once or keep warm, covered, over simmering water.

Makes 4 to 6 servings

n the Hamptons, the Picot's table for family and friends.

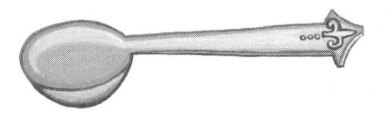

Ratatouille

Ratatouille is a specialty of Provence in the south of France, made in the summer when gardens are bursting with produce and the vegetables are ripe, ripe, ripe. (A similar dish is called caponata *in Italian.) Ratatouille can be served as an appetizer or as a light supper with a platter of salami and another of oil-cured olives, and of course, with roast lamb.*

A French cook would spend hours making a ratatouille, browning each vegetable separately for a long time to bring out the natural sugars; and the tomato paste would be homemade from boiled-down tomatoes and water, which were then passed through a sieve. Some cooks add a drop of vinegar; others a small handful of capers; and many cooks add a handful of chopped flat-leaf parsley and a small, finely chopped raw clove of garlic. At La Bonne Soupe, everyone adores this simple, flavor-plus version.

¼ cup extra-virgin olive oil

1 large onion, thinly sliced

3 cloves garlic, finely minced

1 medium-size red pepper, cored, seeded, and thinly sliced

1 small eggplant (about 1 pound), peeled and cut into ½-inch-thick slices, then quartered

2 medium-size zucchini, ends trimmed, scrubbed, and thinly sliced

2 large tomatoes (about 1 pound), peeled, seeded, and cut into rough dice

⅓ cup chopped fresh basil

¼ cup chopped oregano

1 small bay leaf

½ teaspoon sugar

Salt and freshly ground pepper to taste

Heat the oil in a large (at least 12 inches) heavy, nonreactive skillet over medium heat until hot but not smoking. Add the onion and garlic and cook over medium heat until softened but not browned, 3 to 4 minutes. Add the bell pepper, eggplant, and half the zucchini and cook, stirring occasionally, until the vegetables are lightly browned, 5 to 6 minutes. Reduce the heat to low, add the tomatoes and all the remaining ingredients. Cover and simmer over low heat until the vegetables are tender but not mushy, about 20 minutes.

Check after 20 minutes; if there seems to be too much liquid in the pan, uncover, and cook over medium heat for another 10 minutes until the liquid has reduced a bit. Discard the bay leaf and serve hot, at room temperature, or chilled. It will keep, covered, for up to 3 days in the refrigerator.

Makes 4 to 6 servings

Bread: A tangy *pain de seigle* (rye bread) makes a pleasing foil for the stew.

Lunch: The stew could easily make a meal with a big basket of bread and a platter of cheeses—wedges of runny Brie, a goat cheese (herbed or not) and a Roquefort would be delectable.

Dinner: The stew makes a fine side dish with striped bass baked with a tot of olive oil, freshly squeezed lemon juice, chopped garlic, and lots of parsley.

Dessert: Wedges of freshly baked Lemon Tart (page 160) served with clouds of lightly sweetened whipped cream make a superb windup, especially with cups of double espresso.

Wine: A fruity-spicy Gewürztraminer from Alsace, served well chilled, is delightful with the stew and can be continued with the bass.

Low-Fat Plan: Omit the oil. Add 1 cup of dry white wine (or defatted chicken broth, if you prefer) to the skillet. Proceed with the recipe. Use any low-fat cheese.

Carottes Vichy

GLAZED CARROTS

The reason for the name of these tender, sweet carrot morsels, we've been reliably told, is they're traditionally cooked in the mineral water from the famed Vichy spa. But we'll let you in on a little secret before you run out to look for Vichy mineral water. We think these carrots are just as delicious when cooked in tap water, assuming the tap water is good.

1½ pounds carrots, trimmed, peeled and cut into 1-inch pieces

Pinch of baking soda

1½ tablespoons sugar

½ teaspoon salt

2 tablespoons unsalted butter

Place the carrots in a heavy, 2-quart saucepan, cover with water, and bring to a boil over high heat. Reduce the heat to medium, cover, and cook the carrots until they are tender and nearly all the water has cooked off, 10 to 15 minutes.

Sprinkle the carrots with the soda, sugar and salt and add the butter. Cook, uncovered, over medium-high heat, tossing the pan often, until the carrots are shiny and glazed. Transfer to a warmed serving dish or spoon directly onto dinner plates.

Makes 4 servings

Tomates Provençales de Monique

MONIQUE'S TOMATOES WITH GARLIC AND HERBS

When the Picots are at their country home, and summer's lush, red-ripe tomatoes are at their peak, Monique makes one of Jean-Paul's favorite vegetables: tomatoes cooked, Provençal-style, with olive oil, garlic, and herbs. Lightly browned, they're wonderful with roast chicken, fish, and chops, and add flavor and color as a side dish to omelets. The tomatoes are delicious hot, at room temperature, or even cold.

½ cup extra-virgin olive oil

8 large, ripe tomatoes, peeled and cut in half

Salt and freshly ground pepper to taste

8 cloves garlic, finely minced

½ cup finely chopped fresh flat-leaf parsley or basil, plus an additional ¼ cup for garnish

Preheat the oven to 300°F.

You will need a skillet large enough to hold the 16 tomato halves, or you can cook them in two smaller skillets. Heat half of the oil over medium heat until hot but not smoking. Add the tomatoes, cut sides down, and cook until lightly browned, 10 to 12 minutes. Using a spatula, carefully turn them, drizzle with the remaining oil, season with salt and pepper, and strew with the garlic and parsley. Reduce the heat to low and cook the tomatoes until they lose their liquid and start to become glazed. This will take 30 to 40 minutes. Check the skillet from time to time to make sure they're not burning on the bottom or becoming mushy. You want them to retain their shape, yet transform into a conservelike consistency.

Transfer the tomatoes to a baking dish and place in the center of the oven and bake until fully glazed, about another 10 minutes. Garnish with additional parsley.

Makes 4 servings

Tip: *When Monique Picot prepares garlic she always removes the inner "germ," or budding green part, if there should be one. "This makes the garlic easier to digest," she points out.*

Hot-Oil Tip

A thermometer that clips over the side of the pan is a handy and re gauge of heat. If you don't own one, drop a morsel of bread into hot oil. If it turns golden at once the oil is ready for frying.

Gratin de Pommes de Terre

SCALLOPED POTATOES

The most famous of all gratin dishes is gratin à la Dauphinoise. For this dish, thinly sliced potatoes are layered with grated Gruyère or other Swiss-type cheese and moistened with garlic-infused milk or cream and sometimes eggs. It's then baked until the potatoes are tender and the top is burnished. A similar dish, called gratin de pommes de terre Savoyarde, uses broth instead of milk to moisten the potatoes while they're baking. The milk or cream, needless to say, produces a much richer dish, but a good broth results in a very flavorful gratin that has a lot fewer calories and less cholesterol than the usual recipe, so the choice is yours.

1 small clove garlic
3½ tablespoons unsalted butter
2½ pounds boiling potatoes
1 medium-size onion, finely sliced
Salt and freshly ground pepper to taste
Grating of nutmeg for each potato layer
1 cup grated Gruyère or other Swiss-type cheese (¼ pound)
2 cups milk, Homemade Beef Broth (page 3), or low-sodium canned broth

Preheat the oven to 350°F.

Rub the inside of a shallow 1½-quart baking dish or gratin pan, approximately 12 x 7 x 1½ inches, with the garlic and use ½ tablespoon of the butter to grease the bottom and sides of the dish.

Peel the potatoes and, using a mandoline or a sharp knife, cut them into thin slices—about ¹⁄₁₆ inch thick. Blot the slices with paper towels to absorb some of the moisture.

Spread a layer of potato slices over the bottom of the dish and sprinkle them with salt and pepper, and nutmeg; strew with some of the cheese. Continue to layer the potatoes, seasonings, and cheese until all of the potatoes are used and the top is strewn with the cheese. Pour the milk down the side of the dish. Cut the remaining butter into pea-size pieces and dot over the top. Cover the dish tightly with heavy aluminum foil and place in the center of the oven.

Bake for 1 hour; remove the aluminum foil. Continue baking until the potatoes are tender when pierced with the tines of a long fork and the top is golden brown, 10 to 15 minutes.

Makes 4 to 6 servings

Tip: You can make the gratin a day ahead and reheat it for a next-day meal. Cool the baked gratin, cover, and refrigerate. To reheat, pre-heat the oven to 350° F. Sprinkle 2 tablespoons of broth or water over the top and cover with a sheet of aluminum foil. Place in the center of the oven until heated through, about 10 minutes.

Low-Fat Plan: Omit the butter and use skim milk or, preferably, defatted broth, increasing the amount to 1½ cups. Strew with a low-fat cheese and proceed with the directions.

The Pros and Cons of Gratin Pans

Does one need a gratin pan? The answer, of course, is no. But these classic, mostly oval-shaped dishes are so beautiful and multipurpose. Made of white porcelain, colorfully decorated pottery, copper, enameled cast iron, stainless steel, or aluminum, they come in a wide range of sizes. They're also great presentation dishes for other vegetable, fish, and meat mélanges that require a wide surface to be gratinéed in the oven or over the broiler. A gratin pan is a super gift idea.

Pommes de Terre Roties au Romarin de Monique

MONIQUE'S LITTLE ROASTED POTATOES WITH ROSEMARY

Totally addictive: that's the best description we can give for these crusty-on-the-outside, tender and delightfully mealy inside potatoes. And they are all-purpose: They go with everything from omelets and hamburgers to roasts and all manner of fish dishes.

¼ cup extra-virgin olive oil

¼ cup water

1½ pounds small white or red-skinned potatoes, approximately 1½-inches in diameter, cut in half

1 tablespoon chopped fresh rosemary or 1 teaspoon dried

Salt and freshly ground pepper to taste

8 to 10 cloves garlic, unpeeled

Preheat the oven to 375°F.

Using a little brush, spread the oil and water evenly over the bottom of a shallow baking dish that will hold the potatoes in one layer. Add the potatoes, skin sides down, and sprinkle the tops with the rosemary and salt and pepper.

Bake, uncovered, in the center of the oven until lightly browned, about 30 minutes. When the potatoes have baked halfway, add the garlic in a random pattern and continue to bake until brown and puffy, another 20 minutes longer. Transfer the potatoes to a warmed serving dish.

Makes 4 servings

Pommes Frites

FRENCH FRIED POTATOES

"I can't see a French menu without French fries," says le patron (the owner), Jean-Paul Picot, munching a slender, crispy golden French fry and nodding his approval. "I love French fries myself; that's why we have French fries with the steak, with the hamburgers, with omelets. The French are so used to them and ours are so good! People ask for side orders and Chef Francis Freund keeps frying them to crisp, golden deliciousness."

At La Bonne Soupe the potatoes are twice cooked, which ensures sticks with tender insides and crispy, crunchy exteriors.

4 large Idaho potatoes (about 2 pounds)

1½ quarts peanut oil or other vegetable oil for frying

Salt and freshly ground pepper to taste

Peel the potatoes and cut them into rectangular blocks: Trim off the rounded ends, then cut a slice off on either side lengthwise so that you are left with a chunky block. Cut the block lengthwise into slices approximately ¼ inch thick. Turn the slices parallel to the cutting surface and cut into ¼-inch-thick sticks. Pat the potato sticks dry with paper towels.

Heat the oil in a 2½ quart saucepan until the temperature reaches 350°F. Place about one-third of the potatoes in a frying basket and fry just until they turn a very pale golden, about 2 minutes. Drain on paper towels and continue to fry the remaining potatoes, draining them on paper towels. At this point the potatoes may be piled in a napkin-lined bowl and reserved for later use.

For the second frying, heat the oil until the temperature reaches 375°F. Place the potatoes in the basket or strainer, one-third at a time, and fry until crisp and golden, about 5 minutes. Drain immediately on paper towels, sprinkle with salt and pepper, and serve at once.

Makes 4 to 6 servings

Pommes de Terre Savoyarde de Jean-Paul Picot

JEAN-PAUL PICOT'S PURÉED POTATOES WITH BACON AND CHEESE

The Savoyards really dote on their firm, flavorful potatoes that flourish in the pure mountain air of this Alpine region of France. "Cooking the potatoes in milk enriches their basic goodness," Jean-Paul explains. The cooked potatoes are puréed and blended with bacon, heavy cream, and grated Swiss cheese, then gratinéed until puffed and golden. "It's really a little meal unto itself," he adds, "and makes a nice lunch or late-evening nibble, with a tossed green salad and a glass of country wine."

1½ pounds firm boiling potatoes, such as russets, peeled and cut into quarters

2 cups milk

4 slices bacon, cut into ½-inch slices, diced

½ cup heavy cream

1 large egg yolk

Salt and freshly ground white pepper to taste

3 ounces Gruyère or other Swiss-type cheese, finely grated

Place the potatoes in a heavy 1½-quart saucepan and add the milk. Bring to a boil over high heat. Reduce the heat to medium-high, cover the pan, and cook until the potatoes are tender, about 20 minutes. Transfer the potatoes to a food processor or blender and process until they are puréed. (If using a food processor, process just until blended; don't over process or the consistency will tend to be gluey.) Or mash the potatoes with a potato masher.

Cook the bacon in a small skillet over medium heat until the pieces are nicely browned. Drain the fat and discard and pat the bacon with paper towels to absorb the excess fat. Crumble the bacon. Add the bacon to the potatoes, and stir in the cream and egg yolk, beating with a wooden spoon until they are well incorporated.

Preheat the broiler. Butter a 1½-quart gratin dish or other shallow baking dish. Spoon in the potato mixture and sprinkle the cheese over the top. Place in a broiler, 4 inches from the heat, and broil just until the cheese melts and turns lightly browned, about 2 to 3 minutes.

Makes 4 servings

10

Sauces

Simple, well-seasoned, and quickly prepared sauces are the cook's ace-in-hand. They perk up bland dishes and aggrandize the elegant. You'll find countless uses for Jean-Paul's Zesty Vinaigrette and Chef Francis Freund's Shallot Vinaigrette. The Tangy Tomato Sauce is so multipurpose. Try it with broiled or baked fish, as a great pasta sauce, or with chicken and hamburgers. The Herbed Vinaigrette is a natural for salads. And when you're in the mood for a truly opulent sauce for your filet mignon, roast beef, or fish steaks, Paul Barraud's Tangy Butter Sauce will have your guests asking for seconds!

Vinaigrette de Jean-Paul

Jean-Paul's Zesty Vinaigrette

What a versatile and flavor-filled boon to dress a multitude of salads and vegetables! And, although in La Bonne Soupe's kitchen, this lively vinaigrette is prepared fresh daily, you can store it, tightly covered, in the refrigerator for up to one week, making it a great frazzle-time resource.

- ¼ cup red wine vinegar
- 1 tablespoon Dijon mustard
- ¾ cup extra-virgin olive oil
- Salt and freshly ground pepper to taste

Place the vinegar and mustard in a small mixing bowl and, using a wire whisk, beat until the mixture is smooth and amalgamated. Continue to whisk as you add the oil in a small, steady stream until the sauce is slightly thickened. Season with salt and pepper, whisking until well blended. Alternatively, you can make the vinaigrette in a food processor or blender. Start with the vinegar and mustard and gradually add the oil, pulsing as you continue until all the oil is used and the mixture has thickened.

Makes about 1 cup

Variation: For garlic vinaigrette, add 1 or 2 finely minced cloves garlic to the dressing. It's especially felicitous with artichoke bottoms and bland salads that will benefit from the earthy jolt of garlic.

Vinaigrette aux Échalotes

Shallot Vinaigrette

This is a piquant version of vinaigrette that Chef Francis Freund drizzles over sliced, red-ripe tomatoes as a first course or side dish.

- ¼ cup red wine vinegar
- 2 tablespoons finely chopped shallots
- 1 tablespoon Dijon mustard
- ¾ cup extra-virgin olive oil
- Salt and freshly ground pepper to taste

Place the vinegar, shallots, and mustard in a small mixing bowl and, using a wire whisk, beat until well mixed. Continue to whisk as you add the oil in a small, steady stream, until the sauce is slightly thickened. Season with salt and pepper, whisking until well blended.

It can rest, covered, for several hours, at room temperature to allow the flavors to meld. Store leftover vinaigrette, covered, in the refrigerator. Bring to room temperature before using.

Makes about 1 cup

Vinaigrette aux Herbes

HERBED VINAIGRETTE

You can add any herb of your choice. When using fresh herbs, it's best to add them just before serving. Dried herbs may be added to the vinegar at the start of the recipe to bring out their flavor.

¼ cup red wine vinegar

1 tablespoon Dijon mustard

1 tablespoon finely chopped shallots

¾ cup extra-virgin olive oil

Salt and freshly ground pepper to taste

2 tablespoons finely minced fresh chives, cilantro, or flat-leaf parsley

Place the vinegar and mustard in a small mixing bowl and, using a wire whisk, beat until well mixed. Continue to whisk as you add the oil in a small, steady stream, until the sauce is slightly thickened. Season with salt and pepper, whisking until well blended. Whisk in the shallots and fresh herbs.

Variations: You could also add 1 teaspoon finely chopped fresh tarragon or ¼ teaspoon dried. Or add 1 tablespoon chopped fresh chervil or ¼ teaspoon dried.

Makes about 1 cup

Sauce Café de Paris

TANGY BUTTER SAUCE

"I learned to make this elegant sauce at L'École Hôtelière in Lausanne, Switzerland, from my maître [teacher] Paul Barraud," Jean-Paul says, proudly. "It's an elegant sauce for grilled meat and fish, such as swordfish, halibut and tuna, and it freezes very well."

1 can anchovy fillets, drained

3 tablespoons finely chopped fresh flat-leaf parsley

6 shallots, finely minced

2 cloves garlic, finely minced

1 tablespoon Dijon mustard

1¾ teaspoons ground sage

¼ teaspoon dried tarragon

½ teaspoon sweet paprika

½ teaspoon freshly ground pepper

1 teaspoon freshly squeezed lemon juice

1 pound unsalted butter, softened

Place all the ingredients in the container of a food processor and process until well blended and smooth. If you don't have a food processor, place the softened butter in a mixing bowl and, using a wooden spoon, add all the remaining ingredients, mashing the mixture into a smooth paste.

Shape the mixture into a log, about 1½ inches wide, wrap well in heavy foil or freezer paper and store either in the refrigerator for up to 2 days or in the freezer for up to 2 months.

To use, cut ¼-inch slices, one per portion, and place on top of broiled fish or steak just before serving.

Makes about 1 cup

Sauce Tomate Arômatisée

TANGY TOMATO SAUCE

Here's a simple, fresh-tasting, versatile sauce that enlivens omelets, pasta dishes, broiled fish, and veal. It can be stored, well covered, in the refrigerator for up to 4 days. Or double the recipe and freeze it in 1-cup freezer containers for up to 6 months.

- 1 tablespoon extra-virgin olive oil
- 1 medium-size onion, chopped
- 1 clove garlic, finely minced
- 1 pound fresh ripe tomatoes, peeled, seeded, and chopped
- 1 cup tomato purée
- 1 tablespoon finely chopped fresh basil or ½ teaspoon dried
- 1 tablespoon chopped fresh oregano or ¼ teaspoon dried
- Salt and freshly ground pepper to taste

Heat the oil over medium-high heat in a 1½- or 2½-quart saucepan until the oil is hot but not smoking. Add the onion and cook, stirring occasionally, until it is softened but not browned, 3 to 4 minutes. Reduce the heat to medium, add the tomatoes, and cook until they start to soften, stirring occasionally, about 10 minutes.

Reduce the heat to medium-low. Add the tomato purée, herbs, and salt and pepper, cover the saucepan, and cook until the tomatoes are completely softened, another 8 to 10 minutes. The sauce may be used at once or stored in the refrigerator for up to 6 days.

Makes about 2 cups

Sauce aux Champignons

MUSHROOM SAUCE

Chef Francis Freund uses this deep, woodsy-flavored sauce for his spinach omelet, but it can double as an elegant finish for broiled veal chops, chicken, and meaty fish such as swordfish and halibut.

- ½ pound small white mushrooms
- 2 tablespoons unsalted butter
- ½ cup Homemade Chicken Broth (page 4) or low-sodium canned broth
- ½ cup dry white wine
- ½ cup heavy cream
- Salt and freshly ground pepper to taste

Wipe the mushrooms with damp paper towels, cut off the stems (reserve them for soups) and cut the mushrooms into thin slices.

Heat the butter in a 1-quart, nonreactive saucepan over medium heat until it is hot but not smoking. Add the mushrooms and cook, stirring occasionally, until they turn dark and exude their juices, 4 to 5 minutes. Add the wine and broth, raise the heat to medium-high, and bring to a boil. Continue to cook the liquid until it has reduced by one-half.

Take the pan off the heat and transfer the contents to a food processor or blender. Process until the mixture is smooth and puréed; return to the saucepan.

Heat the mushroom mixture over low heat; gradually add the cream, stirring to blend. Season with salt and pepper and cook just until the sauce is heated through. The sauce may be kept warm over a pan of simmering water if you are not going to use it at once. Or store it in a tightly covered container in the refrigerator up to 2 days.

Makes about 1 cup

11

Desserts

In planning the original dessert menu, Jean-Paul and Monique instantly zeroed in on beautiful basic French crêpes, Caramel Custard, Melting Chocolate Mousse (a runaway favorite), and for apple-loving Americans: Apple Tart. "We thought these are the typical bistro kinds of desserts our diners would go for—and they sure did," Jean-Paul explains enthusiastically. "Of course, we also offered fresh fruit in season, cheese for our French patrons, and a selection of ice creams for our American customers. And since New Yorkers are, or at least were at the time, big cheesecake fanciers, we included a purchased cheesecake. In this business, you've got to go with the flow," *le patron* adds, with a big smile.

Well, you'll certainly have a big smile when you prepare the sweet endings in this chapter. The crêpes are still much in demand, and they are heavenly, with their rich cream and sensuous sauce garnishes. The Apple Tart is so light, flavorful, and easy to assemble, you'll immediately place it on your must list for entertaining. We've also included some super desserts Monique and Jean-Paul prepare at home. We know you'll relish Dr. Vassaux's Rice Pudding, very much in tune with today's healthy lifestyle—it's eggless! And Paul Barraud's tingly tangy Lemon Tart is perfect after a weighty meal. The poached fruits can be enjoyed solo or teamed with all manner of sauces, such as the deep-flavored Rosy Raspberry Sauce. And the Lacy Tile Cookies are superb with fruit and ice cream and just for nibbling. So don't hold back. Do have a sweet ending.

Crêpes au Chocolat

CRÊPES WITH CHOCOLATE SAUCE

Here come the light, tender, basic French dessert crêpes. La Bonne Soupe's diners dote on these delicate, melt-in-your-mouth lacy pancakes, lovingly folded in quarters, topped with ice cream, and sumptuously sauced with chocolate. For more suggestions, see Crêpes with Orange Butter (page 152) and "Other Tasty Crêpe Filling Ideas" (page 154).

1¼ cups sifted all-purpose flour

¼ teaspoon salt

1 teaspoon sugar

3 large eggs

2 cups milk

2 tablespoons dark rum

2 tablespoons unsalted butter, melted, plus additional as needed

6 scoops vanilla ice cream

Chocolate Sauce (page 152)

Sift the flour, salt, and sugar into a large bowl. Using a wire whisk or fork, beat the eggs until well blended in a second bowl. Add the milk, rum, and 2 tablespoons of melted butter to the beaten eggs, stirring to blend well. Slowly pour the liquid mixture into the dry ingredients, stirring until smooth and free of lumps. Cover the bowl and place in the refrigerator for at least ½ hour to help it set and improve the flavor.

When ready to cook, heat a 6-inch skillet brushed lightly with melted butter over medium heat. For each crêpe, pour in 2 tablespoons of the batter, tilting the pan so the batter covers the bottom surface evenly. Cook over medium heat until the underside is brown and bubbles begin to form on the top, 1 to 1½ minutes. Lift the crêpe with a spatula and turn it over. Cook just until brown, about 1 minute. Transfer to a long length of aluminum foil and continue to cook the remaining crêpes, using a bit more butter in the pan if they begin to stick, and stacking them on the foil. The crêpes are now ready to use.

To serve, fold each crêpe in half, then into quarters; place 3 on a plate. Top each serving with a scoop of ice cream and pour 2 to 3 tablespoons of Chocolate Sauce on top.

Makes 6 servings (about 18 crêpes)

Tip: You can cook the crêpes ahead of time, placing a square of foil between each one so they don't stick together. Keep them in the refrigerator until ready to use. Rewarm by placing the foil-wrapped package in a preheated 350°F oven for 5 to 6 minutes.

They also freeze very well. Pack the crêpes in stacks of 6, 8, or 12 and wrap in freezer paper or heavy foil. Thaw them before rewarming. Or place them in a preheated 350°F oven until thawed and warmed through, about 10 minutes.

The Crêpe Pan

If you use a pan with a nonstick surface there's no need to add butter before cooking each crêpe. Otherwise, if the crêpes start to stick to the pan, you may need to add a tiny bit of butter from time to time.

Sauce au Chocolat

CHOCOLATE SAUCE

Dark and sensuously chocolatey, this is a great sauce to spoon over ice cream, poached fruits, and toasted pound or angel food cake squares. Tightly covered, it will keep for several weeks in the refrigerator, ready for instant delight.

- ½ cup milk
- ½ cup heavy cream
- 4 ounces semisweet chocolate, broken into small bits
- 1 tablespoon Curaçao or other orange-flavored liqueur
- 1 tablespoon unsalted butter

Bring the milk and cream to a boil in a heavy, 1-quart saucepan over medium-high heat. Add the chocolate and cook, stirring, until melted and the sauce is slightly thickened and smooth, about 5 minutes. Add the liqueur and butter, stirring until well blended. Remove from the heat and cool to lukewarm before using. Or store in a tightly covered jar in the refrigerator.

Makes about 1 cup

Crêpes au Beurre d'Orange

CRÊPES WITH ORANGE BUTTER

Top a warm compote of plums or prunes with a slice of the orange butter for a special-effects dessert. And, since no sugar is used, you can use it to garnish broiled halibut, swordfish, and tuna steaks. The orange butter may be frozen in its log shape, which allows for cutting off slices and using them as needed. However, allow the slices to thaw before placing atop a warm crêpe.

For the orange butter

- ¼ pound unsalted butter (1 stick), softened
- Grated zest of 1 orange
- Juice of ½ orange
- 1 teaspoon Curaçao or other orange-flavored liqueur

For assembling the dish

- 18 crêpes (page 151)
- Confectioner's sugar

Prepare the orange butter:

Place the butter in a bowl. Add the orange zest, juice, and liqueur. Using a wooden spoon, blend until smooth. Shape the mixture into a log, about the size of a stick of butter. Wrap in foil or plastic wrap and refrigerate until firm, about 1 to 1½ hours, or store in the freezer.

Assemble the dish:

When ready to serve, fold the crêpes in half, then into quarters, and place 3 on each plate. Cut slices about ¼ inch thick from the butter log and place 1 slice on top of each crêpe. Dust with confectioner's sugar and serve.

Makes 6 servings

Getting a Start in Crêpes

"If this is America, it is indeed beautiful," exclaimed Jean-Paul Picot as he stepped from the ferry to the sea-swept shores of Nantucket Island, off the coast of Massachusetts. It was 1969, and it was his first job as manager of one of the branches of the widely popular, New York–based La Crêpe, a 15-unit chain that blossomed in the mid-1960s, becoming a great success. The restaurants featured the lacy, crisp-thin crêpes of Brittany with a choice of some 50 fillings—from cheese and crabmeat to sweet dessert treats—including the classic *Crêpes Suzette* (flamed with orange liqueur). Waitresses wore Bretonne costumes; it was really a picturesque ambiance.

As manager of the Nantucket branch, Jean-Paul Picot ordered the food essentials for the operation and oversaw the kitchen and front-room staff. "It was such a wonderful island, and I saw so little of it," Jean-Paul recalls. "The place was extremely popular with the island's summer people, so from early morning through late evening, my services were very much needed. Oh, I did manage to get in a few swims from time to time, but basically it was a work summer. Luckily for me, Monique and the boys came for the month of August.

"There were some celebrities on the island, of course, but most everyone walked around in very casual attire, and it was difficult to know who was who," Jean-Paul says, remembering one celeb's appearance. "One day, this man in shorts and T-shirt, unshaven and unkempt, came into the restaurant and asked for a table. I was about to show him to Siberia—the areas with the worst tables in the house, near the restrooms or in drafty spots that restaurateurs usually save for unknowns—when one of my waitresses put her hand on my arm and said: 'No, no. This man is a billionaire business magnate. You must show him to the best table in the house.' I gulped, regained my composure and graciously showed him to a royal table. So the financier enjoyed his crêpes and I sweated out the summer much more on the *qui vive!*"

Other Tasty Crêpe-Filling Ideas

- Top the crêpes with coffee ice cream and drizzle with chocolate sauce.

- Place a small scoop of French vanilla ice cream inside each crêpe and serve with raspberry sauce.

- For another ice cream and sauce variation, try strawberry–vanilla or cherry–vanilla ice cream with chocolate sauce.

- Spread each crêpe with butter and sprinkle with sugar before folding it up.

- Spoon some of your favorite jam or Nutella (a chocolate and hazelnut spread) onto each crêpe.

Crème Caramel

CARAMEL CUSTARD

Isn't crème caramel *everyone's most beloved first taste of French desserts? Among La Bonne Soupe's dessert fanciers, it is most certainly a runaway favorite, along with* crème brûlée, *which is much trickier to make. How creamy and comforting, how light and soothing, and what a perfect individually molded golden delight. The little mound of burnished vanilla custard gives the impression that it was prepared just for us. Well, it was!*

For the caramel

1 cup sugar
¼ cup water

For the custard

1 cup heavy cream
1 cup milk
1 teaspoon vanilla extract
3 large whole eggs
3 large egg yolks
Pinch of salt
⅓ cup sugar

Prepare the caramel:

Cook the sugar and water in a 1-quart, heavy saucepan over medium-high heat, stirring, until the sugar melts. Raise the heat to high and cook, uncovered, without stirring until the liquid turns a deep amber color, 4 to 5 minutes. Watch the pan and if it turns dark sooner, remove from the heat and cool immediately by placing the pan in a bowl of ice water.

Quickly and carefully pour about 1 tablespoon of the hot caramel into each of four 6-ounce custard cups and swirl to coat bottoms and sides. Set them aside.

Prepare the custard:

Preheat the oven to 325°F. Combine the cream, milk, and vanilla in a heavy, 1-quart saucepan and scald just until bubbles appear around the edge. Remove the pan from the heat and allow to cool slightly.

Break the eggs and egg yolks into a medium-size bowl and add the salt. Using a wire whisk or a fork, whisk the eggs until they are well beaten. Gradually beat in the sugar until blended and the mixture is smooth and creamy. Very gradually add the hot cream mixture, stirring gently to blend. Do not whisk or beat, or you will wind up with undesired foaminess. Carefully pour the custard into the caramel-lined cups, leaving about ¼ inch of headroom.

If there is any foam on the top, spoon it off.

Set the cups into a shallow roasting pan and pour warm water into the pan until it reaches halfway up the cups. Place the pan in the center of the oven and bake until the custard has set and a small sharp knife inserted into the custard comes out clean, 45 to 60 minutes.

Remove the roasting pan from the oven and, using a pot holder, transfer the custard cups to a wire cake rack to cool. Cover the cups with plastic or aluminum foil wrap and refrigerate until cold, up to 8 hours. To serve, run a spatula around the sides of the cups and unmold the custard into dessert coupes.

Makes 4 servings

Richer or Lighter?

The combination of heavy cream and milk, together with the eggs, makes a smooth, rich custard, but you can use all whole milk or 1 or 2 percent milk, if you'd like a lighter consistency.

Riz au Lait du Dr. Vassaux

DR. VASSAUX'S RICE PUDDING

Monique Picot remembers a very kindly doctor who practiced and subsequently retired in the small town of Saint-Saëns, which was very close to her parents' farm in Normandy. "When I was a small girl, my mother entrusted me with a basket of fresh eggs to take to Dr. Léon Henri Vassaux as a little gift from time to time. In return, the good doctor, by then a venerable man with a long, flowing white beard, would give me a family recipe to take home to my mother, such as his eggless rice pudding, which he prescribed for mal de foie*—the ubiquitous French liver problem."*

*R**ue de Docteur Léon Vassaux in Saint-Saëns, Normandy.*

Each time Monique visited Dr. Vassaux she lingered to admire the beautiful paintings that adorned his walls. On one occasion, Dr. Vassaux pointed to a group of oils and etchings he had hung in a very special room. "These, Monique, are the works of a very great painter, who has been my friend since we were students together at the Collège [high school] de

Saint-Quentin. His name is Henri Matisse."

More recently, Monique was thinking about those paintings as she perused New York's Museum of Modern Art's huge retrospective of Matisse in 1992. Turning a corner, she came upon an etching of a man's head that gave her a start. "Why, it's Dr. Vassaux," she exclaimed. And indeed it was, a wonderful likeness, beard and all. It was titled, Charles Bourgeat (Resemblant Dr. Vassaux) [Resembling Dr. Vassaux], *Paris 1914. Bourgeat was one of Matisse's favorite engravers.*

Charles Bourgeat, a friend and fellow student of Matisse at L'école des Beaux Arts, had a gallery in Paris on the Rue de la Boétie. In 1914, Matisse decided to do a portrait of him, an etching. However, as he was progressing with the artwork, he thought of his childhood friend, Dr. Vassaux, and the final portrait is more like Dr. Vassaux than of Bourgeat, hence its title.

⅓ cup uncooked short-grain rice, such as Arborio

⅓ cup sugar

1 quart milk

2 teaspoons vanilla extract or one 2- to 3-inch piece of vanilla bean, split in half

Preheat the oven to 250°F.

Place the rice and sugar in a 2-quart soufflé or other deep baking dish. Add the milk and vanilla extract, stirring lightly to blend.

Place the baking dish in the center of the oven and bake, uncovered, until the milk has been absorbed by the rice and the top becomes golden and crusty, 2½ to 3 hours. Serve the pudding warm, *tiède* (at room temperature), or chilled.

Makes 6 to 8 servings

Variations: Monique sometimes stirs in ⅓ cup chopped prunes or raisins before baking.

Poires Belle Hélène

POACHED PEARS WITH ICE CREAM AND
CHOCOLATE SAUCE

*For this luscious dessert, pears are poached in
a vanilla-flavored syrup and then topped with
scoops of rich vanilla ice cream and warm
chocolate sauce.*

4 firm, ripe pears, such as Comice or Anjou

Juice of ½ lemon

2 cups water

1 cup sugar

1 teaspoon vanilla extract

4 scoops rich vanilla ice cream

½ cup Chocolate Sauce (page 152), warmed

Peel the pears, cut them in half, and cut out the
cores. Place the pears in a small bowl, cover
with water, and add the lemon juice.

Bring the water, sugar, and vanilla extract to
a boil in a heavy, nonreactive 2-quart saucepan,
stirring, over high heat. Continue to cook over
high heat until the sugar is dissolved, about 5
minutes.

Reduce the heat to medium. Drain the
pears and slip them into the poaching liquid.
Cook the pears until tender, 10 to 12 minutes,
depending on the pear. Remove the pan from
the heat and allow the pears to cool in the
poaching liquid. This can be done ahead of
time, and the pears can be stored, covered, in
the refrigerator for up to 4 days.

To serve, place a pear half, cut side up, in
each compote dish. Place a scoop of vanilla ice
cream on top of the pear half and spoon the
Chocolate Sauce liberally over the ice cream.

Makes 4 servings

Fondue au Chocolat

CHOCOLATE FONDUE

*Chocolate has been rewarded with every cliché
imaginable from decadent, sinful, and wick-
edly rich to seductive, ecstatic, and aphrodi-
siacal. But surely, swirling a fat, luscious
strawberry (and other fruits or morsels of
cake) into a gently bubbling fondue pot filled
with dark, meltingly mellifluous chocolate
sauce, breathing in its alluring aromas, and
tasting the hot, dripping chocolate-robed morsel is one of the ultimate indulgences.*

For the sauce

8 ounces semisweet chocolate, broken into
   pieces

Grated zest of 1 small orange

½ cup heavy cream, heated until bubbles
   appear around the edges

2 tablespoons Grand Marnier or other
   orange-flavored liqueur

Fruit for dipping

1 pint strawberries, hulled

2 Delicious or other tart-sweet apples,
   peeled, cored, and cut into bite-size
   chunks, then tossed with 1 tablespoon
   of lemon juice to keep them from
   turning brown.

2 pears, such as Anjou, Comice or Bosc,
   peeled, cored, and cut into bite-size
   chunks, then drizzled with freshly
   squeezed lemon juice to prevent
   darkening

1 cup bite-size chunks of pineapple

2 cups bite-size chunks of pound, sponge, or
   angel food cake

Prepare the sauce:

Place the chocolate and orange zest in the top of a double boiler or in a heavy, 1-quart saucepan set over a larger pan of simmering water. Cook, stirring, over low heat until melted and smooth, about 5 to 6 minutes. Gradually stir in the cream until smooth and finally the liqueur.

Transfer the pan to a table warmer, chocolate fondue pot, or chafing dish set over a burner with a low flame. Stir in the Grand Marnier.

Prepare the fruit for dipping:

Arrange the fruits and/or cake chunks in small bowls around the pan of fondue and provide guests with long-handled forks.

Makes 4 to 6 servings

Tip: Since we're dealing with a hot sauce destined to reach the lips rather quickly, either caution your guests to wave the chocolate-coated morsel in the air for a few seconds before eating, or provide each guest with a second, regular fork, and little plates on which to rest the dainty before downing.

Tuiles

LACY TILE COOKIES

This is a classic French cookie that gets its name from the curved roof tiles of village houses. After the cookies are baked, they're draped over a narrow rolling pin, bottle, or, dare we mention, a broomstick, to give them their curvy shape. However, if you take them from the cookie sheet and leave them flat, they'll still be delectable.

Whites of 2 large eggs
Pinch of salt
⅓ cup sugar
⅓ cup all-purpose flour
¼ cup ground almonds or walnuts
¼ cup unsalted butter, melted

Preheat the oven to 350°F. Grease and flour 2 large cookie sheets.

In a medium-size bowl, lightly beat the egg whites, salt, and sugar until foamy, about 1 minute. Using a wire whip, whisk in the flour, nuts, and butter until the mixture is well blended.

Using a teaspoon, drop the batter onto the prepared cookie sheets, spacing the mounds at least 2 inches apart. Don't crowd them or they will run into each other.

Bake in the center of the oven until the edges of the cookies turn brown, 8 to 10 minutes. Using a spatula, remove the cookies carefully and place them immediately over a rolling pin or broomstick to harden and cool. If the cookies harden before you can get them off the cookie sheet, return them to the oven for 1 to 2 minutes to soften. Store the cooled cookies in a tightly covered container for up to 1 week.

Makes about 2 dozen cookies

Poires au Vin Blanc

PEARS POACHED IN WHITE WINE

The great thing about these pears, apart from their ambrosial flavor, is their flexibility: They can be made ahead—which is indeed a plus—and they may be dressed down, served just with their light sauce, or fancied up by adding congenial consorts such as crème fraîche, whipped cream, ice cream, and/or slivered almonds.

> 4 firm, ripe pears, such as Comice or Anjou
> Juice of ½ lemon
> 3 cups dry white wine
> 1 cup sugar
> One 2-inch strip of lemon zest

Peel the pears, cut them in half, and cut out the cores. Place the pears in a small bowl, cover with water, and add the lemon juice.

Bring the wine, sugar, and lemon peel to a boil in a heavy, nonreactive 2-quart saucepan over high heat. Continue to cook over high heat until the sugar is dissolved, about 5 minutes.

Reduce the heat to medium. Drain the pears and slip them into the poaching liquid. Cook the pears until tender, 10 to 12 minutes, depending on the pear. Remove the pan from the heat and allow the pears to cool in the poaching liquid. Serve at room temperature. Or store the pears, covered, in the refrigerator and serve chilled.

Makes 4 servings

Variations: For pears in red wine, substitute a fruity red wine for the white and proceed with the recipe. The pears will sport a pretty red blush.

For *poires cardinale,* poach the pears in white or red wine and sugar as directed, but serve with Rosy Raspberry Sauce (page 164) that has been flavored with kirsch instead of crème de cassis and strew each dish with toasted slivered almonds.

Pêches au Vin Rouge

PEACHES POACHED IN RED WINE

When peaches are at their peak, poaching them in red wine makes an utterly enchanting dessert. We like to leave the peaches whole, peeled, of course, but shapely, roseate in color, and totally beguiling in flavor. Use a fruity, inexpensive Beaujolais, French or American Merlot, or blended Bordeaux.

> 4 firm ripe peaches
> 3 to 4 cups red wine, enough to cover
> 2 tablespoons sugar
> ⅛ teaspoon ground nutmeg
> ¼ cup slivered almonds, toasted (see Note)

To peel the peaches, plunge them into a pot of boiling water for 10 to 15 seconds, then drain in a colander and place under cold, running water. The skins will slip right off.

Place the wine, sugar, and nutmeg in a heavy, 2-quart saucepan and bring to a boil over high heat. Reduce the heat to medium, add the peaches, making sure that they're completely covered with liquid. (If they aren't, add more wine or water.) Cook the peaches until tender, about 10 minutes. Using a slotted spoon, transfer the peaches to a bowl.

Raise the heat to high and reduce the poaching liquid to about 1 cup. Cool the liquid and add it to the peaches in the bowl. Cover and refrigerate until cold, at least 2 hours or up to 1 day.

When ready to serve, place 1 peach in each pretty compote dish, spoon the sauce on top, and garnish with the almonds.

Makes 4 servings

Note: To toast the almonds, place them on a baking sheet with sides and bake, stirring once or twice, in a preheated 350°F oven until lightly browned, 6 to 8 minutes.

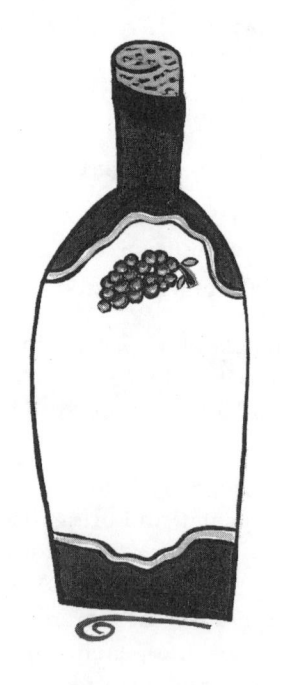

Tarte au Citron

Lemon Tart

Here's another specialty of Jean-Paul Picot's friend and teacher Paul Barraud at the L'École Hôtelièr in Lausanne, Switzerland. "The lemon filling is pleasingly piquant—just tart enough," Jean-Paul explains enthusiastically. "It's a marvelous dessert after a heavy meal." Monsieur Barraud serves a little glass of Malvoisie, a sweet white wine from the Valais region of Switzerland, made from the Pinot Gris grape, a charming complement to the piquancy of the lemon.

For the pastry shell

1 cup sifted all-purpose flour

¼ teaspoon salt

3½ tablespoons unsalted butter, cut into small pieces

3 tablespoons ice water

½ teaspoon white wine vinegar

For the filling

2 large eggs

½ cup plus 1 tablespoon sugar

3 tablespoons unsalted butter, melted and cooled

Grated zest of 2 large lemons

Juice of 2 large lemons (at least ⅓ cup of strained juice)

Prepare the pastry shell:

Place the flour and salt in a shallow mixing bowl. Using a pastry blender or two forks, cut in the butter until the mixture resembles coarse meal. Sprinkle the water and vinegar over the flour mixture and, using a fork, lightly and quickly mix until the pastry holds together. If it seems too dry, add another tablespoon of ice water. Form the pastry into a ball, wrap in plastic or waxed paper and chill in the refrigerator for 20 minutes.

When ready to bake, preheat the oven to 425°F. Roll out the dough on a floured board into a circle that measures about 12 inches in diameter. Transfer the pastry to a 9- or 10-inch pie pan and press lightly to fit. Press the sides so that about 1 inch of the pastry hangs over. (If it hangs unevenly, trim it to an even 1 inch.) Using your thumb and forefinger, flute the edges of the pie shell. Using a fork, prick the bottom and sides of the shell at random to prevent shrinkage. Cut a piece of foil or waxed paper to fit the bottom of the pie shell, place in the shell, and strew with dried beans or rice to weight it down.

Bake the shell in the center of the preheated oven just until it turns light tan, about 10 minutes. Remove the shell from the oven and allow it to cool before filling. Remove the liner and discard the beans or rice.

Prepare the filling:

Using a wire whisk or fork, beat the eggs and sugar in a medium-size bowl until blended and light. Add the butter, beating until well blended, then add the lemon zest and juice and beat until blended. Pour the mixture into the pastry shell.

Bake in the center of the oven until the lemon custard has set and the top is lightly browned, 30 to 35 minutes. Serve *tiède* (at room temperature) or chilled, as you prefer.

Makes 4 to 6 servings

Tip: We find the lemon tart is perfect served as is, in all its tangy golden glory. For those who feel the need for a bit of enrichment, however, top each slice with a puff of lightly sweetened whipped cream.

Some Tart Tips on Lemons

- To extract the maximum amount of juice from a lemon, roll it back and forth on the counter, using the heel of your hand until you feel it start to soften. Then use a juice extractor.

- If the lemons have been refrigerated, immerse them in hot water for a few seconds before juicing them.

- When buying lemons, look for firm, unblemished fruit heavy for its size and completely yellow. A tinge of green indicates the lemon is not quite ripe.

- One large lemon will yield about 3 tablespoons of juice.

- Use the finest part of the grater when grating lemon zest.

- Be sure to avoid the white pith underneath the lemon's yellow skin, which will impart a bitter taste.

Mousse Fondante au Chocolat

MELTING CHOCOLATE MOUSSE

The great gastronome Brillat-Savarin regarded chocolate as a digestif *[an aid for digestion] and a tonic. He also singled out chocolate lovers as happy people who enjoy life to the fullest. Well, let's drink to that!*

Certainly let's savor this voluptuous mousse, with its darkly intense chocolate frothed with airy eggs to a texture as light as hummingbirds' wings. It ranks high on the happiness scale.

9 ounces semisweet chocolate

1 tablespoon unsalted butter

6 large eggs, separated

Pinch of salt

½ cup heavy cream

1 tablespoon sugar

Melt the chocolate in the top of a double boiler or in a heavy, 2-quart saucepan set over a larger pan of simmering water. Cook, stirring, over low heat until melted and smooth. Add the butter, stirring until well blended. Remove the pan from the heat and allow the chocolate to cool slightly.

Place the egg yolks in one large bowl and the whites in another large bowl. Using a wire whisk or fork, beat the egg yolks until they are well blended. Slowly add the beaten egg yolks to the slightly cooled chocolate, beating constantly, until well blended. Return the saucepan to the simmering water or place over very low heat and cook, stirring, for 1 to 2 minutes. Remove from the heat and cool. Transfer the mixture to a clean large bowl.

Add the salt to egg whites and, using an electric beater or wire whisk, beat them until they hold stiff peaks. Using a large, slotted spoon, fold the egg whites into the cooled chocolate mixture, a little at a time, folding until no specks of white are visible. When all the whites have been amalgamated into the chocolate, turn the mixture into either a pretty serving bowl or 8 dessert dishes. Cover and chill in the refrigerator for at least 2 hours and up to 12.

To serve, beat the cream with the sugar until it holds soft peaks. Serve the chocolate mousse with a scoop of whipped cream on top.

Makes 8 servings

Tarte aux Pommes

APPLE TART

When Monique was a little girl living on a farm in Normandy, she always sighed a bit at apple-picking time. It was not among her favorite chores. But when the family sat down to dinner and the pièce de résistance *was her mother's flaky-pastry apple tart, Monique was so very happy to have contributed to the creation of this light, ambrosial dessert!*

Today, Monique makes what she calls "a simple, country pie, with apples that are not too tart and not too sweet." And, since making the rich puff pastry, or feuilletage, *is time-consuming and exacting to make from scratch, she finds the frozen, already multirolled sheets easy to roll out just one time. The resulting crust is flaky and delectable.*

- 1 sheet frozen puff pastry (about ½ pound), thawed according to the package's directions (see Note)
- 1 apple, such as Granny Smith or Golden Delicious (about 1 pound)
- 1½ tablespoons sugar
- 4 to 6 tablespoons crème fraîche or ½ pint vanilla ice cream

Preheat the oven to 450°F.

On a lightly floured surface, unfold and roll out the pastry into a rectangle about 18 x 14 inches and about ⅛-inch thick. Using a paring knife, cut out a 10-inch round and fit it into a 9-inch pie pan. (The pastry will come up about ½-inch on the side of the pan.)

Peel and core the apple and cut into slices about ⅛ inch thick. Arrange the apple slices, overlappping, in one layer in the pastry shell. Sprinkle the apple with the sugar.

Bake the tart in the center of the oven until the crust is golden and edges of apples are lightly browned, about 20 minutes. Serve the tart warm with a scoop of crème fraîche or ice cream.

Makes 4 to 6 servings

Note: *Frozen puff pastry is available in supermarkets' frozen food cases in packages that contain two sheets. It is much easier to handle than phyllo and strudel dough, whose tissue-thin layers are piled one on top of the other.*

Variations: A luscious pear tart using ripe but firm pears, such as Anjou or Comice, sliced very thin, is another of Monique's favorites.

Sauce Framboise

Rosy Raspberry Sauce

Here's a sauce you'll never want to be without. Teamed with fruit, ice cream, sherbet, or frozen yogurt, it's an instant dessert. Spooned over poached fruit and angel food cake, it's heavenly. In fact, our advice is to double the recipe. It will keep in the refrigerator in a tightly closed jar up to one week. If you're using fresh raspberries, you can store the sauce in the freezer up to one month.

Keep a couple of packages of frozen raspberries in your freezer, ready to turn into this quickly made, beguiling sauce.

One 12-ounce package frozen raspberries or 2 cups fresh raspberries

¼ cup sugar

Dash of ground nutmeg

1 tablespoon crème de cassis (black currant liqueur) or other fruit-flavored liqueur

Place all the ingredients in a heavy, 1-quart saucepan and cook, stirring occasionally, over medium heat until the sugar has melted into the berries, 2 to 3 minutes. Cool slightly.

Purée the mixture in a food processor or blender. Push the sauce through a fine-mesh strainer to eliminate the seeds.

Serve either warm or cold. Covered tightly, the sauce will keep in the refrigerator for up to 1 week.

Makes about 1 cup

Fraises au Vinaigre

Vinaigered Strawberries with Ice Cream

If the idea of macerating strawberries in vinegar strikes you as outré (outrageous), we quickly assure everyone that the touch of red wine vinegar and sprinkling of black pepper intensifies the flavor and lifts the succulent berries to a lofty, palate-pleasing plateau. Spoon the strawberries over chocolate ice cream for a simply sensational dessert.

2 cups fresh, ripe strawberries, hulled

½ cup sugar

¼ cup premium-brand red wine vinegar, such as Dessaux

1½ teaspoons cracked peppercorns

1 pint rich chocolate ice cream

Place the strawberries in a large bowl. Sprinkle with the sugar, vinegar, and peppercorns. Shake the bowl gently to distribute the marinade evenly. Cover and refrigerate for at least 1 hour.

When ready to serve, place a scoop of ice cream in the center of 4 dessert coupes and encircle with the berries.

Makes 4 servings

12

Wines and Cocktails

"La Bonne Soupe is my baby," says Jean-Paul Picot. "I go there the way I'd go to a social club, which it is, really; and it's fun. Someone comes in, goes straight to the bar, orders a glass of wine, beer, or a cocktail, and I join in with an espresso or water. I don't drink wine or hard liquor in the restaurant. But my patrons do! Which is as it should be."

Jean-Paul Picot, the proprietor of this social club, is sitting at one of the three red-topped bar stools, the most coveted trio of seats for many of La Bonne Soupe's regulars. At noon, it could be Maurice Galli, the jewelry designer of Tiffany's, who comes for chat and a glass of wine and who enjoys one of the *plats du jour* right at the bar. He's followed by others throughout the day and evening. It's a hot spot. "That's why I hang around there so much," Jean-Paul admits. "I get to see everyone coming and going. And I can keep tabs on what wines and other drinks are popular with the diners."

Wine is the most frequently ordered beverage at La Bonne Soupe, along with a sprinkling of trendy cocktails and Perrier. "Do you know that when we opened in 1973, a glass of house wine was 45 cents?" Jean-Paul beams as he remembers that he made a better percentage on that 45-cent glass than he does on the current dollars-plus glass.

Since the beginning, Jean-Paul decided to offer an American wine as the house wine. "First of all, I decided we're in America so we should serve the wine of the country, *n'est-ce pas?*" And it always went over big. My customers love it. In fact, once, when I tried to change to a French wine, it was a disaster. People said: 'What did you do to the wine? We want the same wine you've always had.' So we went back to the Mondavi. We go through 25 cases (12 liter bottles per case) every two weeks. That's a lot of wine!"

But, of course, there are French wines at La Bonne Soupe. "We've recently added Fortant de France, a nice country French wine from the Languedoc [southwest France], which is going over very well," Jean-Paul Picot says. The wines are listed on discreet table cards, which give the types—Chardonnay, Merlot, and Cabernet Sauvignon—a description of the wine, and the price (which is reasonable).

There is a proper wine list, and most of the French diners do ask for and order a bottle from this list. Among the reds, there are a Beaujolais-Villages, Château Simard from Saint-Émilion, and a French country wine (which at the moment is Buzet). White wines include a Mâcon-Villages from Burgundy and Muscadet de Sèvre-et-Maine from the western Loire Valley; for Champagne, it's Taittinger. The sparkling white is Kriter.

"We get orders for that great French favorite, pastis," Jean-Paul adds. Pastis is an anise-flavored spirit that mimics the color, flavor, and character of absinthe, the sale of which is illegal in the United States and other countries. People generally drink pastis with water to cut the aggressively licorice taste. They also enjoy it in popular French mixed drinks, such as *Ricard Tomate* and Autumn Leaves.

For Generation X-ers, there are margaritas, piña coladas, and frozen daiquiris, which are especially popular in warm weather.

When the weather is kind, the minioutdoor terrace that abuts the upstairs dining room is a popular spot—for munching and people watching.

Ricard Tomate

The color of this French apéritif is rosy and its anise flavor is from the Ricard—France's best known brand of pastis. There's a hint of almond provided by the orgeat syrup.

- 2 ounces Ricard or other anise-flavored liqueur
- 1 teaspoon grenadine
- ¼ teaspoon orgeat syrup (see Note)
- Water and ice to taste

In a tall collins glass, combine the Ricard, grenadine, and orgeat. Add ice to taste and fill the glass with water, stirring to blend well.

Makes 1 serving

Note: Orgeat syrup is a sweet, almond-flavored nonalcoholic syrup available in specialty food stores and Italian groceries. If you cannot find orgeat, use a dash or two of almond flavoring.

Feuilles Mortes

AUTUMN LEAVES

A song by the same name, sung by the renowned celebrities Yves Montand and Juliette Greco in the 1950s and 1960s is the inspiration for this cocktail. Its color, naturellment, resembles autumn leaves!

- 1½ ounces Ricard or other anise-flavored liqueur
- 1 teaspoon grenadine
- 1 teaspoon crème de menthe
- Ice and water to taste

In a tall collins glass combine the Ricard, grenadine, and crème de menthe. Add ice to taste and fill the glass with water, stirring to blend.

Makes 1 serving

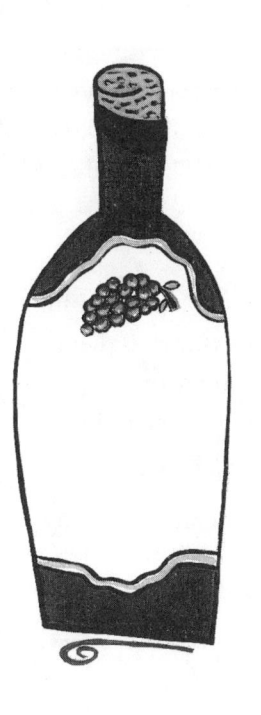

Piña Colada

This is among the most frequently ordered drinks young bistro aficionados enjoy ordering and sipping.

2 cups crushed ice
½ cup pineapple juice
3 tablespoons cream of coconut
3 ounces light rum

Place the crushed ice in the container of a blender, add the pineapple juice, cream of coconut, and rum and blend at high speed until frothy, 15 to 20 seconds. Pour into a chilled collins glass and serve with a straw.

Makes 1 serving

Frozen Strawberry Daiquiri

Rum and strawberries have a wonderfully synergistic effect, judging from the diners who clamor for a frozen daiquiri, especially during the warm weather.

2 cups crushed ice
1 ounce freshly squeezed lime juice
1 ounce strawberry liqueur
1 teaspoon superfine sugar
4 or 5 strawberries, hulled
2 ounces light rum

Place all the ingredients in a blender and blend at high speed until well blended and frothy, 15 to 20 seconds. Pour into a chilled collins glass.

Makes 1 serving

Margarita

Honore Pochat and Daniel Lagarde, who alternate tending La Bonne Soupe's tiny bar, agree that their tequila-based Margarita sticks pretty much to the classic recipe, "which is the way our guests like it!"

Juice of ½ lime
Coarse salt
Juice of ½ lemon
1½ ounces tequila
½ ounce Cointreau or other orange-flavored liqueur
1 cup crushed or cracked ice
1 slice of lime for garnish

Moisten the rim of a cocktail glass with the lime juice, and dip the rim into coarse salt.

Place the juices and spirits in a cocktail shaker or blender, add the ice and shake well or blend until well mixed, 15 to 20 seconds. Strain into the prepared glass and garnish with the slice of lime.

Makes 1 serving

Index

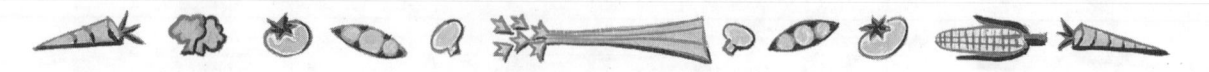